Praise for
The Invention of Design

"A stunner. In a series of absorbing, well-crafted episodes, Maggie Gram both lures you into the world of design and poses hard questions about it. This book goes down easy but packs a wallop."
—Daniel Immerwahr, author of *How to Hide an Empire*

"A sharp, perpetually surprising, connection-filled excavation of how 'design' came to rule our present. You won't look at your phone, your chair, or the horizon the same afterward."
—Hua Hsu, Pulitzer Prize–winning author of *Stay True*

"This book is the secret history of the twentieth century. Gram introduces us to a cast of characters whose names you have never heard, but whose ideas produced the user-friendly look and feel of our world. Her approach is beautifully balanced. She distinguishes the ingenuity from the hype—and there was a lot of hype. But she shows us that although design alone will not cure all the inequities of life under capitalism, it can help."
—Louis Menand, Pulitzer Prize–winning author of *The Metaphysical Club*

"With *The Invention of Design*, Gram has created something I did not think was possible: A sweeping account of the world of design that will engage curious readers who know nothing about the subject, and, at the same time, surprise readers who think they know everything about it. It is expansive, erudite, skeptical, optimistic, and an absolute blast to read. I only wish my mom had lived long enough to read it, so she could finally understand what I do for a living."

—Michael Bierut, partner and graphic designer, Pentagram

"This is a book I've been waiting for. Gram effortlessly synthesizes across histories of industry, geopolitics, craft, and social movements, animating each with characters both known and obscure—the dreamers, pragmatists, revolutionaries, bureaucrats, and CEOs who all shaped the big tent known as design. Erudite, ambitious, and plainspoken, *The Invention of Design* is an ideal companion for the reader who wants to see design made newly strange and contingent."

—Sara Hendren, designer and author of *What Can a Body Do?*

"A lucid, humane, and consistently fascinating history of the concept of design told through the lives and ideas of some of its most talented exponents. A knowledgeable practitioner and a beautiful writer, Gram skillfully illuminates design's critical role in the shaping of modern society."

—Nikil Saval, author of *Cubed*

THE
INVENTION
OF DESIGN

The
INVENTION
of DESIGN

A Twentieth-Century History

MAGGIE GRAM

BASIC BOOKS

New York

Copyright © 2025 by Maggie Gram
Cover design by Chin-Yee Lai
Cover image DNY59 / E+ via Getty Images
Cover copyright © 2025 by Hachette Book Group, Inc.

Hachette Book Group supports the right to free expression and the value of copyright. The purpose of copyright is to encourage writers and artists to produce the creative works that enrich our culture.

The scanning, uploading, and distribution of this book without permission is a theft of the author's intellectual property. If you would like permission to use material from the book (other than for review purposes), please contact permissions@hbgusa.com. Thank you for your support of the author's rights.

Basic Books
Hachette Book Group
1290 Avenue of the Americas, New York, NY 10104
www.basicbooks.com

Printed in the United States of America

First Edition: June 2025

Published by Basic Books, an imprint of Hachette Book Group, Inc. The Basic Books name and logo is a registered trademark of the Hachette Book Group.

The Hachette Speakers Bureau provides a wide range of authors for speaking events. To find out more, go to hachettespeakersbureau.com or email HachetteSpeakers@hbgusa.com.

Basic books may be purchased in bulk for business, educational, or promotional use. For more information, please contact your local bookseller or the Hachette Book Group Special Markets Department at special.markets@hbgusa.com.

The publisher is not responsible for websites (or their content) that are not owned by the publisher.

Print book interior design by Amy Quinn.

Library of Congress Cataloging-in-Publication Data
Names: Gram, Maggie, author.
Title: The invention of design: a twentieth-century history / Maggie Gram.
Description: First edition. | New York: Basic Books, 2025. |
　Includes bibliographical references and index.
Identifiers: LCCN 2024044117 (print) | LCCN 2024044118 (ebook) |
　ISBN 9781541600638 (hardcover) | ISBN 9781541600645 (ebook)
Subjects: LCSH: Design—Social aspects—History—20th century.
Classification: LCC NK1390 .G73 2025 (print) | LCC NK1390 (ebook) |
　DDC 306.4/7—dc23/eng/20250127
LC record available at https://lccn.loc.gov/2024044117
LC ebook record available at https://lccn.loc.gov/2024044118

ISBNs: 9781541600638 (hardcover), 9781541600645 (ebook)

LSC-C

Printing 1, 2025

For Glory and Nan

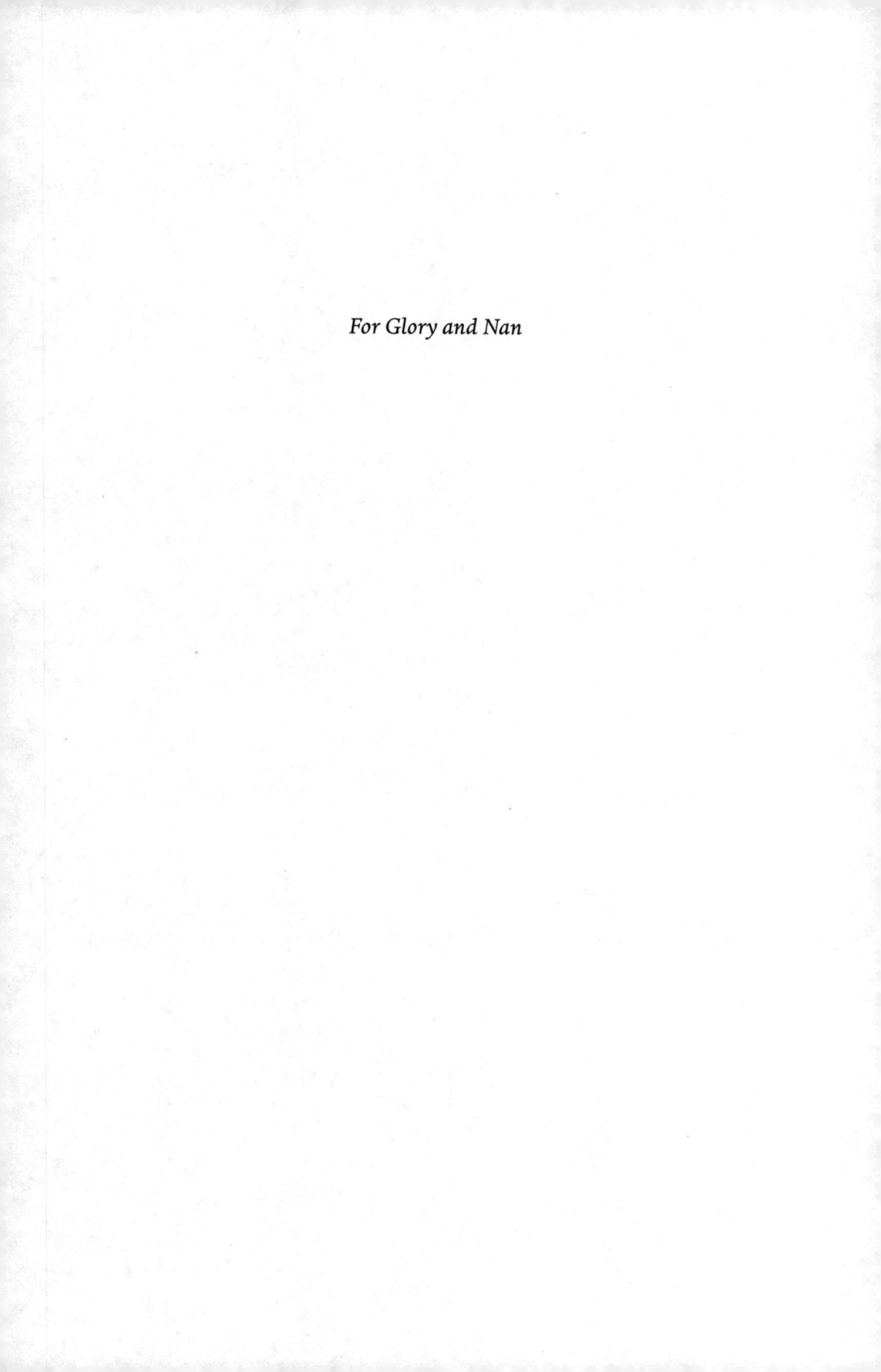

CONTENTS

Preface	1
Introduction	7
Chapter 1. Beauty	19
Chapter 2. Function	51
Chapter 3. Problem Solving	87
Chapter 4. Human-Centeredness	125
Chapter 5. Experience	169
Chapter 6. Thinking	209
Afterword	249
Acknowledgments	*259*
Notes	*263*
Index	*309*

Preface

This book is about how people constructed one of the ideas that shapes the world we live in. Over the period from about 1890 through about 2010, people around the globe came to understand a set of previously unrelated concepts—beauty, function, problem solving, human-centeredness, experience, even thinking itself—as components of one single megaconcept. They invested faith and capital in this megaconcept, made it meaningful and valuable, and used it to shape first consumer objects and then institutions and systems. In English, they called it "design."

This could have happened only in the twentieth century. By the 1890s, the changes we now call the Industrial Revolution had transformed Great Britain, most of Europe, and the United States from agrarian and handicraft economies into machine-driven industrial ones. Meanwhile, the "invisible hand" of the market—largely unconstrained by states—had come to dominate everyday life. Industrialization and unregulated markets were uprooting people, degrading their working conditions, squeezing their leisure time, exploiting their children as workers, polluting their rivers and air, and alienating them from the products of their labor.

Now a battle played out over what to do about it. In the 1930s, in response to a global economic crisis and to workers' demands, Western governments regulated markets and built safety nets: social democratic institutions like redistributive tax regimes, social insurance systems, and labor laws. Then, in the 1970s—after business leaders revolted, and as Westerners obsessed over the perceived existential threat of Soviet communism—nation-states from the United States to Indonesia to Chile systematically dismantled these regulatory constraints and safety nets. Their dismantling opened doors to globalization: the rise of fast-moving global markets dominated by sprawling, effectively unregulated networks of corporate actors, all of which dissolved national identities and subordinated local preferences and needs. The dismantling of regulatory constraints and safety nets also enabled financialization: the displacement of traditional material production, as the chief driver of economies, by complex financial engineering. And it drove a resurgence of wealth inequality across the globe.[1]

People all over the world tried to ride these waves in ways that might preserve their own dignity and power. Our contemporary idea of design—that hopeful amalgam of a concept—was born in the process. Inventing design helped people imagine reversing some of the damage wrought by the Industrial Revolution. It helped people convince themselves that capitalism fundamentally served human interests; that positive social change could be achieved without politics and government action; that problem solving could be both generative and profitable. And it enabled people of substantial power and privilege to imagine themselves as benevolent actors. "Design," in short, made capitalism feel, both to its participants and to its subjects, less brutal and inhumane—less destructive, in Joseph Schumpeter's terms, and more creative. It seemed to give them a way to reclaim the things they'd made and to re-embed them in a human order.[2]

No one person decided that all those smaller concepts—beauty and function and human-centeredness and the like—should become one thing. No one person invented the idea of design. Countless people participated, and they did so not intentionally, exactly, but through their everyday conversations and decisions and purchases and writing and labor. What they said and made and sold and bought—and the ideas and beliefs and rules that emerged in the process—constructed the idea of design. Design was invented, in large part, through discourse.

This book is a history, then, of the discourse of design. The word "discourse" comes from the Latin verb for "to run to and fro," and from another Latin word for "argument." So a discourse is, figuratively, as the critic Sarah Williams Goldhagen has put it, "a bunch of people running about having an argument—or more correctly, a series of arguments and debates, which are related to one another and governed by a set of underlying concerns or principles." These arguments are everywhere, and they never end. Discourse is the word cloud we live in, the conversation so inexhaustible we start to hear it as baseline white noise.[3]

Discourse matters because it helps construct reality. When Steve Jobs tells the *New York Times* that "design is how it works," his remark contributes a tiny but meaningful change to the overall consensus regarding what counts as "design." At this point, quite a lot counts. And what counts as "design" helps determine what goods and services people need and want and how much it all costs to obtain. It helps determine what's taught to students in colleges and graduate schools, what it feels like to visit a museum exhibit, and who gets to participate in a growing subset of lucrative careers that afford affluent, propertied lives. It decides who's authorized to lead some of our most powerful institutions. Perhaps *least* consequentially, it determines how designers actually make the things we buy and use.[4]

Like any history of discourse, this book is also a history of power. It focuses on the most privileged people. This is both by necessity and (forgive me) by design. Among the members of any society, it's the most powerful—often white men like the industrial designer Walter Teague, the computer scientist Herbert Simon, the entrepreneur Steve Jobs—whose voices get amplified. Their words get published, their biographies get written, their archives get preserved. Often they get to decide who else speaks and is heard. Their discourse has disproportionate impact. They aren't the only ones whose voices matter, and they aren't the only characters in this book. But they do dominate.

This is also a mostly American story. The contemporary discourse of design, particularly in English, was produced by German and Japanese and Scandinavian and Soviet and American (and a world of other) designers and consumers and businesses. But in the end, the twentieth century was, in fact, the American century. The United States was where power lived. Much of design discourse passed through US publications, US television, the corporate guidelines of US-based companies. Americans got to determine the bounds of the global conversation, including the conversation about "design." Almost all of the characters in this book are either immigrants or the children of immigrants, but most of them end up in the United States.

◖◗

This is not a history of all the cool things that people have designed in the history of the world. There's a place for such dead catalogs, but I don't find them very interesting. What I do find interesting is the weirdness—and the relative newness—of the idea of design as a unitary concept and driver of value. So this book's subject is that concept, and the world that that concept has made.[5]

This book also is not an argument about what design *really is*—if it has any such transhistorical essence—or what it should be. I don't care whether "design" exists in some transhistorical way, independent of anyone thinking or talking about it. I care when and why we started *believing* it does.

I wrote this book for two reasons. One was, roughly, political. In the past few decades, a lot of institutions have embraced design as an approach to problem solving, from cities like Los Angeles and Helsinki hiring "chief design officers" to universities paying lavishly for "design thinking" engagements. This made me uneasy. I worried, for reasons I couldn't fully articulate even to myself, that relying on this newly fashionable idea to improve social, economic, and political relations might result in more unequal and unjust relations than we began with. I hoped that understanding "design" historically, taking the idea apart into a set of constituent elements born of particular times and places and ideological contexts, might help me make sense of my own unease, and—more idealistically—might strip "design" of a bit of its runaway imaginative power.

The other reason was personal. I run a small team of designers at an American multinational corporation and technology company. And I teach design, on and off, in universities. I think what I do is interesting and challenging and sometimes worthwhile. But I don't think it's coherent. Designers do a wild array of kinds of work, from organizing data to creating modular systems of pixels to writing reader-friendly text. Very little of it seems organically related to its other parts. So what, I've found myself asking, *is* design? This book begins to answer this question—not with a definition (I don't think there's any single right definition), but at least with an explanation of how we got here.

So those were the impulses that led to the book. Now that I've written it, though, there's another reason I'm glad to have lived with it for so long: writing it has reconnected me with the history of twentieth-century political economy and with the ways that this history has helped define our cultures. I hope reading it does a bit of this for you, too. I hope the book reminds its readers that our seemingly natural cultural forms are, in fact, so many artifacts of the specific histories that made it possible to imagine them. Only when we see our institutions and cultural forms as contingent, after all—only when we see them as historical rather than inevitable—does it become thinkable to try to change them.

Introduction

> "That's a great deal to make one word mean," Alice said in a thoughtful tone.
> "When I make a word do a lot of work like that," said Humpty Dumpty, "I always pay it extra."
> —**Lewis Carroll,** *Through the Looking-Glass, and What Alice Found There* **(1871)**

> Design is one of the terms that has replaced the word "revolution"!
> —**Bruno Latour, "A Cautious Prometheus? A Few Steps Toward a Philosophy of Design" (2009)**

Design Within Reach was founded in 1998, when a potter-turned-Stanford-MBA named Robert Forbes Jr. realized he could make money by providing wealthy Americans with opportunities to buy furniture that had been overtly "designed." Before then, buying an object designed by a famous modern designer—say, an Eames lounger, or a Mies van der Rohe chair—usually meant finding an architect or interior designer with access to trade showrooms, since manufacturers, who were often in Europe, had minimum order requirements that exceeded the requirements of an individual or small-business buyer in the United States. Rob Forbes bought twenty containers of high-modern furniture inventory and hired the prestige graphic design firm Pentagram to design a logo. Then he set up an online store, publicized it with a newsletter, and sent out a direct-mail catalog to about 240,000 recipients. Within five years, Design Within Reach had gone public. The stock market valued the company at $211 million.[1]

One explanation for the success of Design Within Reach is that it took advantage of consumers' emergent passion for "provenance." Around the end of the twentieth century, luxury markets—for everything from coffee to textiles to restaurant food—began to tilt toward brands and branded objects that lay explicit claim to specific historical origins. Consumers chose these "heritage brands" because they believed they offered higher quality and perceived their goods to be more "authentic." Design Within Reach rode the beginning of that wave. It enabled the American consumer to buy not just a chair but a story.[2]

But there's another interpretation for the company's success: the turn of the twenty-first century was a good time to be selling not just any provenance story but a *design* story. The magazine *Wallpaper** had been founded in London in 1996. *Grand Designs* started in 1999, *Dwell* in 2000, *Project Runway* in 2004, *Domino* in 2005. Roman Mars launched his podcast *99% Invisible*, focused on "the hidden world of everyday design," in 2010, after he noticed that "people on the internet were already talking about design in a different way than [he] had ever experienced before." By the beginning of 2014, the show was one of iTunes's top fifty podcasts. Target launched its Made by Design line in 2018. It was, and it remains, a designy time.[3]

Introduction

All these businesses and shows and magazines and product lines understand "design" in a particular way: as the marriage of aesthetics with function. Designed things, in this view, are things that are exceptionally beautiful and work exceptionally well. We could call this a "modernist" concept of design, since it's roughly what midcentury European and American designers and design consumers meant when they talked about design.

As of 1998, design, as an idea, was still inextricably bound up with that modernist ideal. But it had also come to mean more than that. People associated it with the idea of "problem solving." It was often described, approvingly, as "human-centered." And it was taking on new meanings all the time. In 2021, for instance, as the young New York gallerist Emma Scully told the *New York Times*, design was welcoming "a new wave."

What was this new wave? Chris Shao, who'd recently opened his Objective Gallery in Shanghai, described group design shows that were less formal thematic investigations and "more of a vibe." Stephen Markos, who had curated pop-up exhibitions and an Instagram feed before opening his Chinatown gallery Superhouse in 2021, emphasized that the works he showed were meant to be touched, heard, smelled, encountered. In an age of social media, the *Times* reporter concluded, tastes had skewed toward the unique, the eclectic, the participatory. Design could still be beautiful, be functional, solve problems, be human-centered—but it should also be an *experience*.[4]

Design was also becoming a way of *thinking*. The design agency IDEO began using the phrase "design thinking" in 2003 to refer to the use of design methods, by both designers and nondesigners, to solve problems outside design's traditional purview. By 2009, the Stanford design school was treating "design thinking," in cofounder Robert Sutton's phrase, "more like a religion than a set of practices for sparking creativity." Whereas IDEO had once specialized in industrial and interaction design, the *New York Times Magazine* noted in 2016, "now its projects include 'redesigning' such abstractions as the school lunch (for the city of San Francisco) or the vote (for Los Angeles County), experimenting with how to lace in 21st-century technology elements and shed out-of-date practices." "Design thinking" had become "a reigning ideology in which every object, symbol or pool of information is just another design problem awaiting some solution."[5]

In 2009, the French philosopher and social scientist Bruno Latour marveled at "the extraordinary career" of the term "design" over the twentieth century. "Design has been extended from the details of daily objects," he wrote, "to cities, landscapes, nations, cultures, bodies, genes, and . . . nature itself." The little word "design," Latour continued, "could offer a very important touchstone for detecting where we are heading." Indeed, he continued, society's obsession with change by design was a sign that human beings had stopped believing in other forms of change: "To put it more provocatively, I would argue that design is one of the terms that has replaced the word 'revolution'!"[6]

I, too, have been mystified by my own and other cultures' outsized investments in design. Since around 1900, in the affluent regions of the globe, people have endowed the idea of design with layer after layer of meaning and value. At the beginning of the century, "design" was most

Introduction

often associated with beauty; soon it was also about function. With the end of World War II and the beginning of the Cold War, it also became a mode of problem solving. By the second half of the twentieth century, "design" had become a way of understanding and serving *people* better (I call this "human-centeredness," for lack of a better term); then a way of centering and enhancing "experience"; and finally—at the turn of the twenty-first century—a way of thinking. Today, the idea of "design" mediates decision making among global executives and elites. You can find "human-centered design" and "design thinking" and "chief design officers" in the upper reaches of corporations and governments and universities in the English-speaking world and beyond. What we now call "design" is, in short, a very popular—and very freighted—amalgam of optimistic human values.

Historians agree that the impulses behind design modernism—the historical movement that peaked around the middle of the twentieth century—were utopian, in the sense that they were hopeful and even idealistic. Le Corbusier ended his 1923 modernist manifesto *Vers une architecture* (commonly translated as *Towards a New Architecture*) by suggesting that design—he specifically refers to architecture—could itself enact the kind of transformative social change that otherwise could be achieved only by revolution:

> Society is filled with a violent desire for something which it may obtain or not. Everything lies in that: everything depends on the effort made and the attention paid to these alarming symptoms.
> Architecture or Revolution.
> Revolution can be avoided.

Le Corbusier's statement—at least the "Architecture or Revolution" part—became a foundational maxim of modernism, whose architects and other designers hoped their new buildings and new objects would usher in a better world.[7]

But it isn't just *modernist* ideas of design that are utopian. In fact it's the very *idea of design itself*, as that concept was defined over the course of the long twentieth century. Contemporary ideas of design—as beauty, as function, as problem solving, et cetera—are about more than just improving products and processes: they are idealistic visions of how people might live in the wake of the Industrial Revolution and amid the destabilizing forces of markets. Each came into being through discourse among creative people who were experiencing some kind of crisis in political economy, whether the Great Depression or the Cold War or the 1970s "rediscovery of the market" or the late twentieth-century rise of finance. In each case these people responded by reimagining "design," a set of ideas and practices at the crux of economy and creativity, as a tool for fixing broken aspects of market society from within. And so "design" has become the hero of many of our most hopeful stories—dreams, fantasies, utopias—about how we might better live with capitalism.

Soon after its launch, Design Within Reach expanded from the web into the brick-and-mortar world. It opened its first retail store in 2000, in an elegant three-story historic building on San Francisco's leafy, sun-dappled Jackson Street. By the time the company went public a few years later, it had eighteen retail locations ("studios") around the United States, and it was profitable. The average customer order came to $917.[8]

Introduction

And the brand had become authoritative. Shortened to "DWR" and affectionately nicknamed (for its exorbitant prices) "Design Not Quite Within Reach," it was becoming a household name. "We're like Volvo or Saab," Forbes told *Newsweek*. The logo was increasingly familiar, and the product lines were covered regularly in the *New York Times*. And the appeal went beyond the highbrow. DWR received prominent placement as a supplier of home furnishings and decor on Bravo's *Queer Eye for the Straight Guy*—in which, as one commentator put it, "slobs get their apartments redone using furniture you formerly might have seen only in Scandinavian hotels"—and TLC's *Trading Spaces*.[9]

And yet sustained success was elusive, particularly once shareholders got involved. After it went public, Design Within Reach started opening new "studios" even faster. "The mantra was, 'Let's open more stores, so we can make our revenue numbers, in order to achieve our growth,'" Forbes told the *New York Times*. But the costs of real estate and staff made it difficult for DWR to sustain a profit. Forbes resigned as CEO in 2007. Sales plummeted in 2008; in 2009, a venture capital firm called Glenhill, judging correctly that DWR was "running out of money," bought 92 percent of the company. By the end of 2009, DWR's sales hovered at around $30 million—almost 85 percent down from peak—and its stock price, once about $18 a share, had fallen to about twelve cents.[10]

One reason was the 2008 crash. But there were other problems. In 2009 *Fast Company* reported that DWR had "veered from one ill-advised strategy to another, ranging from a craven knockoff program to a baroque pursuit of brand extensions." The knockoffs were particularly egregious, diluting, as they did, DWR's claims to that ever-important (if elusive) virtue of authenticity. At least two companies, including the

New York–based Heller and the Minneapolis-based Blu Dot, had filed suit against DWR for trademark infringement. (Blu Dot alleged that DWR had even used a photograph of a Blu Dot table to market its own version.) Forbes himself acknowledged that knockoffs had been part of the company's strategy. "I was always reluctant personally," he told the *Times*. "But the business metrics were so compelling."[11]

Things did stabilize, eventually, for Design Within Reach. In 2014, the furniture manufacturer Herman Miller—which owned many designs that DWR already retailed—announced that it would buy DWR for $154 million. The acquisition would provide Herman Miller, which intended to expand from the office-furnishings business into consumers' homes (establishing itself as a "premier lifestyle brand"), with a "complete consumer-focused infrastructure" through which to retail its products. And it would protect Design Within Reach from some of the exigencies of the market. "With a stable parent," *Bloomberg* wrote, "DWR will be rescued from the ups and downs."[12]

Meanwhile, "design" continued to roll down the hill of history, picking up kinetic energy as it went: new meanings, new markets, new forms of value. McKinsey & Company bought Lunar Design; Accenture bought Fjord; the electronics manufacturing company Flextronics International took an equity stake in frog design, which later was acquired by Altran, which itself was taken over by the consulting firm Capgemini. DXC bought Argodesign, itself a spinoff of frog. Fuseproject bought BlueFocus. Capital One bought Adaptive Path. Steelcase Inc., one of Herman Miller's chief competitors, had for a time owned a majority share in IDEO, the design firm that popularized the idea of "design thinking." Now, in 2016, Steelcase invited Tim Brown, IDEO's former CEO, onto its board, and in its public statements it adopted the idea that design was not just a set of practices for enhancing beauty and function but its own way of thinking. Today, Steelcase's website offers a plethora of content about, to quote the title of one post, "Design Thinking and Its Role in the Creative Process."[13]

Design Within Reach had banked on "design" resolving some of capitalism's internal contradictions. It didn't—at least not fast enough to keep DWR itself from being chewed up and spit out by the stock market, which wanted DWR to be a better financial instrument, a more rapidly accelerating vehicle for making money, than it was. Even after its acquisition by Herman Miller, though, Design Within Reach evolved with "design" as the concept morphed and morphed again for the new late-late-capitalist era. Most recently, it's embraced the idea that design is about creating "experiences." A circa 2018 ad campaign by an agency called Language Dept. showed three middle-aged white people in deep discussion in the DWR Nashville studio, with the headline "Good design is to be experienced."

It was more than a slogan: it was a strategy. In early 2024, DWR moved its flagship "studio" to a new, 1920s-era, fifteen-thousand-square-foot industrial warehouse that had once been home to the California Caster and Hand Truck Company. DWR gave the space a deep renovation—preserving, of course, the historic woodwork—and opened it that spring as a kind of experiential playground on the theme of design. Two thousand square feet were given over to rotating display areas called "the Gallery," which showcased work by designers like the French architect Jean Prouvé, and "the Case Study Apartment," a callback to the experiments in American residential architecture that *Arts & Architecture* magazine famously sponsored at midcentury. The new DWR space also featured a vinyl collection curated by Haight Street's Amoeba Music and publications selected by City Lights. These site-specific touches made the space an experience in itself, noted one architect who visited the space for an opening party: "I can imagine our younger colleagues and design students treating this space as an extension of the other cool stuff that's happening nearby."[14]

Other critics agreed. "DWR is such a gem of a brand," remarked the San Francisco–based designer Susan Work at an opening party for the studio, "in part because it keeps reinventing itself." Hope—embodied in that ever-adapting idea of "design"—springs eternal.[15]

Here's a spoiler: none of the ideas of "design" in this book get very far in actually resolving the contradictions or repairing the damages wrought by capitalism. To generalize some lines from Meyer Schapiro's May 1932 review of the Museum of Modern Art's "International Style" show: "Without the will to apply it for a common end," design—which, as Schapiro notes, is itself a product of industrial capitalism—"will remain a means for exploitation, or the newest fad of the richest class, the symbol of a profitable, spectacular efficiency." Today that faddishness manifests as a kind of techno-utopianism—an obsession with the new and its capacity to improve, enhance, optimize—that manifests in private spaceflight, Tesla cybertrucks, and the collective fixation on artificial general intelligence as, in OpenAI CEO Sam Altman's words, "magic intelligence in the sky." We may be hurtling toward planetary demise, but we're not *irreversibly* subject, our richest class seems to believe, to the whims of biology or the limitations of the human mind or the fragility of our planetary ecology. No: individual human "makers" can change our course and build a better future. It all seems to me a powerful self-delusion.[16]

So this story isn't all that strategically instructive. And in fact some people think that all utopian thinking—the category into which I'm casting design—is inherently antiprogressive. The critic Fredric Jameson, a historian of utopian ideas, notes that older Marxist thinking denounced utopianism as unstrategic, idealistic, in fact "structurally averse to the political as such." Older Marxists saw utopianism as so fantastical as to lack political utility and even potentially to forestall real transformative politics.

There's something to this. And yet even I have to admit that the idealism of "design" probably has more practical political value than it seems to have on its face. "At its core," the critic and civil servant Nikil Saval has written, "design is an inherently futurist medium." It's about imagining a future that's different from the present. To believe in design, in other words, is to believe—foolishly or not—that human society can change for the better.[17]

For those who desire democratic political change, this is a good thing. In times when part of what holds us back is the belief that, in Margaret Thatcher's words, "there is no alternative" to industrial and postindustrial capitalism, half the battle is simply to begin imagining a society that looks different from this one. If we can use design to help us conceive at all of alternative possibilities, then we should.[18]

Maybe the key is not to suppose that, because of design, "revolution can be avoided." It's to prevent design from becoming a compensatory and purely aesthetic fantasy, one that stands in for and obviates political action, whether revolutionary or reformist. I think uneasily of Margaret

Cavendish's 1668 text *The Description of a New World, Called the Blazing-World*, in which "spirits" convince a duchess that, rather than being troubled with worldly governance and politics, she should create a fantasy realm in which she can do whatever she pleases. "Why should you desire to be Empress of a Material World, and be troubled with the cares that attend Government?" the spirits ask, "when as by creating a World within your self, you may enjoy all both in whole and in parts, without controle or opposition; and may make what World you please, and alter it when you please, and enjoy as much pleasure and delight as a World can afford you?" That temptation—to retreat into design and to "make what World you please" there—ought to be avoided. Better to muck around, I think, in the messy and troublesome and slow and sometimes dispiriting and genuinely efficacious business of actual politics.[19]

So "design" isn't a bad idea. I'm glad the twentieth century invented it. My hope, though, is that seeing the idea of design historically, as this book does—taking the concept apart into its constituent elements, each born of its particular time and place and ideological context—will help us both to understand it better and to recognize its limits. And doing that might help us decide what to do *with* design, both as a space for social dreaming and as a real set of tools, from here.

Chapter 1

BEAUTY

The ceramicist Eva Zeisel was born in 1906, in Budapest, as Eva Polanyi Striker. She was the daughter of a bourgeois Jewish family of some wealth and standing in Hungarian society. Her mother's family, the Polanyis, were historically minded, socially connected (her grandmother had run a famous Budapest salon for decades), and deeply engaged in social democratic politics. Her mother, Laura Polanyi Striker, was an activist and teacher who had been the first woman to earn a doctorate in history at the University of Budapest. One of Laura's younger brothers, Michael Polanyi—Eva's uncle—would become widely known as a scientist and philosopher of science. Another younger brother, Karl Polanyi, would become one of the twentieth century's preeminent theorists of political economy.[1]

When Eva was born, the Polanyi Strikers were at home in Budapest, then a rapidly growing, cosmopolitan city. They were assimilated, Hungarian-speaking, Jewish intellectuals in a city where 25 percent of the population was Jewish and where many Jews were assimilated, Hungarian-speaking intellectuals. From a young age, Eva thought of herself as "modern." Later, she remembered identifying strongly with a children's book meant to be the memoir of "a modern doll," a toy that felt overwhelming pride at having been born at the end of "the superb nineteenth century." It was a time "of miracles, of the triumphs of technology." To the six-year-old Eva Striker, modernity made everything seem possible.[2]

As for herself, she planned to become an artist. She was good at drawing, and even better—strikingly original—at painting. In 1923, at the age of seventeen, she entered the Képzőművészeti Akadémia, the Hungarian Royal Academy of Fine Arts, in Budapest, where she learned from distinguished symbolists and impressionists, including the Paris-trained Hungarian modernist János Vaszary. She focused on portraiture. A self-portrait painted in those years shows a solemn young woman rendered in blacks and creams and blue-greens, wearing an artist's jacket, trying on the artist's piercing gaze. She seems poised to embrace her vocation as a painter.[3]

But she lived in strange times. Hungary was half of the Austro-Hungarian Empire, an experimental "dual monarchy" that, upon its creation by a compromise in 1867, had been the first of its kind. The 1867 compromise had positioned the benevolent and multilingual emperor Franz Joseph, of the House of Habsburg in Vienna, as the ruler of two separate entities, united by their government but constitutionally distinct. Franz Joseph was a liberal, and for Hungary his reign facilitated rapid economic growth: industrial and commercial

Eva Zeisel, self-portrait, ca. 1920s. Presumed oil on canvas. Photo by Brent C. Brolin.

development surged, industrialists built scores of highly productive new factories, and national revenue grew fast. But even as Hungary's cities became modern, most of the country remained feudal. It was made up largely of peasant towns. It was split between ethnic Hungarians (known as Magyars) and more recent settlers of other European ethnic origin (particularly Slovaks, Serbs, and Germans), all of whom tended toward linguistic and cultural autonomy. And at the turn of the twentieth century, nationalist and separatist feelings among all these groups—the Magyars, the Slovaks, the Serbs, the Germans—had begun to grow.[4]

As Eva Striker approached school age, Hungary experienced mounting waves of political and social crisis, driven largely by these internal ethnic tensions. In 1912, the Social Democratic Party organized major demonstrations and a general strike; the state police killed six participants, wounded nearly two hundred, and arrested three hundred. That year the Striker family left Budapest for Vienna. They would stay there through World War I, the death of Franz Joseph, and the full disintegration of the Austro-Hungarian Empire.[5]

The Polanyi Strikers returned to Budapest in 1918, but their old life was gone. Eva's father sold his factory and entered a series of unprofitable ventures. The family took heart when the new liberal bourgeois government of the Hungarian Democratic Republic (1918–1919) took power; Eva's mother, Laura, mounted a campaign for a parliamentary seat. But then the new government collapsed, the election never took place, and the short-lived communist Hungarian Soviet Republic instituted an extremist regime involving repressive violence against its opposition. Within six months, that government, too, had collapsed, this time felled by an anti-Semitic, anticommunist right-wing coup.[6]

The family's peaceful social and political world had fractured. Eva's uncles Michael and Karl emigrated to the United States; so did many others in the family's circle. The Polanyi Strikers remained in Budapest, their circumstances diminished. Eva's father experimented with ways to make the family more self-sufficient—he brought home cows, pigs, and other farm animals, hoping they might provide milk and meat—but the family didn't know what to do with them ("The pigs ran off and ate the grapes," Eva recalled). As for Eva herself, she decided to find a way to provide for herself independently in a world that felt unstable. She would not "starve in the garret," as she put it later, like most artists did.

Instead, she would learn a craft, and she would use that craft to find employment and support herself independently for the rest of her life. She would put her training in aesthetics, in other words, into the service of capitalism.[7]

Once, a young Hungarian person with the aspiration to learn a craft—presumably a young man—would have presented himself to a guild to be educated. Hungary was relatively slow to industrialize, and guilds dominated its economic life as late as the middle of the nineteenth century. The number of factory workers in Hungary in 1847 was around 23,400, whereas the number of guild workers and apprentices, around 78,000, was more than three times that many. The prototypical guild dictated the terms of a craft and provided support for its members. It enabled a close-knit group of artisans to serve and protect their own collective interests. It trained apprentices, conducted quality assurance, controlled pricing, and even provided some poverty relief and political education for its members. Our notional young male aspirant would have approached a guild to ask to be taken on as a trainee. Over time, he would have developed the skills, credentials, and protections that would enable him to practice his craft.[8]

Now, though, the guild system was on its way out. Throughout the 1800s, the new industrial interests taking hold in Europe had worn down its systems of feudal privileges and power. Guild codes were replaced, gradually, with laws; crafts and trades gave way, in many cases, to factory production. By 1923, Hungary's guilds were nearly extinct. But Eva Striker wanted to learn a craft, and she found one of the last guilds in Budapest: the Hungarian Guild of Chimney Sweepers, Oven Makers, Roof Tilers, Well Diggers, and

Potters. There, a potter named Jakob Karapancsik agreed to take her on as an apprentice.[9]

"Ladies didn't pot," she said later, "but my mother let me do it anyway." Karapancsik had a shop in the basement of his apartment house, in a working-class district of Budapest, where he made pitchers, pots, and tiles. Eva Striker dressed each day in waterproof pants, a bright orange vest, and a red head kerchief. She mashed the clay with her bare feet after it came in from the hillside, and she kneaded it to prepare it for throwing. She threw pots herself, and she applied glaze. She went from house to house with Karapancsik installing the tiled stoves that Hungarians used for domestic heating. She and Karapancsik's son watched the pottery kiln through the nights.[10]

When she finished her training, Striker was tested by and admitted to the guild, becoming at age eighteen the first female journeyman potter in the guild's history. She commandeered what had been a gardener's shed in her family's backyard and turned it into her pottery studio. There she began making pots: throwing them on a wheel, then firing them underground with pine logs. The product was a form of Hungarian folk art known as "black pottery." She sold her pots in the markets in Budapest.[11]

Striker's time as a craftsperson turned out to be brief. The Budapest pottery workshop Kispester-Granit was building the first mass-production pottery factory in Hungary, and the following year Striker visited it; she asked so many questions that the proprietor offered her a job. And at the Kispester factory, Striker's work changed. She shifted from crafting objects for individual use to making prototypes to be used for mass production. Having transitioned from art to craft, she was now transitioning again into industry.

It was an era when many artists in recently industrialized societies followed that same trajectory: from art for art's sake, at least ostensibly, to art for hire in the service of industrial mass manufacturing. (Some took a pit stop, as Striker did, in craft.) And what industrialists hired these people to do was, for the most part, what we might call "beautification." They wanted a decorative sheen to differentiate their manufactured products from the growing competition. To be sure, the artists they hired often ended up doing much more than this: what Eva Striker did at Kispester-Granit, for instance—making prototypes that would be copied in molds for mass production—involved not just beautification but planning for everything from aesthetics to materials to manufacturing. The "design" Striker did there, in other words, seems in retrospect to have included *problem solving* and attending to *function*, two concepts that later would become strongly associated with the idea of design. But beauty, and beauty alone, was what her generation of artists was originally hired into industry to deliver.

By the early twentieth century, the flow of visual artists into industry had begun to accelerate, and fast. When a *Collier's Weekly* reporter asked Henry Ford, in 1914, "Do you care for art?" Ford responded that he "wouldn't give five cents for all the art in the world." Likewise, Ford put little stock in beauty and beautification; his company made just one model; he boasted that any customer could have one painted "any colour that he wants[,] so long as it is black." That same year Ford spoke to *Colliers*, though, *Colliers* itself was running an advertisement for cars from Packard, a competitor to Ford, reading "Beauty is a human necessity." The words sat alongside a picture of an elegant cab-sided limousine; it looked like something a person would want to buy, and people did.

Between 1924 and 1930, the aesthetically sophisticated Packard became the top-selling luxury automobile brand. Meanwhile, the upstart General Motors—which had also invested in visual styling—overtook Ford in the mid-priced market.[12]

By the 1920s, the idea that hiring artists could be a major differentiator for a manufacturer had become mainstream. In 1927, the American advertising executive Earnest Elmo Calkins published in the *Atlantic Monthly* an essay titled "Beauty: The New Business Tool." Calkins told a story of human progress. "We passed from the hand to the machine, we enjoyed our era of triumph of the machine, we acquired wealth," he wrote. And then, he continued, "we began to miss something in our cheap but ugly products. Efficiency was not enough. The machine did not satisfy the soul." The answer was to introduce beauty into consumer objects of all kinds, from radios to automobiles to kitchens. "Beauty is the natural and logical next step," Calkins wrote. "It is in the air."[13]

What these artists were called—what their job titles were, how they referred to themselves—is, on one level, irrelevant: they are the beginning of the story of the modern idea of "design," in that their work became the foundation of the discursive universe of concepts now known by that term. Starting early in the twentieth century they were indeed called, sometimes, "designers." The word was an import from the visual arts in which most were trained, which were then known as the "arts of design." That phrase comes from sixteenth-century Italy. The Renaissance art theorist Giorgio Vasari wrote with highest admiration about the practice of sketching and visual outlining that often preceded visual art; he called that practice *disegno*, and he referred to the arts that began in *disegno* (architecture or painting or sculpture) as the "arts of design." When industrialists began to hire the practitioners of those "arts of design," they referred to those practitioners either as "industrial artists" or as "designers."[14]

Today, we often think of "design" as something visual. This is because it began in visual art. But given that it so quickly became more than that, why do most people still think of design as beautification? And why are so many designers themselves still legitimately obsessed with beauty?

●◐

Eva Striker spent the end of the 1920s as a designer in Germany. She worked in the southern Black Forest region, as the sole designer for a mass producer of domestic goods called Schramberger Majolikafabrik, and then in Berlin, as a freelancer for Germany's second-largest maker of ceramics. Her job for that second company, Christian Carstens KG, was exclusively to prototype objects for mass production, both by sculpting the models herself and by sketching and drafting. In the latter cases, a professional modeler would use Striker's sketches and drawings to create formal three-dimensional prototypes. She came to collaborate so closely with her primary modeler, the redheaded Hermann Fuhlbrügge—whose home base was seven hours away at the Carstens factory in Hirschau—that eventually she rented a room for him in the apartment building where she lived so that they could work together without needless travel.[15]

As she established herself as a designer, the style of Striker's work was changing. Her earliest products, from that preindustrial pottery shed behind the Striker family home, look like traditional European stoneware, decorated with flowers painted in rough strokes or with festive dots or stripes. (She had been influenced at the time by the work of other well-known potteries that were themselves influenced by folk traditions and the Arts and Crafts movement.) Then, as she progressed through her earlier roles in industry, her designs became more geometric, more angular. She seems to have been influenced more and more, during this period, by the emergent "modern movement": the rise, in the decorative arts, of a new vision and style that rejected nineteenth-century ornament and eclecticism and instead embraced simplicity, order, and machine production.[16]

Later, Striker would describe the modern movement—by then called "modernism"—as a fundamentally *negative* crusade. Modernism was known by then for its social optimism, its evangelical revolutionary zeal. And yet, she observed, modernist manifestos seemed to want nothing so much as a "violent break from the past." Its practitioners embraced strictly geometric forms not for their own sake but because they rejected ornament and romance. They loved the new not for its new ideas or aesthetics but because they opposed the old. Striker saw modernism's dictums as rigid, and she saw its principles as reactionary. They made her feel constrained.

At first, though, she found much in modernism to admire. She admired the Deutscher Werkbund—the German association of artists, architects, and industrialists who sought to build connections between craftwork and machine production and advocated for quality and vernacular style—and read *Die Form*, the Werkbund's monthly magazine. She held in high regard Ludwig Mies van der Rohe's Barcelona Chair, as well as Marcel Breuer's "esoteric interiors," as she described them, "where lovely furniture seemed to float in shadowless space." With her mother, she traveled to Paris to see the 1925 International Exposition of Modern Industrial and Decorative Arts, where she admired the "festive, holier-than-thou simplicity" of Le Corbusier's model home Pavillon de l'Ésprit Nouveau. The "pure, simple lines of Le Corbusier's construction," she remembered later, "seemed so untouched, clean, and elegant that I felt I had entered a realm beyond my everyday untidy ways."[17]

Striker's divergence from modernist orthodoxy can be traced through the ceramics she made. Her early designs for Schramberger are relatively geometric, hewing close to what she would later call her early "compass-and-ruler aesthetic": the lines of an elegant brandy service, for instance, are either perfectly round or perfectly straight, and the service is decorated with Mondrian-esque black lines and color blocks. ("I played with geometry," she said later, "because this was the fashion.") But as Striker designed in Berlin, for Carstens, her work began to look curiously organic. For its early marks of this turn, consider her 1932 "T" tea service (*Kugelservice*), each piece perfectly round but for the handles, which are shapely little ears. Still more elegant is her "S" tea service, its pitchers

Eva Zeisel, *Kugelservice* (for Christian Carstens KG), 1930. Porcelain. Photo by Brent C. Brolin.

swelling outward not once but twice, at the hips and the shoulders, while broad, ribbonlike handles arch over the gentle waists at their midsections.[18]

Striker also began to insist, in her writing and speaking—as well as in the objects she made—on her points of difference from modernist orthodoxy. She associated modernism with clean minimalism, dogma, and—above all—function prioritized over pleasure. When the journal *Die Schaulade* asked her, in 1931, for an essay on contemporary design, she distanced herself from exactly these principles. Of course, she wrote, "one must ask what the practical use of the object will be," as modernism dictates. But such basic functionalism should be table stakes, the place good design started from rather than where it ended. No, great designers should aspire to something higher than just making things work better, Striker wrote. "We must make soul contact with our public."[19]

● ♥

When Eva Striker wasn't working, her Berlin was a gay and glamorous world. She and her brother had rented a huge, white-walled, high-ceilinged, light-filled apartment and studio at Tauentzienstrasse 8, a five-minute walk from that famous artists' and bohemians' gathering place called the Romanisches Café. At the café she socialized with other progressive and leftist intellectuals, often inviting them home for house parties with as many as one hundred people spilling out the doors and windows. She conducted brief romances with other politically engaged artists and scholars, including with each of the two men she would later marry. Berlin was "buzzing with contradictions," she felt: "Science, design, politics, starving mothers and children, the fat bourgeois with his cigar, the drab, impoverished, declasse officeholders and pensioners hiding their poverty and resentments, the brutal, ugly paintings of the German Expressionists, the sugar-white modern architecture that was beginning to proliferate, and high unemployment." It was a city "obsessed with modernity and urgency."[20]

It was, she remembered later, "the most elegant, the only elegant, time of my life." And yet she also felt a certain bleakness in the air in Europe, an atmosphere of despair and disgust. Berlin in particular was becoming "more and more politically complicated and jittery": even before Wall Street crashed in October 1929, Germany was struggling under hyperinflation and widespread unemployment, and Joseph Goebbels had begun to rally Berliners in support of the Nazi Party. The future, both of design and of political life, seemed to be elsewhere.[21]

It made Eva curious about the country that was organizing itself in opposition to Europe and its principles: the Soviet Union. She knew something of Soviet art. She admired children's books and theater from the country and had read novels by Wassily Kandinsky and Vladimir Tatlin. She wasn't a Communist, but she was interested in Communist ideas and Communist energy. It all seemed to originate, she thought, "from a vigorous healthy source, an unknown, faraway country striving towards a utopia where justice would finally reign." And so she decided to "look behind the mountain to see for [her]self." She left Berlin in January 1932, at age twenty-five, for a visit to an old friend and lover, Alexander Weissberg, in the Soviet Ukrainian city of Kharkov.[22]

Although she'd arrived in the Soviet Union as a visitor, Striker quickly found work. As the country neared the end of its first five-year plan (1928–1932), its leaders were focused on rationalizing industrial production, including ceramics, and they were eager to recruit a young ceramicist as a "foreign specialist." Two weeks after leaving that high-ceilinged, white-walled Berlin flat, she recalled later, "I was traveling in traditional sleds, covered by a huge fur cape through the endless snow-covered steppes, with wolves howling in the distance," to visit and inspect factories in the rural locality of Baranovka for the Ukrainian Porcelain and Glass Trust. Soon she was designing prototypes for the dishware that the Soviet state would distribute to its citizens. Hermann Fuhlbrügge, her modeler from Berlin, joined her in Russia so that they could continue to collaborate. She moved full-time to Leningrad, where she worked in the "Artistic Laboratory" of the Lomonosov State Porcelain Factory, and then to Moscow.[23]

By 1935, Eva Striker had become art director of the State China and Glass Industries of the Russian Republic. In a photograph from this period, one journalist writes, "there is a group of males in suits, brows beetled, eyes staring, mouths drawn downward, chests thrown out—and Eva, a lithe, dark young woman in a simple dress, relaxed and companionable." An industrial designer in a rapidly industrializing country, she was in high demand. Her Soviet years would be some of the most productive of her life. She aimed to "rationalize" ceramic tablewares: to make them hygienic, cost-effective, sturdy, stackable in both kilns and cupboards, and easy to distribute. They would be mass-produced for a country of 160 million people, many of whom had never before owned a plate.[24]

Even with these functional mandates, Striker found ways to make her Soviet ceramics beautiful. Whereas previously she'd designed only earthenware ceramics, she now worked primarily in porcelain—a more difficult ceramic material, because it must be fired at such a high temperature as to come close to melting, but also a delicate and elegant medium. Some of her tablewares were painted to evoke the art deco and modern art movements; some were patterned with designs based on decorative Soviet peasant textiles; some were clean, white, and unpatterned. Striker's goal in every case, she would write later, was to marry modernism's clean lines to "sensuous, classic shapes," informed by history and by humanity.

･･

Eva Striker had cared about aesthetics from the beginning of her time as a designer. But "beauty" as such seems to have become the organizing principle in her life's work sometime around May 1936, when she was twenty-nine years old. One day that month, Striker arrived suddenly at what would be, "for a long time," "the end of my good life."[25]

It was 4 a.m. when the Soviet police arrived at the door to Striker's Moscow flat. Striker stood wide-eyed, in a green flannel housecoat, as the large group of policemen searched her letters and photographs. They seemed to be enjoying themselves. They paused on an enlarged snapshot of Striker herself lying on a beach, her eyes closed to the sun, utterly relaxed. She watched the officers smile suggestively at one another as they passed it between them. The photo looked like a mask, Striker thought: a mask of her own dead face.[26]

The officers put her in a car and drove her through Moscow to Butyrka prison, then transferred her to a train that took her to Kresty prison in Leningrad. (In the compartment of the transport train she caught a glimpse of her modeler, Fuhlbrügge, who had come with her to the Soviet Union from Berlin. He had also been arrested, and now his face was aflame with fury.) When they arrived, she was booked into a solitary-confinement cell. She would stay in prison for the next sixteen months. The charge, she would learn, was that she had plotted to kill Joseph Stalin.[27]

Prison was a crisis. At first Striker was in shock ("It had a great feeling of unreality. . . . I mean, I was a designer of china; I was not in the business of killing Stalin"). Then she felt tormented by the passage of time, the minutes' unbroken unmeasured mass. Sound, too, became a kind of torture: "In the emptiness of the cell, the slightest and quietest noise became mountain-high, gruesome, disturbing." It felt like a form of cruelty.[28]

Striker was sure she would be executed. Under the shadow of that seeming inevitability, the waiting was excruciating. The halls echoed with shouts and with the sounds of whipping. From a grid on the wall of the prison shower, Striker had learned how to knock on the walls to communicate with people in neighboring cells; she taught the knocking alphabet to her neighbor, and they conducted a slow, wry correspondence about prison life through the wall. But another neighbor, a former dentist, went crazy and began viciously biting her own hands. Striker herself felt a "gruesome, dumb depression." She remembered saying to herself, "I have closed my life. I have had a wonderful time, but I have nowhere to go from here."[29]

And yet she wanted to stay alive, and staying alive required a certain cast of mind. In more strategic moments, she felt that if she thought of her mother, or of her past self—"the skipping girl looking at the sun"—her heart would break. So she did mental gymnastics, trying to identify and to contemplate only those thoughts that would keep her alive. She could survive, she decided, only by entirely disregarding any hope of a future, as well as any memories of her happy past. She must live solely in the present.[30]

How to stay in the present? The one reliable way, she came to believe, was to meditate on beauty. "In me was all the power for beauty and dignity and strength," she wrote, and so "I sat down on my bench and started to think a beautiful thought." From there, she learned to turn her focus intentionally toward beauty. She might admire a spider web's ephemeral elegance, or inhale the scent of a lovely and fragrant pink soap obtained from a former cellmate. She might watch a ray of sun entering her cell and spending an hour moving slowly over the floor and wall. When she was with beauty, she felt—natural beauty, sensual material beauty, moral beauty—she was present. And so beauty was a way to stay alive.[31]

Years earlier, in 1929, when Striker lived in the south of Germany, her employer had sent her on a work trip to Paris to learn about trends in design. While there, she had looked up a friend from her kindergarten in Budapest: the writer Arthur Koestler. They'd become lovers. One night they'd eaten at an expensive restaurant, and at the end of the meal Koestler had abandoned Striker at the table while he drove around the city asking friends to lend him money to pay the bill. She had thought of marrying him. But then she'd moved to Berlin, ending their love affair as suddenly as it had begun. She and Koestler had remained correspondents, and Koestler had often visited her in Berlin, where she became, his biographer writes, "the chief catalyst" for Koestler's "lurch to the left."[32]

Koestler's misadventures during the Communist years that followed were documented in his now classic novel *Darkness at Noon* (1940), which is widely known to have been modeled on his own imprisonment and solitary confinement in 1937 by Francisco Franco's forces during the Spanish Civil War. Less known, though, is that *Darkness at Noon* also draws deeply on Eva Striker's experiences in her Soviet prison cells. Soon after Striker's release, she wrote to Koestler about the mental agony she had experienced, her belief that she was simply waiting to be killed, a false confession that she had made under duress, and her experiences knocking messages to her neighbors through the walls. Koestler was shocked to learn that she had been imprisoned—and then shocked by the overlap between her experiences at the hands of Communists and his own experiences at the hands of Fascists. Unable to reconcile Striker's revelations with his own (already strained) ideological convictions, he left the Communist Party. Then he wrote Striker's psychological anguish, and many of her specific experiences, into his bleak new novel of ideas about a party member in solitary confinement.[33]

Koestler's novel was published two years later to international acclaim. In the decades after her release, Eva Striker was largely silent about her time in prison, reluctant to revisit its emotional content and afraid that speaking about it publicly might still endanger her or her family. But *Darkness at Noon* contains the shadow of her torment.[34]

It's clear now that Eva Striker's arrest was a sham. She was caught up in the "Great Purge" (also called the "Great Terror"), Joseph Stalin's campaign between 1936 and 1938 to consolidate his power over the Soviet state and its Communist Party by purging the Soviet people of alleged enemies within, including the entire Bolshevik old guard and any politician or civilian who had criticized Stalin. A former colleague of Striker's from the Dulevo porcelain factory had pointed a finger at her, telling investigators that she had opposed Stalinist power, to escape his own punishment and perhaps execution for alleged treason. Eva Striker certainly never plotted to kill Joseph Stalin.[35]

But Striker's road out of prison was an odd and winding one. Additional charges were fabricated and brought against her. A young interrogator convinced her to sign the aforementioned false confession; when she realized what she had done, she tried to kill herself by cutting her wrists with a sharpened wire. When her suicide attempt failed, she retracted the confession. She was sent back into solitary confinement. Then, suddenly—in September 1937, after eighteen months' imprisonment—she was called from her cell and put on a train to Vienna. There, to her staggering surprise, she was released without explanation.[36]

Striker found herself in a collapsing Europe. Hungary had been Fascist since 1919; Italy, since 1922; Germany, since 1933. In March 1938, as the Nazis entered Austria, Eva Striker took one of the last trains out of Vienna for Switzerland. From Switzerland she traveled to England, where in July of that year she married an old acquaintance, Hans Zeisel, a Left Social Democrat with degrees in law and economics. (He would become an eminent lawyer and sociologist, known for pioneering quantitative legal work and scholarship on American juries.) In the fall of 1938, one year after Eva's release, she and Hans left Europe. Sponsored by a cousin of Eva's in Iowa, they sailed for New York.[37]

By Hans's count, between them Hans and Eva Zeisel lost thirty-eight relatives in the Holocaust. Meanwhile, safe in the United States—in a city full of other émigré artist-intellectuals from central Europe—Eva experienced a deep, debilitating depression. In her final six months in prison, she had experienced "the unappetizing image of [her] body as a soon-to-be rotting thing." Now, not rotting but living, at the dawn of the 1940s, she found herself exhausted. She felt "completely frigid." The arbitrariness of her own survival—the knowledge that "I from Cell No. 4 am out but people in Cell No. 2 and No. 3 are there"—haunted her. Feeling unable to care for herself, believing herself to have been "put too fast into daily life," she handed all decision making to Hans. "When I was asked a question, he answered," she remembered later. "I did anything I was told."[38]

She found her refuge in work. Arriving in New York in 1938, she and Hans had $64 between them. She'd been prepared to take work cleaning apartments, but on her way into the city she saw the facade of the New York Public Library on Fifth Avenue, and the next day she visited it. She pulled off the shelf copies of trade publications on industrial design, copied down names from their mastheads, and found addresses associated with the names. Then she visited each one, making the case that they recommend her to prospective employers.

Soon she received a commission, and then another, designing small items: giftware, a miniature tea set, a watch. She also found a job at Brooklyn's Pratt Institute teaching ceramics, which she treated not as a handcraft but as a variety of industrial design, teaching students to fashion not one-off items but prototypes for machine production. She arranged for her students to work in the factory of New Jersey's Bay Ridge Specialty Company, designing prototypes for the company and then learning from seeing their designs through production. It was a happy match. Pratt had just begun to develop courses in industrial design, a new academic subject. (The first known course in industrial design in the United States had been offered just five years before, in 1934, at the Carnegie Institute of Technology, now Carnegie Mellon University.)[39]

Zeisel's first child, Jean, was born in 1940. That same year, she held an exhibition of work by her Pratt ceramics students; among the attendees was the young modernist architect and designer Eliot Noyes, who had been named director of the new Department of Industrial Design at the Museum of Modern Art (MoMA). After the exhibition, Zeisel invited Noyes to a lecture on handicraft and mass production that she was giving to a meeting of the New York Society of Ceramic Arts. He attended. Soon after, he recommended her for a major commission with the MoMA and Castleton China. The idea was to design a line of dinnerware of excellent quality and peak design credentials. It should be both stylish enough to ignite consumer desire and highbrow enough for museum display.[40]

After four years of collaboration between Zeisel and her sponsors at the MoMA and Castleton, the Castleton "Museum" dinnerware collection was produced in 1946. It was a breakthrough. Zeisel had been given a mandate to design a formal dinner service for an institution, the MoMA, that was the country's foremost advocate of Bauhaus modernism: modernist geometry, modernist minimalism, modernist machine aesthetics. In response, she had created a white porcelain collection that broke all the modernist rules. Every shape was organic, curvilinear, seamless, and undulant, prioritizing nothing so much as its own beauty. The creamer swelled upward and inward, without separate handle or spout, as if it had grown that way. The ribbonlike teacup handles, *Art News of America* reported, conformed perfectly to the fingers. "I wanted to design a service of real elegance," Zeisel told the *New York Herald Tribune* that spring. She had transcended her

Eva Zeisel, Castleton "Museum" collection, 1946. Porcelain. Photo by Brent C. Brolin.

own earlier "compass and ruler era," as she put it, and found her calling in "lyrical" forms. She sought the "poetry of communicative line."[41]

The MoMA, that monument to high modernism, embraced the "Museum" collection, exhibiting it upon its release at a one-woman show, "New Shapes in Modern China: Designed by Eva Zeisel" (1946), the museum's first-ever exhibition of a solo female designer. Later, the MoMA included Zeisel alongside Le Corbusier and Mies van der Rohe in the museum's popular 1950–1955 "Good Design" exhibitions, through which curator Edgar Kaufmann Jr. aimed to educate the public on the value of high-quality industrial design. Meanwhile, "Museum" was also finding success—despite the high prices at which Castleton was retailing it—on the mass market. It remained in production for almost forty years, until the late 1970s. In 1959, *Fortune* magazine published a list titled "The 100 Best Designed Products"; the "Museum" collection was number fifty-three.[42]

"Museum" was a triumph of Zeisel's version of the beautiful. And it signaled the beginning of what would be her lifelong commitment to beauty as a kind of organic biomorphism. Later in the 1940s Zeisel designed the "Town and Country" set for Red Wing Pottery, which had asked her to channel a "Greenwich Village vibe." This collection, too, takes organic forms, but it feels more immediately familiar and connective than her more formal "Museum" collection. Similarly, "Tomorrow's Classic" (1952), her most commercially successful collection (its sponsor Hall China Company advertised it as "America's fastest-selling modern dinnerware"), seemed designed to reach out to the user and connect. In New York City it was stocked in all the leading department stores: Macy's, B. Altman, Gimbels.[43]

The longer she worked as an industrial designer, the more confident Zeisel became about her commitment to what she described as "the playful search for beauty"—and the more ardent became her self-distancing from high modernism. She described modernism variously as "untouched," "soulless," "cold," "highfalutin," "dictatorial," and "elitist," one colleague and friend remembered. She felt modernism offered neither "amusement nor beauty." She recoiled from what she saw as its rejection of history, its insistence that design could be "rationalized," its insistence on the extinction of style and ornament. And most of all, she loathed "the ridiculous idea that form followed function."[44]

What instead? Beauty, yes—but what did that mean? For Zeisel, one thing it meant was organicism: the use of natural rhythms and patterns, from rounded edges and undulating curves to motifs resembling piles of rocks, to try to promote harmony between natural and human-made elements. In her dedication to organic forms, Zeisel shares territory with her contemporary Alvar Aalto, the Finnish architect who brought sensitivity to natural materials, attention to landscape and light, and an organic visual vocabulary (topographic shapes, radiating fans, weathered surfaces) to Scandinavian architecture. Frank Lloyd Wright, Charles and Ray Eames, and Russel Wright are also known for work that feels closer to nature than that of more rational modernists. As for Zeisel, she helped bring to ceramics in particular, as the curator Paola Antonelli later told the *New York Times*, the "organicism and elegance and fluidity that we expect of ceramics today," in particular by inventing new forms for a wide range of ceramic objects with popular appeal and accessibility. "It's easy to do something stunning that stays in a collector's cabinet," Antonelli said. "But her designs reached people at the table, where they gather."[45]

But there was an element of Zeisel's conception of beauty that went beyond organicism—one to which Antonelli's remarks also speak, if only implicitly. For Zeisel, beauty was about *connection*. She had bridled at high modernism's rules and principles because she felt they "silenc[ed] communication between the maker of things and his public." She believed, on the contrary, that beautiful things could facilitate "soul contact" between their creators and their users. It was an almost literal principle, this idea of "soul contact," and Zeisel emphasized the importance of her designs' "touchability" by their users. Elsewhere, she emphasized that what facilitated soul contact was beauty itself: "I tried to design for my audience. . . . I thought that my feeling of what was beautiful was a tie between us."[46]

I come closer to understanding Zeisel's intentions when I hold her work in my hands. Her 1983 "Granit" collection was reproduced in 2009 by Design Within Reach. Its pieces

Eva Zeisel, "Town and Country" tableware (for Red Wing Pottery, Red Wing, Minnesota), 1945–1946. Earthenware, cast. Photo by Brent C. Brolin.

feel soft and smooth, almost anatomical; I find myself stroking the pitchers' little backs, running my fingers over the rims of the teacups, with a furtive intimacy. It isn't much of a reach to think their designer wanted to make "soul contact" through their shapes. Or take her "Town and Country" line, which became popular enough to help visually define an era in American ceramics. All of its pieces have a rounded, organic, connective kind of beauty; some of them are so anthropomorphic as to make almost literal the idea of connection through line and form and color. The nestled salt and pepper shakers, called the "Shmoos," are like mother and child, their cocked heads mutually curious and mutually assured of their need to touch.

Zeisel's career would rise and fall and rise again through the decades that followed. She worked seven days a week until she died, at age 105, in 2011. In 1987, interviewing Zeisel for a *New Yorker* profile, writer Suzannah Lessard first perceived the eighty-one-year-old ceramicist as "a dignified, foreign-seeming person sitting upright in a black dress, white hair brushed back from a high forehead." Within a few minutes, though, Lessard saw Zeisel differently: both playful and absolutely authoritative, Zeisel "had acquired an uninhibited, lounging physicality and confident openness that left me with the afterimage of a near-naked, pipe-smoking Mama-chief of an island tribe."[47]

She had never become bitter toward the Russian people, or even deeply opposed to the Soviet Union. Until the fall of the USSR, she never spoke publicly of her time in prison. She remained afraid of retribution, but she also felt little acrimony. Unlike her friend Arthur Koestler or her uncle Michael Polanyi, she never became stridently opposed to communism; she was not an anti-Communist at all, she told a reporter who profiled her in the late 1980s, but a "former non-Communist." She understood her traumatic imprisonment, in the reporter's gloss, as "a painful revelation not about systems of government but about a paradox in human nature—the capacity of ordinary, decent human beings to participate in atrocities."[48]

Above all, she hoped passionately that American and European anticommunism would not lead to more war. She wrote many pleading letters urging Koestler, Polanyi, and other close contacts to reconsider both their strident anticommunism and the interventionism that so often came with it. Russia, she argued in her letters, "was a huge, backward, Oriental country," and it made "no sense to judge it by Western standards." She feared that US intervention to try to halt or reverse Soviet expansion would be disastrous, leading to escalation and the use of the atom bomb. Once Koestler's *Darkness at Noon* became widely read as an interventionist text, Zeisel asked him not to use her name in connection with it, despite the fact that her own experiences had inspired it. Ultimately they disagreed so strenuously on the topic that they stopped speaking to one another for several decades.[49]

Over the course of the twentieth century, as functionalist modernism became the dominant influence on global design aesthetics and values, Zeisel's emphasis on beauty went out of fashion. "Beauty" came to seem trivial or even counterrevolutionary as a focus of designers' attention. "I am surprised how rarely we speak about beauty nowadays," Zeisel told an interviewer in the early 1980s. "The word 'beauty' is used self-consciously if at all." But Zeisel remained committed to beauty, and to creating beauty with design, through the end of her career. She continued to insist that beauty connected people. "Things speak to us," she wrote in 2004. "They talk to us through their shapes, contours, color, weight, temperature, surface, sound, and most clearly, their associations." Beautiful objects transported their users out of time with them, inviting them to think neither of past nor future, to simply experience pleasure.[50]

In 1982, the Hungarian government awarded Zeisel the "Order of the Star," the highest honor the country can give to a noncitizen who is not a head of state, for "a lifetime of achievement, a life of merit." In 1984, the Brooklyn Museum mounted a retrospective exhibition of her pioneering life's work, "Eva Zeisel: Designer for Industry," containing 154 items of tableware and culminating in the 1946 Castleton "Museum" collection, which the curators described as "one of the most beautiful and influential achievements of modern design." Zeisel insisted that she "couldn't care less" about the exhibition. She was deeply proud, though, of the letters she had received over the years from her customers and other admirers. The letters tended to focus on the writers' affective relationships to the objects Zeisel had designed. "The word 'love' appears over and over in these letters," she said. "It's the 'love' that I am so proud of."[51]

Eva Zeisel's younger uncle, the economic anthropologist Karl Polanyi, wrote *The Great Transformation* in Vermont in the early 1940s. It is one of the major works of twentieth-century political economy. Like his brother Michael and much of the rest of the Polanyi family—including Eva Zeisel herself, with whom he was close—Karl was in exile from Hungary, which had joined the Axis powers in November 1940. He wrote *The Great Transformation* in part to try to understand why the peace of the nineteenth century had exploded into the world wars and economic catastrophe of the twentieth. These paroxysms had destroyed the milieu of his and Eva's childhoods and had spun the Polanyi family centrifugally across the globe. Polanyi wrote to explain to himself the disintegration of their world.

He found his explanation in the rise of "market society" and the social dislocations it had caused. Markets themselves were an old phenomenon, as he saw things; they weren't the problem. They could be brief, bounded, harmless events, a gathering every Saturday in the town square. But with the Industrial Revolution, Western civilization had embraced the idea that markets should be ever-present and self-regulating. Nation-states had facilitated the rise of these unbounded markets, and economies and cultures had risen around them. This was what Polanyi meant to describe with the phrase "market society." He believed it had led, over time, to the implosion of European and Asian and American life.[52]

So *The Great Transformation* was a historical explanation. But it was also a kind of elegy: an elegy for human life as it had been organized, to Polanyi's mind, before the markets took over. "Economics" is, at its Greek root (οἰκονομικός), the science of "household management," and, in Polanyi's account, there had been highly effective ways of doing such management before markets became dominant. People had traded things according to principles of reciprocity, Polanyi wrote; they'd shared resources and made sure their neighbors were fed. A person acted not "so as to safeguard his individual interest in the possession of material goods" but "to safeguard his social standing, his social claims, his social assets." People's lives had been organized not by the market but by custom, community, and social life. *Oikonomikos* had been *embedded* within the social fabric. Now nation-states had torn *oikonomikos* apart from that fabric, and the fabric had been left in tatters.[53]

Eva Zeisel was less engaged than Karl Polanyi as a critic of capitalism. But she, too, had a strong historical consciousness, and she, too, was nostalgic for times and places when the collective interest took precedence over individual gain. She had become a potter by seeking out a guild; "under the guild system," Karl Polanyi wrote, "as under every other economic system in history, the motives and circumstances of productive activities were embedded in the general organization of society." She had gone to Russia hoping to find people acting genuinely in the collective interest, and her memories of Russia were indeed of a kind and generous people who treated their neighbors with equanimity and patience. She remembered the famine of 1933 in Ukraine, for instance, but from that time she recalled more vividly "the hopeful, beautiful dreams of utopia." On a bus around the time of the famine, she recalled, some peasant women had seen the red silk lining of her own jacket, and she heard one exclaim, with genuine delight, "Look at what sumptuous material we already have!" She never forgot the woman's use of "we."[54]

And Zeisel was never a wholehearted enthusiast of capitalism. Despite having what we might describe as an entrepreneurial nature—and despite her extensive work designing for mass production—she was not primarily a businesswoman, regarding her dishes not as commodities so much as "a collection of beloved little pets." She was as interested in history as in design or craft, and she stopped designing for decades in the middle of the twentieth century when the history taking place around her came to feel more urgent (in "the years of the peace marches and Martin Luther King," she said, "modern design somehow ceased to be interesting or relevant"). And she was unconvinced, as a historical thinker, that contemporary capitalism had enabled greater autonomy and creativity than what came before it. Like Karl Polanyi, with whom she was raised, she thought market society had produced a coldness, an absence of that generosity she associated with Russia. Modernist machine aesthetics was the apotheosis of this phenomenon: cold, calculated, without warmth or connection. Market society was perhaps better than the alternatives, but she regarded it with no particular admiration.[55]

Beauty, though, could make a difference. By re-embedding the objects of industry and commerce into social life—by making those objects, as Zeisel saw it, into social subjects— beauty might be able to reverse some of that coldness, some of the disintegration that market society had wrought. Recall her emphasis on *connection* through her objects; her investment in their touchability; her desire to enable "communication between the maker of things and his public." Recall her ideal of "soul contact": "I tried to design for my audience. . . . I thought that my feeling of what was beautiful was a tie between us." Beauty, she believed, created a connection between an object's designer and its user, and in so doing it might begin to repair the fabric that capitalism had torn apart.[56]

It is itself a beautiful idea—a genuinely utopian idea—if not a particularly convincing one. On the one hand, who doesn't want to heal the rift between economic and social life under capitalism? On the other, though, who really believes that holding a beautiful pitcher—whether Zeisel designed it for Sears, or for Design Within Reach, or for Crate & Barrel, or for the Museum of Modern Art—will make the difference? What we need is not symbolic reintegration but structural change—perhaps starting with the reintegration of markets into social life and the reorganization of our economy around the impulse Polanyi called "redistribution." But that kind of transformation requires more than just beauty. It would mean throwing a wrench in the gears.

Chapter 2

FUNCTION

Walter Dorwin Teague went to New York in 1903, at the age of nineteen, because he wanted to make things beautiful. He wanted to paint or draw, and he wanted to make money by doing it for business. The term people used for this, in those days, was "industrial artist."[1]

Teague had come from Indiana. His father was a circuit-riding Methodist minister: an itinerant preacher who rode horseback around a radius of "unsettled," unchurched frontier. Walter was bookish and was not interested in being a frontiersman. As a teenager, he had read an architecture book in the library, admired its illustrations, and begun dreaming of drawing and painting himself. Now he stepped off the train in Manhattan with $35 in his pocket, moved into the YMCA, got a job checking hats, and enrolled in a school on West 57th Street called the Art Students League of New York.[2]

He would take night classes there for five years: courses with names like "Portrait," "Antique," "Life," "Anatomy," "Illustration & Composition," "Perspective." During the days, he used his art skills to make money. From hat checker, he became sign painter. Then he was an illustrator for a mail-order catalog, drawing shoes and neckties. Then, in a breakthrough, he was hired as an illustrator for an advertising agency.[3]

By 1912, when he was twenty-seven, Walter Teague was operating a small "industrial art" agency of his own. His business was drawing ornamental borders around advertisements. Advertising was a growth industry at the time; advertisements were just becoming, as the historian T. J. Jackson Lears has put it, "part of the iconography of everyday life." Teague's border drawings were ornate, almost baroque. For Arrow Collars or Murad Turkish Cigarettes or Phoenix Hosiery, he would draw intricate designs with flowers curling through a trellis, or a pair of Romanesque emperors with some vegetation spilling out of a horn. They were just pen-and-ink drawings encircling advertisements, but they were beautiful enough to make those advertisements seem highbrow. They made people feel good about buying things.[4]

In the early twentieth century, English-speakers used the word "design," whether noun or verb, in a few different ways. The word had a generic meaning: it referred to planning something out, like God was supposed to have done with the Earth or like an engineer or a craftsperson did with their works. It also had some specific meanings. It could refer to any visual art, like painting and sculpture, that began with

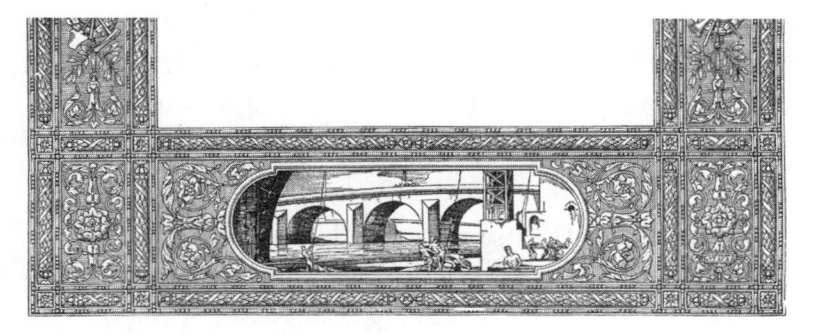

Walter Dorwin Teague, untitled borders (clients unknown), 1919, 1920, 1920. Pen and ink on paper. Public domain.

drawing. Or, emergently, it could refer to a newer practice: using artistic skills to add polish to industrial products.[5]

When he arrived in New York City, Teague became a practitioner of design in both these more specific senses. He went to school to learn design as visual art: drawing, sculpture, painting. But as he moved into business contexts, he began practicing design as the application of his visual art skills to enhance the products of industry.[6]

He could have made a whole career doing it. He was a success. New York City advertising men began referring to decorations surrounding advertisements as "Teague borders," whether Teague had designed them or not. He opened offices on Madison Avenue. In 1925, he was invited to give a talk at the Upper East Side's prestigious Art Directors Club of New York; he delivered a lengthy paean to ornament, of all kinds, in art and design. Ornament, he proclaimed, was both the foundational element of design and the aspect that brought originality to any particular work. It was the most democratic form of art expression: "It rises almost to the dignity of a human instinct. . . . Everything we make and everything we use[,] we adorn."[7]

Business was booming, and life was affordable. By 1929, when Teague was forty, the productive capacity of the US economy was at an all-time high. National income had shot up—even accounting for inflation—over the first three decades of the century, and workers were taking home the highest wages in US history, all while working less than they had when the century started. Teague found himself living with his wife, two sons, and a daughter in a five-bedroom house with a sun porch in the idyllic planned neighborhood of Forest Hills Gardens, Queens. There were curving streets— the neighborhood's landscape architect had been Frederick Law Olmstead—and a tennis club within walking distance. The Teagues' living room was decorated with French and English antiques. In the front hall, a player piano performed classics and ragtime by itself.[8]

And yet it wasn't enough. Teague had a sense that what he was doing—his now famous "Teague borders"—was not the future of industry. And so in 1926, at forty-two, Walter Dorwin Teague put his clients on ice and shut down his office. He left his family behind, and he boarded a steamship to Europe.

⬛⬤

There was something happening in the European art world that wasn't happening in the United States. The French government had just held an exposition in Paris—the same 1925 exhibition that the young Eva Striker and her mother had attended, where Eva had admired a Le Corbusier building's "festive, holier-than-thou simplicity." The exposition had been a spectacle. European art, glass, jewelry, furniture, and architecture were submitted to the world's gaze. The purpose, the organizers said, was to display and celebrate "the new modern style."[9]

It was also meant to honor the Allied countries of World War I, so the organizers had offered the United States a prime spot. But Secretary of Commerce Herbert Hoover had declined the invitation. The organizers had asked participating countries to contribute works of decorative or industrial art that showed "new inspiration and real originality"— rather than "reproductions, imitations, and counterfeits of ancient styles." Hoover wrote, in response to the invitation, that he had consulted American art experts, but to no avail: the experts felt their country couldn't meet the criteria. Americans didn't do "new" or "original," at the moment, in the arts or decorative objects. "Modern" design did not exist in the United States.[10]

This turned out to be an embarrassment. Sixteen million people attended the exhibition in 1925. The *New York Times* covered it weekly, sometimes daily. Critics called it groundbreaking. It launched the luxurious but geometric new

French art deco, then called *le style moderne*, to international renown. It also opened the door to other early modernisms: a clean, geometric Bauhaus modernism, a warm and organic Scandinavian modernism, and the many other global modernisms that they inspired.[11]

Hoover sent a formal delegation to report back, but his gesture seemed paltry. The exhibition was a major global spectacle, and the American absence seemed bizarre and conspicuous. Henry Creange, US commissioner for the Department of Commerce, spoke uneasily at an exhibition lunch: "Americans have not realized the immense strides designers and producers have made over here." He urged Americans to come to Paris to "study the possibilities" and to "take some fresh inspiration back." American steamship travel to Europe that summer broke records.[12]

Walter Teague didn't make it to the exhibition itself, but by summer of the following year, 1926, he was on his way to France. His steamship travel across the Atlantic likely took about five days. In Paris, he visited buildings by the designer whose work had most electrified exposition visitors: the young Swiss architect and painter Le Corbusier. Le Corbusier's exposition building, Pavillon de l'Ésprit Nouveau—made in collaboration with his cousin (and fellow Swiss architect) Pierre Jeanneret—was a stark modern house with a tree through the roof. It had seemed so unconventional, so nearly feral, that the exposition organizers had at first tried to contain it with a fence. Le Corbusier's permanent structures in Paris included the Maison Ozenfant (1922), a reinforced-concrete house and studio designed for a collaborator and friend, and the Maison La Roche (1923–1925), a disorienting cubist villa and gallery designed for a Swiss banker and collector. Teague stood in front of structures like these—lifted on Le Corbusier's slim signature *pilotis* (stilts), using strip windows or large pane glass to convey the feeling of weightlessness—in wonder. He was seeing, he felt, a new style, enabled by new ways of making and building, with a new purpose. Later, he read Le Corbusier's manifesto, *Vers une architecture* (1923; translated in 1927 as *Towards a New Architecture*), describing a house as "a machine for living in," and found it mind-altering in its vision of how to organize society for the machine age. Le Corbusier, he wrote, was "a major prophet."[13]

Le Corbusier, Maison Ozenfant (for Amédée Ozenfant), Paris, France, 1922. Glass, concrete, steel. © F.L.C. / ADAGP, Paris / Artists Rights Society (ARS), New York 2024.

Teague went on to Italy, where he was stopped in his tracks again by an exhibition of the work of Walter Gropius, the German architect, and Gropius's art school, the Bauhaus, then based in Dessau. When Teague came home to New York, he began his own research into what these people were doing. He had brought home armfuls of French design magazines—*Mobilier et Décoration*, *Art et Industrie*—and catalogs and booklets on the Bauhaus and its predecessor, the Deutscher Werkbund. Now he compiled a huge folio of clippings documenting the new "modern" ways of making: a photo of construction workers climbing the structural beams of a skyscraper-in-progress, illustrations of modern home interiors, art nouveau *New Yorker* ads for Parisian perfumers, stark black-and-yellow German book covers, a photo of the Eiffel Tower.[14]

The style of Teague's two-room agency office, on Madison Avenue and 36th Street, was "period French." (He had long harbored, as one journalist had put it, a deep "sympathy for classical forms.") Now he had the office's interior torn out. He would remake it in the new, simple, modern style: clean straight lines, lacquered white walls, tubular chairs. Then he would restart his career. Beginning that fall, there would be no more ornamental borders. The new way was about removing ornament, not adding it. But what instead? What was a *modern* industrial artist, a modern designer—in 1926, in America—supposed to do?[15]

"Modernism" is as slippery a concept in design as in any other context. It's easiest to cognize as a recognizable visual architectural style: flat roofs, strip windows, stilts (those aforementioned *pilotis*) that lift buildings off the ground. The architecture critic Sarah Goldhagen has noted that visual style is what linguists and philosophers have called a "basic-level category": a concept that naturally evokes mental images rather than something more abstract (a "superordinate category"). "Vegetable" is a basic-level category; "nutrition" is superordinate. Asked to imagine nutrition, we're likely to picture a vegetable; asked to imagine modernism, we tend to picture a style. We know it's more complicated than all that, but we still think first of the *pilotis*.[16]

European design modernism arrived in the United States, accordingly, in the form of images of modernist style. It came on the fronts of postcards home from those who visited the 1925 Paris exhibition. It came in black-and-white architecture books like Gropius's *Internationale Architektur* (1925), untranslated but visually legible, featuring images of Peter Behrens's AEG assembly hall in Neubabelsberg (1912), of J. J. P. Oud's clean and balanced Hoek van Holland housing blocks in Rotterdam (1924–1927), of Mies van der Rohe's soaring glass office towers in Berlin (1921). It arrived in tourists' drawings of the early villas (1922–1927) of Le Corbusier, with their *pilotis* and flat roofs and strip windows.[17]

But the modernism that came to the United States wasn't only a style. It was also a set of ideas. "Modern" architecture and industrial art, its practitioners and critics proposed, should take advantage of and respond to new methods of construction. It should reject historical reminiscence or imitation, focusing solely on needs and experiences in the present. It should respond to the ways that the machine, that new invention, was impacting human life and culture. And it should prioritize function over form. As Louis Mumford put it in his 1928 essay "Towards a Rational Modernism," modernism was "the emphasis of function and structure." Its canon was "simplicity and directness." The idea that modernism meant "living in glass houses and sitting in steel chairs" or "producing couches of tricky shapes and cabinets of oddly matched woods" gave the lie to the "essential canon" of respecting and prioritizing the function that the house or the object was meant to serve.[18]

All of these modernist ideas struck Walter Teague as revelations. He loved the idea of embracing and responding to the rise of the machine, both as the icon of the age and as the mechanism that would produce his designs. (Indeed, he felt such response was inevitable; "the forms which fit our needs and our machines," he would predict early in the 1930s, would arise inevitably from "the preferences and prejudices of this age.") But that final idea about *function*—the idea that modern design must focus less on whether something was beautiful than on how it worked for the people who would use it—was the one that would change Teague's life.[19]

Attending to the exigencies of function wasn't a wholly new idea. The Roman architect and engineer Vitruvius wrote in *De architectura* around 25 BCE that builders must aim for "firmitas, utilitas, venustas" (firmness or structural stability, spatial adequacy or utility, and, finally, beauty); *firmitas* and *utilitas* can be read together as something like "function," to which the triad gives primacy over aesthetics. The German architect Heinrich Hubsch wrote in 1828 that buildings should be organized not around "unnecessary adjuncts" ("flutings," "leaf work on capitals") but around structural fundamentals. The Boston-born sculptor Horatio Greenough, a professor at the Academy of Fine Arts in Florence, in the 1840s and 1850s criticized the "false beauty" of "embellishment" and praised the design and construction of sailing ships, which took their form, he believed, in direct response to the functional needs of people at sea. The French architect and archaeologist Eugène-Emmanuel Viollet-le-Duc wrote in the 1860s that "purely artistic questions," like decorative styling, must be considered secondary to "fulfill[ing] exactly and simply the conditions imposed by need."[20]

These ideas had been making their way to the United States in dribs and drabs for a long time. Greenough's critique of embellishment and romance of the sailing ship inspired both Ralph Waldo Emerson and Walt Whitman—contributing to their nascent ideas about utilitarian American aesthetics—and, through Emerson and Whitman, a generation of Americans compelled by transcendentalism and pragmatism. The architect Louis Sullivan's belief that "form ever follows function," articulated in his 1896 essay "The Tall Office Building Artistically Considered," influenced the young Frank Lloyd Wright's turn toward organicism, which Wright embraced out of enthusiasm for nature's perfect selection of the forms most suited to organisms' vital functions. Later, what would become the bible of modern architecture, Le Corbusier's crisp and passionate polemic *Vers une architecture*, found its way into the hands of designers from Walter Teague himself to the young Eliot Noyes, who would go on to revolutionize design for IBM. *Vers une architecture* champions what has been called a "functionalist" ethic: the idea that a building or object should be judged in large part by how it functions, how it uses its materials to do its job for its occupants or other users. Beauty is also important to Le Corbusier—a building becomes "architecture," he writes, only when it "touch[es] my heart"—but performing its function well is a necessary precondition.[21]

It wasn't until Walter Gropius started the Bauhaus, though—and until Bauhaus dicta began to spread around the globe—that functionalism arrived in the United States in full force.

◖◗

The most commonly told story about the Bauhaus is a story of rise and fall. Gropius founded his art and design institute, the Staatliches Bauhaus (Bauhaus State School), in 1919, out of the German artists' and industrialists' association called the Deutscher Werkbund. The Bauhaus began in Weimar, then rose to prominence following its 1925 move to Dessau. And then it declined with the rise of Nazism, finally closing in Berlin in 1933.

But of course that story is too simple. In fact, the Bauhaus also changed over time. For one thing, although the school (like the Deutscher Werkbund before it) was always invested in marrying art with industry, its strategy for achieving that goal changed profoundly over the fourteen years of its life. At first, "industry" was a very abstract idea—little more than a hypothesis—to the students and faculty of the Bauhaus. And then it became something much more concrete.[22]

What changed was the Bauhaus's business model: its way of keeping itself afloat. The Bauhaus had been founded not as a private institution but as a state school: the *"Staatliches* [State] Bauhaus in Weimar,*"* financially and politically dependent on the support of the (then–social democratic) Thuringian state government. The original curriculum was organized not around practical principles for use in technology or industry but around the building blocks of art and handicraft: basic forms, primary colors, aesthetic principles. Students progressed only later, if at all, to learning more practical, functional skills: metalworking, weaving, typography, pottery, cabinet making. But over the course of the Bauhaus's decade and a half of existence, as the German art historian and Bauhaus archivist Magdalena Droste has shown, its sponsorship shifted—and, accordingly, its curriculum changed. Conflict arose between the school and its government sponsors, who saw the modern art and design developing at the school as Bolshevist or left-wing. The increasingly right-wing-dominated Thuringian state, in which Weimar was located, began to exert major political pressure on the school's leadership. The Bauhaus, wrote former public education minister Max Greil, was being "slowly but surely strangled to death."[23]

Gropius responded to this pressure by formally dissolving the Bauhaus's contractual relationship with the Thuringian government and relocating it from Weimar to Dessau. He also sought alternative sources of funding. He had already begun exploring founding a limited company that would sell Bauhaus products, with the idea of freeing the school from its state dependence. Now he sought partnerships with other businesses as well. And as the Bauhaus moved away from state funding and toward various forms of business, its focus changed. Its students became practitioners of artistic techniques applied to industrial production. And accordingly, although the basic aesthetic principles remained important to the curriculum, the curriculum became dominated, as Droste puts it, "by the concepts of *type* and *function* and the confrontation with *technology* and *industry*." In short, Bauhaus classes became less about pure aesthetics and more about using machines to mass-produce objects that *worked*.[24]

There was some resistance to the transition. As one historian has put it, faculty and students "felt compromised by Gropius's new commodity fetishism." The painter and Bauhaus instructor Lyonel Feininger wrote to his wife, Julia, "We now have to aim at earnings—at sales and mass production!

But that's anathema to all of us and a serious obstacle to the development process." But Gropius pressed forward. Upon his own resignation as director in 1928, he chose as his successor the radical functionalist Hannes Meyer, an architect with little patience for aesthetics and art instruction. Coincidentally or not, it was at this time that the Bauhaus began to call itself a "design" school. "Design" as a marriage of art and industry, and relatedly as a marriage of aesthetics and function, thus entered popular discourse out of the ashes of state patronage and as part of a transition to private partnership.[25]

As went the Bauhaus, so went much of the rest of the globe. "Houses and even whole housing settlements are being built everywhere," the Hungarian art critic Ernő Kállai wrote in 1930, "all with smooth white walls, horizontal rows of windows, spacious terraces, and flat roofs. The public accepts them . . . as the products of an already familiar 'Bauhaus style.'" Throughout Europe and the United States, the Bauhaus—through its publications, exhibitions, news coverage, and advertising—had become a household name, and not just its style but also its ideas were coming to seem familiar. (That process would accelerate when the school closed, upon which its former affiliates founded Bauhaus-influenced institutions on many continents.) The Bauhaus was bringing design as "how it works," as Steve Jobs would put it much later, to the world.[26]

● ♥

Bauhaus functionalism first arrived in the United States during the Great Depression. That crisis in capitalism threatened to kill "industrial art," as an emergent stand-alone profession in that country, altogether. Industrial manufacturers, on whose business the new designers relied, cut their output by 42 percent in the first four years of the Depression. Most industrial artists either closed up shop or came close to doing so.[27]

But around 1933—just as the American banking system shut down before Franklin Roosevelt's election and the global economy slid deeper into Depression—business began to turn around for the new profession. Why? For one thing, raising the overall quality of American manufacture was coming to be seen as a civic mandate, a way to boost consumer spending by rendering American products more attractive to Americans themselves. American politicians and businessmen had turned away from the problems of "producers" and become interested in "consumers." As the idea of the consumer became more central to American politics, the historian Alan Brinkley has written, "it became the basis of an almost universal political language." Consumer spending, businessmen and politicians believed, was what propelled the economy— and so businesses must optimize their products for consumer desire. More compelling than civic virtue, though, was profit, and hiring designers had also come to seem like good business at the level of the individual enterprise. Citing remarks by Metropolitan Museum of Art associate in industrial arts Richard Bach, the *New York Times* explained in 1934 that these days every object manufactured and advertised "must carry a promise of marketability, for there is no margin to finance flights into the unknown." And design promised marketability. "If products could look more graceful, more efficient, and more dependable," one *Atlantic Monthly* commentator explained— referring implicitly to a concept of design that included both beauty and function—"people would desire them more."[28]

Before long, it was clear to critics and commentators that the market for industrial art had begun to expand again.

Sales curves arced upward, buoyed by the new appearances and features enabled by industrial artists. And industry took note. Having tamed the problems of production cost and mass distribution, many "alert minds in American industry," as Teague himself put it, had begun "casting a critical eye on the products they were making. Conscious of the competition they faced constantly, more and more American manufacturers began to wonder whether their products themselves possessed all the appeal they might have." They sought out industrial artists to boost that appeal.[29]

And so it was that the Depression began to *drive* design's growth rather than to suppress it. The historian Jeffrey Meikle has shown that, around 1933, Teague's and his colleagues' books of business either stabilized or began to grow significantly. Manufacturers had begun to see designers' services as a tool for making their products stand out to choosy, cash-strapped American buyers. By the mid-1930s, it was clear that the Depression's very conditions of scarcity had enabled the new industrial art—now increasingly called "industrial design"—to take off. And as industrial design flourished, so did its functionalist *concept* of design.[30]

That year, 1934, the *New Yorker* ran a profile of Teague. He was fifty-one years old, and he worked sixty hours a week at his own design firm. The author described him as "faintly stout and a little more than faintly bald." He was still "quiet and studious," although apparently also in the habit of going "discreetly nudist" while relaxing with his family at their lake house in New Hampshire.[31]

And he had figured out for himself what a "modern" designer did. His focus now was design for physical products: Pyrex ovenware, Eastman Kodak cameras, Corning cocktail glasses, a "Stormoguide Weather Station" barometer-thermometer for Taylor Instrument. But he also had transformed his methods. He had stepped away from focusing on how things looked—away from decoration, ornamentation, and aesthetics in general—and begun focusing on how they worked.[32]

Gilbert Seldes's *New Yorker* profile led with an anecdote that demonstrated the change. It told the story of Teague's redesign of something called the "gas compressor." If the word "compressor" makes your eyes glaze over, you are not alone: "The public is unaware of their existence," Seldes wrote, "and even if informed, would be totally indifferent to their appearance." (For what it's worth, a compressor is a mechanical device that moves natural gas forward through pipes by increasing the gas's pressure.) So why, Seldes asked, would a company bring in a designer to work on a compressor, given that a consumer will likely never see one? "There would seem to be no reason in the world for the manufacturers of these engines to redesign them," the writer reasoned, "if design is considered as a superficial layer of attractiveness applied to a commercial product."[33]

The answer was that the Walter Teagues of the world were changing what design was "considered." Before the compressor's redesign, Seldes wrote, it had been an octopus of indecipherable and chaotically interlocked pipes and parts. In the new compressor, Teague had created "a proper organization of the machine for its maximum of efficiency." In short, Teague had improved the compressor's function. A modern designer still cared about "handsomeness," to be sure—but to the manufacturer and to Teague, "the fact that the new compressor is a handsome machine is secondary." A modern designer's primary job was to improve function. *Design is how it works.*[34]

In his writing from that era, Teague himself articulated his own relatively newfound functionalism by distinguishing it from what had come before. "It was not so long ago," he wrote in 1938 in a trade publication, "that we merely covered our products with ornament. Our homes and office buildings, resembling nothing so much as a French pastry, bulged from cellar to attic with gingerbread furnishings. Even such humble articles as stoves and furnaces could not escape the blight of crawling ornament." But now ornament was out. "Today," Teague wrote, "we find that people choose to surround themselves with products which are simple, frank and undisguised." And designers—particularly the new "industrial designers"—were hired not to decorate those products but to make them work from the inside out.[35]

Even as Teague thrived, the reporter Gilbert Seldes noted a certain frustration in him—one that many other practitioners and enterprise customers of "industrial design," and then of design conceived broadly, would come to share. Teague was frustrated, Seldes wrote, with the state actors known as "the New Dealers."[36]

It would have been hard, in 1934, not to have some opinion or another about the New Deal. President Franklin Delano Roosevelt's domestic program to bring economic relief and prosperity to the American people, via reforms to the structures of American capitalism and the creation of a social safety net, was profoundly expanding the scope of federal government activity. By three months into his presidency—mid-1933, a year before Seldes's profile of Teague was published—Roosevelt's administration had sent fifteen presidential messages to Congress and signed fifteen bills into law, establishing the Works Progress Administration, the National Recovery Administration, the Civilian Conservation Corps, the Agricultural Adjustment Administration, the Federal Art Project, the Federal Writers' Project, the Federal Theatre Project, the Federal Emergency Relief Administration, the Tennessee Valley Authority, and a host of other new state-funded bodies. For the people of the United States, the New Deal was changing what "government" meant.[37]

In historical hindsight, the New Deal was good for business. It installed institutions and processes that made the American economy more stable and more predictable. It made the country a healthier place to do business transactions, specifically by making those transactions more reliable, establishing controlled competition in the markets most important to industry, and facilitating relatively ordered relations between management and labor. And it created a safety net for those whom capitalism left behind, thereby forestalling the kind of rebellion that might force capitalism itself to change in any fundamental way. As the historian Alan Brinkley has put it, the New Deal was a promise by the American government, to American business, that the state "would not reshape capitalist institutions." Instead, it would do something less threatening to business: it would "reshape the economic and social environment in which those institutions worked."[38]

In the first few years of the 1930s, though, the New Dealers did seem intent on genuinely changing how those capitalist institutions worked. Brinkley notes that the beliefs "that something was wrong with capitalism" and "that government should find a way to repair it" were central elements of liberal thought. Many early New Dealers were preoccupied with the problem of monopoly, and they advocated for reversing industrialization's increasing centralization of economic power.

And many, like their British Labour Party counterparts, advocated what had come to be called "planning": a term encompassing various ways of giving the state, and in particular the national government, more power over social and economic life. They hoped to curb corporate power by increasing the power of the state apparatus to actively manage the economy. To be sure, many of these critiques and reformist intentions would soon give way, especially in the United States. (They would hold on for much longer across the Atlantic, as Tony Judt has shown, with the shared "belief in an enhanced role for the state in social and economic affairs" becoming "the political religion of post-war Europe.") But from the perspective of 1934, it seemed possible that American capitalism would change profoundly before the Roosevelt administration had left office.[39]

And so the early New Deal felt threatening to American business. It was dismantling the freedom from oversight that corporations had previously enjoyed. Its "planning" could feel heavy-handed: the National Recovery Administration, established in 1933, encouraged business leaders to engage in "industrial cooperation"—establishing production quotas and fixing prices and wages—to address "the excesses of cut-throat competition." (It also guaranteed workers the rights to organize and to bargain collectively.) Later measures like the 1935 tax on undistributed corporate profits seemed aimed at antagonizing industrialists. "The excessive centralization and the dictatorial spirit," the journalist Walter Lippmann wrote, "are producing a revulsion of feeling against bureaucratic control of American economic life."[40]

The sheer pace of change also scared businessmen. Many felt themselves to be living in a world so fraught with short-term uncertainty for their kind—what might Roosevelt reveal next?—as to be paralyzing. "Business is now hesitant about making long term plans," wrote the head of the New York Federal Reserve Board that year to Marriner Eccles, chairman of the Federal Reserve Board, "partly because it feels it does not know what the rules of the game are going to be." Franklin Roosevelt's New Deal America felt like a world of too much government carrying out too much activity in private-sector affairs. Capitalists wanted a return to a world where capitalists, not the federal government, seemed to be making the rules.[41]

That was Walter Teague's feeling: that the New Deal was too much government meddling much too freely in corporate affairs. By the end of the 1930s, Teague was campaigning for Roosevelt's opponent, the 1940 Republican presidential nominee Wendell Willkie. In a letter soliciting votes for Willkie, Teague wrote that he himself believed in "the great future of America under a system of free enterprise." But after ten years of Democratic rule, Teague continued, the United States was stalled on "the greatest frontier of all: the frontier beyond which lies a land of diminishing ugliness and disorder where our people can live decently, wholesomely and graciously." Willkie, by limiting governmental action and re-empowering "free enterprise," could restart the country's engine and lead it into that great beyond.[42]

Seldes's *New Yorker* profile had noted that Teague was a kind of techno-utopian: he believed that society would improve progressively through technology and innovation rather than through politics and government and social programs. "His Utopia," Seldes wrote, "obviously rises out of his admiration for the technical perfections of industry." It was an apt description. Now, in his Willkie election letters, Teague described the ability of designers and other innovators to see over the horizon to the future. These inventive men had already "made forays into this promised land," he wrote, "and brought back samples of its fruits." They had made "charts and maps" to the new territory, and they could lead the United States there once the Republicans were back in power.[43]

Teague was ready for that future. He had had quite enough of the New Deal United States. Meanwhile other American designers—themselves also frustrated associates of frustrated industrialists—had their own discontents with the US government, as well as their own dreams of perfection through design and technology. They voiced them in design books. In *Magic Motorways* (1940), Norman Bel Geddes, who—alongside Teague and the industrial designers Henry Dreyfuss and Raymond Loewy—is now considered a founder of industrial design in the United States, suggested that the top-down New Deal 1930s had left Americans in an inertial slump ("MEN, MACHINES OR SHEEP?" read one caption). The book outlined a coming technological utopia of super-expressways and personal flying machines. In *Ten Years of Industrial Design* (1939) and *Designing for People* (1955), a third founding father, Dreyfuss, laid out a vision of a future that was similarly marked by its embrace of progress through design and technology.[44]

It's worth pausing on the most famous among these books, Dreyfuss's *Designing for People*. Dreyfuss pitched it to his publisher in 1946 as a paean to the industrial designer as "the artist of democracy." While to this day *Designing for People* remains a classic (and rightfully so; it is funny, endearingly illustrated, and wise), the designer never emerges—never even masquerades—as an "artist of democracy." The designer of *Designing for People* doesn't craft American democratic life through politics or collective participation. Rather, he *innovates*, specifically in the field of consumer goods. He optimizes Americans' travel, communications, nutrition, and culture. He improves the consumer's health and comfort, expands the consumer's leisure time, and strengthens the consumer's security. As for collective life (rather than just individual flourishing), it rarely comes up. Democracy, in Henry Dreyfuss's America, doesn't seem particularly necessary at all.[45]

Harcourt, Brace and Company published Walter Teague's own design book in 1940. By that year, Teague's professional legacy was secure—he'd just promoted two colleagues to partner in his thriving firm—and his children grown. Teague had been speaking at universities and conferences, and writing articles and letters, long enough that he could patch the book together on train, plane, and car trips to client sites. What emerged was a manifesto about how much design could do. Design could remake everything, the book explains. And the future would be better if design were handed the reins and allowed to do that job.[46]

The vision of the future in Teague's book, *Design This Day: The Technique of Order in the Machine Age*, was—like the fantasy in the Willkie letter—a vision of a land where inventive individuals, from scientists to designers, led society forward. But since *Design This Day* was a *design* book, Teague took the time here to flesh out the key quality of design in particular that would enable its practitioners to lead. That quality was design's ability to intervene in function: to improve how things worked. A person wielding the tools of design could renovate not just objects but environmental and economic and social life from the inside out. In the future, then, designers would remake not just consumer objects but everything. "This is the job of design," Teague wrote: the "rebuilding of the world," the "vast task of world-building."[47]

The alternative, to Teague's mind, was "world-building" via governmental means. It was, in *Design This Day*, an ugly vision. Teague railed against Roosevelt and Secretary of Agriculture Henry A. Wallace's 1933 "Farm Bill," which addressed alleged overproduction by paying farmers *not* to produce crops and livestock. Limiting production, Teague wrote, was the wrong way to rebuild prosperity. But the deeper problem, Teague argued, was looking to the state for any solution at all. Americans, he wrote, should rely for their well-being not on cooperative institutions but on resourceful individuals. They should not be so foolish as to hand over their affairs to the "group of harassed men known as 'government,'" imagining that "then, by some miraculous extension of human power, all our affairs will be run satisfactorily."[48]

To Teague, in short, the federal government was incompetent and rapacious, and it both depended on and perpetuated the fantasy of a communal interest that didn't actually exist. "'Masses' are a fiction," Teague wrote; "only individuals exist, suffer, and enjoy." (One hears an eerie precursor to Margaret Thatcher's much later remark that "there is no such thing as society. . . . There are individual men and women and there are families, and no government can do anything except through people and people look to themselves first.") Foolish government collectivism must step aside, Teague proclaimed, so that the radiant individual innovator—the designer, remaker of worlds—might bring renewal.[49]

The functionalist concept of design continued to gain force, in the United States and Europe, as more and more artists became "industrial designers." The fashion illustrator Raymond Loewy took work designing copiers and refrigerators. The young theater-set painter Henry Dreyfuss designed suspender buckles and cosmetics bottles, then a new washing machine as a commission for Sears, Roebuck. Then came World War II, and suddenly there was enormous demand for design in fulfillment of war contracts. Manufacturers hired industrial designers to design uniforms for new recruits and medical devices for injured soldiers. The work brought the new field prestige, cash, and the security inherent in long-term government contracts.[50]

Despite Teague's reservations about big government, he seems not to have hesitated to embrace war work, collaborating with Loewy and Dreyfuss, for instance, on the full design of a strategy room for the Joint Chiefs of Staff of the US Army and Navy. Teague's office also made usability improvements to naval artillery controls, fitting them to users of different bodies and abilities. Perhaps war, to Teague's mind, was the right kind of state action, whereas social security and the regulation of business—efforts to re-embed markets, in Karl Polanyi's terms, in social life—were the wrong kind.[51]

It was around this time that American industrial designers began to discuss the pros and cons of "professionalizing" their field, particularly by pursuing a system of professional licensing like the one required of architects. It was a topic of conversation at the 1946 "Conference on Industrial Design: A New Profession," hosted by New York's Museum of Modern Art and organized by its industrial design head, Edgar Kaufmann Jr., himself an architect and architectural historian. A host of designers, educators, and others came together for the two-day conference, excited to discuss what it meant for a designer "to be a member of a profession in the modern world."[52]

The conference consisted mostly of speeches and discussion. But Teague and his fellow designer Loewy also performed an impromptu skit, which kicked off a conversation about designers' responsibilities to clients. Teague played a client who wanted a designer to redesign his product by taking a look at it and making some freshened-up "sketches." Loewy, playing the designer, had to break the hard truth to his client: good designers didn't just sketch up better-looking images of their clients' products. A designer wasn't, primarily, an artist. He needed to understand the problem to be solved, the function to be improved, the market to be conquered, Loewy explained, before he did "any fancy designing."[53]

It had been twenty years since Teague, returning from Europe, had decided to address his attention to function rather than just aesthetics. But now the audience laughed knowingly. Explaining to the uninitiated that design was more than just how something looked had become part of what industrial designers understood to be their vocation. Watching a fellow practitioner trudge through that familiar explanation strengthened their collective belief in themselves as legitimate practitioners, as participants in a socially important collective project, as professionals. Explaining that design was "how it works" was part of the handshake of their tribe.[54]

And it came, as we've seen already, with a politics. At that same conference, Pratt Institute dean James C. Boudreau suggested that the "crux of the question of professional standing" was professional licensing by a regulatory body. (Designers "must address [their] desire to be a profession to legal organizations such as the city, the state, the federal government," he insisted; these were the bodies "constituted with the power to say that [they were] a profession.") And that proposition—getting the government involved as anything other than a client—turned out to be, in the analysis of the other conference attendees, a bridge too far. Several participants stood up to express their utter disgust at the very notion of government recognition. Designer George Sakier stood to declare that design was not a profession and that he hoped that it never would be, because "the thought of licensing industrial designers is revolting to me."[55]

That was the end of the conference's discussion of professionalization. The idea of inviting external governance of a trade or field tends to be contentious no matter what that trade or field is; as Louis Menand has observed, "All professions aspire to be self-governing, because their members believe that only fellow-professionals have the expertise needed to make judgments in their fields." But for industrial design, it was a particular nonstarter. Professionalization would have meant government recognition or even regulation, and imposing any government intervention on society's innovators was "revolting." The designers at that conference—the industrial designers of the 1940s—were happy to sacrifice a conversation about professionalization if it meant keeping the government out of their game. (Industrial designers are not licensed in the United States to this day.)[56]

●▼

In the quarter century that followed World War II, industrial design became a standard function in the American and European manufacturing processes. As the field developed, Teague, now often called the "Dean of Industrial Design," thrived. In 1959, the year before his death at seventy-six years old, reporters for two magazines visited what one called Teague's "palazzo of offices" at 415 Madison Avenue in order to profile the designer and his agency. Teague had trained and promoted six partners by that point, and he employed a staff of more than one hundred. They worked over four divisions: product design, graphic arts, architecture and interiors, and engineering.[57]

The firm's clients were diverse. Eastman Kodak, which in 1928 had been among Teague's very first industrial design customers, had renewed its contract for each of the thirty-two years since. (For the first twelve of those years, Teague said, he had designed all Eastman Kodak cameras and packaging himself, spending one week in Rochester, New York, each month to work closely with the company's engineers.) Teague also worked with DuPont, Servel Refrigerators, Ford, General Electric, Polaroid, and Texas Instruments. His firm had a permanent Boeing task force and had just designed the interiors of Boeing's new 707 Stratojet airliners. It was designing guided missiles for the US Navy. And it had just welcomed twelve thousand residents into the new $60 million "academic city" that it had designed near Colorado Springs for the US Air Force Academy.[58]

But Teague had gone even bigger than cities. An industrial design journal reported in the 1950s that Teague had been offered a job redesigning the export economy of Greece. The country was receiving American aid, and the hope, as the reporter put it, was that a talented industrial designer might help "build up a practical future which would make such aid unnecessary."[59]

Teague took the job. He had no qualms about state "planning," it seemed, when he himself was pulling the strings. He advised changing the standard width of Greek

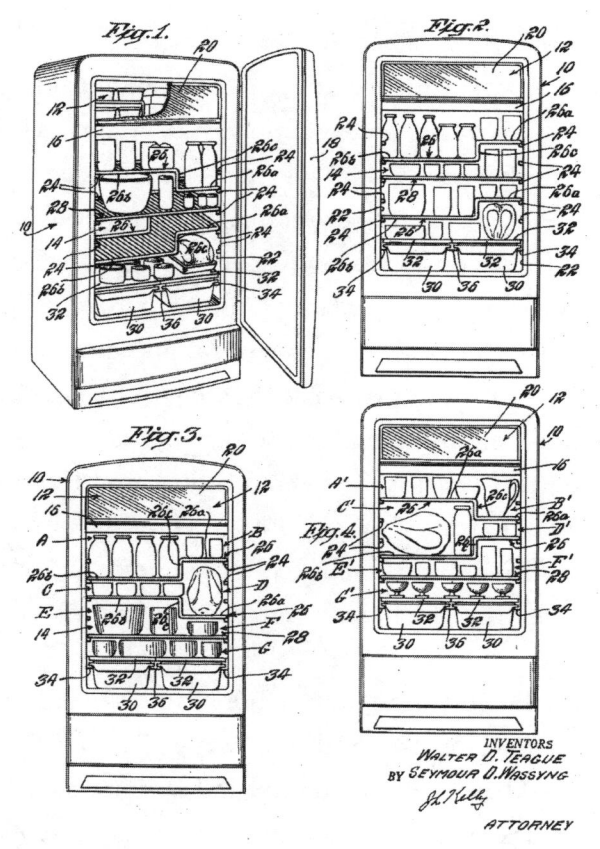

Walter Dorwin Teague, untitled sketches for customizable refrigerator shelves, 1955. Media unknown. Teague patent for Servel, Inc., Patent 2,717,189, US Patent and Trademark Office. Public domain.

handicraft textile looms from thirty to forty-eight inches, supplied advice about the training of weavers, and altered the specifications for pottery. He was "fully exploiting," the reporter wrote, "the modern supremacy of the designer," that master remaker of how literally everything worked. He was carrying out, in his own words, the "vast task of world-building."[60]

Design historians associate the word "function" with modernism. After modernism, according to the canonical narrative, came postmodernism, and postmodernist designers—Robert Venturi, Frank Gehry, Philip Johnson—proclaimed the death of functionalism and did not mourn it. Some professed commitments to design for its own sake rather than for vulgar functionality. Some proclaimed the return of ornament, which modernism had tried to banish, and embraced ornamentality at function's expense. Some—think of Memphis, the 1980s design and architecture group founded by Italian designer Ettore Sottsass—rejected utility, and the homogeneity that could result from prioritizing it, in favor of play, of whimsy, of unconventionality, of garishness, of style itself. Memphis chairs draw the eye, but they do not look comfortable to sit in. (I've never tried.)[61]

In the real world, though, functionalism lives on. "The frequent pronouncements of its death," writes the critic George H. Marcus, are "based on the outlook and output of a privileged echelon of designers." Belying those pronouncements, functionalism remains, Marcus observes, "a benchmark against which much design is judged."[62]

And he's right. Functionalism's basic premise—that making an object function ought to be first among its designer's concerns—has become a foundational aspect of the idea of "design" itself, at least as held by designers and design critics and some corporate executives. Some people, of course, still make "the mistake of thinking design is what it looks like," said Apple CEO Steve Jobs to the *New York Times* in 2003. "People think it's this veneer—that the designers are handed this box and told, 'Make it look good!'" But that wasn't what design meant at Apple, Jobs explained. "It's not just what it looks like and feels like. Design is how it works."[63]

The "design is how it works" mindset is highly compatible with twenty-first-century market liberalism, of which the techno-utopian spirit—with its unsubtle libertarian undertones—is a constituent part. Many technologists and consumers of technology believe that inventive individuals, with their tools of design and technology and innovation, unfettered by collectivist values and rules, can make things work better than government can. It makes a kind of sense—given that key aspects of the very idea of design arose from the promise of escape from the harder work of enacting change by democratic governmental means. Forged in the fires of New Deal conservative resistance, this discourse positions design as a powerful alternative tool for social change. Turn to design to make things work better, it promises, and you don't need to do the dirty work of deliberative politics. Conceived as a practice of making things work, design is disruption with none of the drudgery of bureaucracy, none of the discomfort, none of the drag.

It's a romantic idea, this idea of change by design. In the late 2010s and 2020s, it seemed to hold particular sway in Silicon Valley, where the discourse of design as a tool for optimizing social arrangements seemed to sing in one voice with discourses of explicit resistance to government intervention in economic and social life. See, for instance, PayPal founder Peter Thiel's avowal that "the founding vision of PayPal centered on the creation of a new world currency, free from all government control and dilution," or Elon Musk's insistence that the right way to rescue twelve Thai boys and their soccer coach from the Tham Luang cave in northern Thailand was bringing in Tesla engineers to design and build a mini-submarine. Thiel and Musk don't speak for all tech entrepreneurs, whose politics overall skew left-liberal (pro–redistribution of wealth, pro-immigration, pro–social services). But the Valley's Thiels and Musks are loud and influential. *Government is quaint,* they seem to argue, *but everyone knows design and innovation are where the power is.*[64]

But it isn't true. For one thing, it misprizes governments' own capacity to innovate. Karl Polanyi observed in *The Great Transformation* that states had *created* our apparently self-regulating national market economies. More recently, the political theorist Marianna Mazzucato, in her two widely admired books of economic theory, *The Entrepreneurial State* (2013) and *The Value of Everything* (2018), has dismantled, as a *New York Times* reviewer put it, "the long-accepted binary of an agile private sector and a lumbering, inefficient state," showing that in fact the US government—in addition to being the leading customer of design and related offerings—*has itself been the country's leading innovator.* While the twin ideas that the state and innovation exist on separate sides of a hostile divide and that economic growth comes from unregulated markets have become deeply entrenched in contemporary media, history shows the opposite.[65]

Much of the evidence comes from before World War II. Until that war, the US government was by far the most intrepid and capable entrepreneurial body driving the country's economy, innovating through risk at the frontiers of science and technology. Even in the postwar era, though, the US government has been the "investor of first resort" for private-sector scientists and technologists, playing a leading role in aviation and space technologies, pharmaceuticals and biotechnology, nanotechnology, and the emergent green technology sector. In all these cases, Mazzucato writes, the state "dared to think—against the odds—about the 'impossible'": making huge initial investments in a new technological opportunity, empowering a decentralized network of researchers to explore it, and then betting on multiple developers and commercializers of the new technology to ensure that it would be brought to market in the most dynamic and widely beneficial possible way.[66]

There's a specific reason that the state is better positioned to drive innovation than is any one private company. That reason is that inventing new technologies requires that the inventor and the sponsoring body accept enormous uncertainties and cost—enormous risk—over enormous spans of time. The sponsor has to provide, in Mazzucato's term, "patient capital." Private companies cannot in most cases bear this kind of risk, both because the rewards are so uncertain and because the timelines are so long. Mazzucato thus makes the case for a state empowered, as "lead investor and catalyst," to accept this responsibility: "a targeted, proactive, entrepreneurial State," a state that can take risks, a state that can create a "highly networked system of actors" to "harness the best of the private sector" to advance the national good over time.[67]

Mazzucato's ideas have been widely praised, and not just from the left. The chief economics commentator for the fiercely neoliberal *Financial Times*, in a review in that newspaper's pages, called *The Entrepreneurial State* "brilliant" and acknowledged that its argument—that "the entity that takes the boldest risks and achieves the biggest breakthroughs is not the private sector; it is the much-maligned state"—is "basically right." And yet Mazzucato faces an uphill battle. "The notion of the State as a mere facilitator, administrator and regulator may have first started to gain widespread currency in the 1970s," she notes, "but it has taken on newfound popularity in the wake of the global financial crisis [of 2008]." As a result, the very state agencies that have enabled the technological revolutions of our past half century—such as the National Institutes of Health and Defense Advanced Research Projects Agency (DARPA) in the United States—have seen their budgets shrink. In real-dollar value, DARPA funding declined between FY2005 and FY2021 by 11 percent.[68]

Mazzucato believes in the power of discourse. She thinks that talking about and illustrating the state's capacity to drive innovation is one of the best ways, under late capitalism, to defend the state's very existence. She argues that we must change "the way we reason about the State, its role and its structure" if we are to continue to thrive in collective life. The idea that design and innovation are private powers is a major part of the reasoning that needs to change. It is simply not true, and it is debilitating.[69]

We need not look far for evidence. This book was born during the coronavirus pandemic. It was an era when nature made clear that human civilizations needed not just free markets to organize them but also robust and entrepreneurial governments. ("There are no libertarians," wrote *Atlantic* staff writer Derek Thompson, "in a pandemic.") But it was also clear that it was, at least for the United States, in some ways too late. The essayist and novelist George Packer described "a federal government crippled by years of right-wing ideological assault" and "politicians and donors who wanted government to do as little as possible for the common good," which together had left government powerless against COVID-19:[70]

> Every morning in the endless month of March, Americans woke up to find themselves citizens of a failed state. With no national plan—no coherent instructions at all—families,

schools, and offices were left to decide on their own whether to shut down and take shelter. When test kits, masks, gowns, and ventilators were found to be in desperately short supply, governors pleaded for them from the White House, which stalled, then called on private enterprise, which couldn't deliver. States and cities were forced into bidding wars that left them prey to price gouging and corporate profiteering. Civilians took out their sewing machines to try to keep ill-equipped hospital workers healthy and their patients alive. Russia, Taiwan, and the United Nations sent humanitarian aid to the world's richest power—a beggar nation in utter chaos.

We'd been living in an era that wanted not government action but private-sector action, not government ideas but business ideas, not government making things work but market-driven innovation making things work. In this context, as of this writing, it feels very clear that the idea that design makes things work better than more traditional collective practices can—one of the ideas on which design was founded, and part of the reason it's so widely celebrated—is no small part of the problem.[71]

Chapter 3

PROBLEM SOLVING

In the middle of the Great Depression, Peretz Rosenbaum remade himself for the new world of commercial design. A young Orthodox Jewish man born in Brooklyn, he enrolled in night classes at Brooklyn's Pratt Institute and then Manhattan's Parsons School of Design. Then, like Walter Dorwin Teague before him, he found the Art Students League on West 57th Street. There he studied with the German painter George Grosz, from whom he learned about the European modernists. Alexander Calder, Joan Miró, Pablo Picasso, and Paul Klee became his guiding lights.[1]

Two years later, at twenty-one, he changed his name to Paul Rand. He rented a pillbox-sized studio on East 38th Street, declared himself a freelance graphic artist, and began walking around New York City knocking on famous designers' doors to ask for work. By 1936, at age twenty-two, he was an art director for *Esquire*. Five years later, he joined William H. Weintraub's new Fifth Avenue advertising agency, where for over a decade he would produce glossy, highbrow advertisements for the likes of Ohrbach's department store and Revlon, Inc.

He became a master. "In the decades following World War II," one group of critics has written, "Paul Rand, more than any other single designer, was responsible for defining visual culture in America." Rand went on to create corporate identities for IBM (1956–1992), Westinghouse (1960), UPS (1961), ABC (1963), and many others, as well as to teach graphic design for decades at Yale. He received the AIGA Gold Medal (1966) and the Type Directors Club Medal (1984), and he was named a "Royal Designer for Industry" by the Royal Society of London (1973). His logo work and other graphic design—magazine covers, movie posters, book covers—are astoundingly crisp and vivid works of communication.[2]

Rand had always had a talent for shape-shifting. He is remembered for bringing modernist aesthetics to American graphic design: cut-paper collage, primary colors, minimalist

Paul Rand, logos for UPS (1961), ABC (1963), Atlas Crankshaft (1964), Bureau of Indian Affairs (1968), IBM (1972), and NeXT (1986).

layout, ample white space, typography set in striking asymmetry on the grid of the page. But of course "modernist aesthetics" was at the time, given modernism's functionalist dogma, ostensibly a contradiction in terms: "At the height of modernism's hegemony," the critic Pat Kirkham has written, "it was difficult to admit simply liking the look of something." So when Rand spoke or wrote about design, he tended not to talk primarily about his aesthetic choices. Sometimes he talked instead about the unity of how things looked with how they worked: visual communication, he wrote in 1947, "should be seen as the embodiment of form and function: the integration of the beautiful and the useful." More often, though, he attempted to leave that binary behind entirely in favor of talking about design in a third way. Design, Rand would explain, was an act of problem solving.[3]

He began to write down his ideas in the half decade after World War II. In the early essay "The Designer's Problem"—included in his 1947 monograph *Thoughts on Design*, which he published at thirty-two and which the design historian Steven Heller has called "the bible of modern practice"—Rand described graphic design as a battle between a designer and his client's problem. The problem was a kind of artistic substrate, the key material with which the designer began and on which he built his work. And of course the problem was also the designer's greatest challenge: the obstacle he must surmount in order to succeed.[4]

Rand's point in "The Designer's Problem" isn't just that design begins with a problem; it's that design, as an act of problem solving, is a wholly rational process. Design is logical; it's methodical; it's repeatable. The first step in the design process is analysis. The designer breaks down the problem "into its simplest components . . . the how, why, when, and where." Next is reformulation: as in all likelihood the given problem is "inadequate, vague, uninteresting, or otherwise unsuitable for visual interpretation," the designer reorganizes and restates the material until it's clear and compelling. Finally, once the problem has been analyzed and reformulated, the designer creates and synthesizes. He gathers and incorporates insights from inside the problem and beyond it; he interprets those insights, improvises, brainstorms, upturns, and recombines. In the end he arrives at a solution. The solution is a single concept, abstracted from the problem "by association and analogy," in symbolic visual form.[5]

Rand lived out his belief that every good design was the sole solution to its problem. He did not design corporate identities in iterative partnership with clients; instead, he worked with his client to establish the problem, then retreated to address the problem alone and to formulate and deliver one single perfect solution. For a 1968 logo design project for the US Bureau of Indian Affairs, for instance, the problem was to design a symbol reflecting the bureau's "continuous striving toward worthy goals" such as "economic self-sufficiency of Indians" and "full participation of Indians in American life." The actual process itself was solo, contemplative. The result was a logo mark comprised of three elements, each conveying, in Rand's words, "a universal quality and positive implications": the sun (symbolizing "life-giving force" and "unity"); an arrow (evoking "Indian," "progress," "aspiration," and "optimism"); and a star (for "American," "patriotism," and "hope"). It is not a logo for the 2020s, but it does its best to square the circle of conveying both Indian dignity and autonomy and white American paternalism.[6]

Upon completing each logo-design process, Rand submitted to his client a booklet that restated the problem, explained the process by which the solution had been found, and presented the outcome. The booklets read like geometric proofs. Take, for example, the one for the machining company Atlas Crankshaft (1964):

> **Problem:** To design a trademark for the Atlas Crankshaft Corporation, incorporating the name "Atlas" as an integral part of the mark. The design should be of a non-descriptive and general nature, not limited to a particular product, but reflecting the qualities of precision, speed, power, and dependability. Its form should, therefore, be abstract and/or geometric, avoiding any representational connotation. . . .
>
> [**Solution:**] The mark presented here serves a double purpose: it is a trademark (symbol) as a complete unit, as well as a logotype (group of letters). Its design is based fundamentally on the use of the triangle as an abstract shape and as a letter form. It may be read not only as a triangle (symbol of precision and strength) but also as the letter "A" (symbol of priority and quality).

The client, to Rand's mind, had no choice but to accept the solution. Steve Jobs commissioned Rand to design the logo for his company NeXT. (It was spelled NEXT at the time; Rand changed the orthography.) Early on in the project, Jobs asked Rand to see "a few options." Rand, Jobs recalled, flatly refused. "If you want options, go talk to other people," Rand said. This relationship had different terms. It was premised on a belief in design as a rational process that addressed a problem by finding the single best solution. "I will solve your problem for you," Rand told Jobs. "And you will pay me."[7]

The idea that design is problem solving is not new, exactly. It's implicit, in some way, in the concept of the "architectural brief" (or "architectural program," or "design brief"), the statement that often inaugurates the formal relationship between an architect and a client. An architectural brief is a statement of the client's requirements. It states the problem to be solved. And it's as old as architectural patronage itself. The word "brief" seems to have come into use in English only in the late nineteenth century, but long before that, architects and designers made regular reference to the needs, desires, and intentions of their patrons and clients as the basis for their architectural decisions. Describing the challenge he faced in designing the Royal Hospital for Seamen at Greenwich, built beginning in 1696, the English baroque architect Nicholas Hawksmoor noted that Queen Mary, "who had a great Passion for Building," wanted "to build the Fabrick with great Magnificence and Order." You could call that a problem to be solved.[8]

And surely we might find earlier examples of problem articulation: in written communications between patrons and the architects they hired, in messages from those architects to their subordinates, in legal contracts. By the time Vitruvius wrote *De architectura* (probably around 30–20 BCE), architectural patronage was an established social arrangement and practice in Rome. Before that, early Egyptian, Mesopotamian, and Iranian architects were designing structures for government, nobility, and royalty, beginning long before the invention of written language around 3000 BCE.[9]

But must everyone who starts with requirements think of those requirements as *problems*? Must they think of their process as *problem solving*? The idea of problem solving as such—as a concept, a kind of broad abstraction, and, ultimately, a celebrated practice and capability—is much newer than all this.

The concept originated, somewhat unsurprisingly, with math. Mathematics has long used the language of the "problem" and its "solution." The 1570 English translation of Euclid's *Elements*—the first English edition of what Albert Einstein later referred to as the "holy little geometry book"—stated, "A Probleme, is a proposition which requireth some action, or doing"; in a preface to the same translation, the British mathematician and astronomer John Dee referred to "the famous Probleme of doubling the Cube." The word has been in use among mathematicians for a long time. And by the mid-nineteenth century, they were talking about "problem *solving*," too.[10]

More importantly, though, math is interested in problems *as* problems: it has a *concept* of the problem. Mathematicians have long tried to establish reliable approaches to characterizing different kinds of problems and to solving them as such. In 1945, the Hungarian mathematician George Pólya rendered this interest widely accessible by publishing a little book called *How to Solve It*. (Born in 1887 in Budapest, Pólya was a product of the same Hungarian system of public secondary schools, the "gymnasium" system—during the same years—as Eva Zeisel's uncles Karl and Michael Polanyi. The remarkable generation that came out of that system, nearly all of Jewish descent, is sometimes called "the Martians," after a group of physicists remarked that the weird overflow of genius emerging from Hungary at midcentury could be explained only by the conclusion that the country was a front for aliens from Mars.)[11]

How to Solve It is written from the perspective of a teacher—having left Europe during the war, Pólya was now a math professor at Stanford—who wanted to harness his students' curiosity and excitement. So it began by celebrating the very joy of problems themselves. "Your problem may be modest," Pólya wrote, but "if it challenges your curiosity and brings into play your inventive faculties, and if you solve it by your own means, you may experience the tension and enjoy the triumph of discovery."[12]

How to Solve It is a practical manual and encyclopedia of problem-solving approaches. Specifically, it's a book of what mathematicians call "heuristics." The idea of the heuristic—a generalizable method or rule of thumb, like "work backwards" or "guess and check," that can be used to solve a problem—had been around for a long time, but Pólya wanted to "revive" it in a modern form. He felt it would empower people: give confidence to students, "challenge [their] curiosity," and enable them to "experience the tension and enjoy the triumph of discovery."[13]

The book did revive heuristic analysis. It sold over a million copies and was translated into seventeen languages. The computer scientist Allen Newell wrote decades later that the book "put heuristic back on the map of intellectual concerns." It also changed how math was taught. "For mathematics education and the world of problem solving," the math education researcher A. H. Schoenfeld wrote in 1987, "it marked a line of demarcation between two eras: problem solving before and after Pólya."[14]

For all that impact, though, it's a relatively modest book. It starts by laying out a general four-phase framework for problem solving, beginning with (1) understanding the problem, then proceeding to (2) devising a plan, (3) carrying out the plan, and (4) looking back. The rest of its pages are devoted to (often relatively vague) descriptions of procedures—operations worth trying, rules of thumb, *heuristics*—that might be applicable to any given problem. Faced with your specific problem, for instance, you might look for a different, related problem and solve that one first. Or you might restate your problem in different terms. You might try solving a little part of your problem before trying to solve the whole thing. You might collect all the data you have toward your problem and see what you can make of it. And if none of that works, there are many more heuristics to try.[15]

That design was problem solving became a commonplace thanks in large part to what President Dwight D. Eisenhower in 1961 called the "conjunction of an immense military establishment and a large arms industry": the US military-industrial complex.[16]

One major conduit was Herbert Simon. As of 1945, he was an obscure twenty-nine-year-old professor of political science. Born in 1916 in Milwaukee to a family of Czech and German Jewish descent, Simon had earned a full scholarship to the University of Chicago, graduated with a political science degree, and gone to work for an "operations research" group at the University of California, Berkeley. In 1943—as Allied forces invaded mainland Italy and as the mass murder of Jews proceeded at Auschwitz—Simon, rejected from combat service because he was color-blind, received his PhD and began his term as an assistant professor of political science at the Illinois Institute of Technology.[17]

Simon loved Illinois Tech because it was an engineering school. The Milwaukee of his childhood had been an industrial town, and his father, the German-born Arthur Simon,

Keystone Press / Alamy, untitled photograph of Herbert Simon, 1978. Keystone Pictures USA / ZUMAPRESS.

had been an electrical engineer. Herbert had grown up watching his father build things—including the neighborhood's first radio—and accompanying his father on Saturday "Engineers' Society" visits to area steel mills and research laboratories and to the factory that made the generators for the Hoover Dam. As an adult, he still felt most at home among people who made things.

Simon also had a quantitative inclination. During his years at the University of Chicago, he'd become committed to the philosophy he originally called "logical positivism": that metaphysical speculation was meaningless and that only scientific knowledge was real. Later he would call it "empiricism," but the idea was largely the same. Everything worth thinking about could be experienced through the senses, verified, measured, and quantified.

At Chicago, Simon had shared this conviction with several friends, including the psychology major Harold Guetzkow, another Milwaukeean. They had met on the Interurban Electric North Shore Line en route to Freshman Week, carrying trunks and bags, and become friends for life. "If Harold and I had visions of changing the world," Simon wrote later, "it was by way of understanding it, of contributing to the scientific knowledge that could point to solutions of some of the world's problems."[18]

It was a vision born of their environment. Empiricism also was, and remains, the overall outlook and dogma of the University of Chicago, still known as a tough-minded and nontheistic and rigorously logical institution. And the university's political science department, Simon's disciplinary home, was particularly committed to the faith. The field of political science was, in the early twentieth century, not about observation or description or data; Western political science was primarily a branch of moral philosophy. But under the vanguard leadership of the young chairman Professor Charles E. Merriam (now considered the founder of the behaviorist approach to the study of politics), Chicago's department had become committed to the proposition that, as Simon put it later, "political science is science." Simon was a true believer, and he devoted himself to understanding political behavior through experimentation, quantitative data, and statistical and mathematical analysis.[19]

Now, as a young professor, Simon applied these methods to a relatively humble topic: the people, the "administrators," who ran "organizations." Drawing on his earlier research assistantship and his doctoral dissertation, he published his first solely authored book, *Administrative Behavior: A Study of Decision-Making Processes in Administrative Organization*, in 1947. "Administrative behavior" is not a sexy topic. But Simon was finding that organizations as such—companies, governments, nonprofits, associations—were the perfect environments from which to gather data that might change scholars' most fundamental ideas about how people made decisions.[20]

Administrative Behavior attacked the neoclassical economic model that imagined rational people pursuing rational preferences by making rational choices to achieve outcomes that maximize their self-interest. Administrators, Simon's data showed, turn out to be much less tidily rational than all that. But what model *did* explain their choices? In 1949 Simon left Illinois Tech for the Carnegie Institute of Technology, the school that would later become Carnegie Mellon, and there he began to answer that question by recruiting an old friend: the Milwaukeean Harold Guetzkow, the one he'd met on the Interurban Electric North Shore Line on the way to Freshman Week at Chicago. Guetzkow had gone on to complete a doctorate under the guidance of Norman R. F. Maier, a Gestalt psychologist who specialized in human thought. Now Guetzkow joined Simon on the Carnegie faculty.[21]

For Herbert Simon and his colleagues at Carnegie Tech, working with Harold Guetzkow—and with the field of psychology—would change the discursive frame. Specifically, as they worked together on a Ford Foundation–funded project studying decision-making processes at specific companies, Simon and his colleagues noticed that Guetzkow's way of thinking and speaking about decision making—or something like it—was different from theirs. Specifically, Guetzkow talked not about *decision making* as such but about *problem solving*.[22]

On some level, it was just a change in vocabulary. But it opened the door to new ways of thinking about the decisions people made. For Simon, it opened new worlds.

For the field of psychology, "problem solving" was—and remains—a tricky concept. It's hard to define what counts: What form of thinking is *not* problem solving in some sense? And psychologists, for their part, have never been consistent about the question. The concept of problem solving, the psychologist K. Anders Ericsson observed in 2003, "does not correspond to a single well-defined phenomenon" in human cognition. Rather, it's changed continuously over the course of the twentieth century, transforming in tandem with the field of psychology itself. And it hasn't gotten any clearer. The more the field of psychology has come to understand about thinking in general, Ericsson wrote, "the harder it has become to distinguish problem solving as a separate phenomenon with its unique processes and mechanisms."[23]

It doesn't help that it's invisible: it takes place inside the mind. Immanuel Kant thought that thinking in general could never be studied using scientific methods for exactly this reason. Many European and American psychologists came to share his conviction during the late nineteenth century, as they strove to transform their broader discipline into a legitimate experimental science. In 1879, the world's first psychological laboratory was founded in Germany, and most psychologists turned their focus to phenomena that were explicitly observable and manipulable inside a lab. Their work now focused on very concrete cognitive phenomena, like sensory perception and responses to physical stimuli. One simply could not study, they believed, what one could not see.[24]

Psychologists' allergy to investigating thinking became nearly absolute around the 1910s, particularly in the United States, with the rise of the psychological school known as behaviorism. Behaviorists made a dogma of the idea that only concrete, observable behavior was worth studying. They saw people and animals as machines that responded automatically to external stimuli, without any cognitive processes worth considering. Behaviorist ideology dominated psychological theory and method in the United States for about fifty years.[25]

Not until the emergence of another psychological movement, the Gestalt School, did the study of thinking become widespread. It's hard at first to say what about Gestalt theory made this possible; we associate "Gestalt" today with the word's literal German-language meaning, which is something like "organized configuration" or "integrated whole." But the Gestaltists saw integrated wholes not only on spatial planes (a page of squares, a group of lines) but in the mind. They understood cognition as a dynamic field of events to be studied not only in its behavioral manifestations but in its entirety. And that meant investigating not just discrete, easily observable human behaviors—reflexes, responses to stimuli, actions—but also thoughts.[26]

In the United States, the Gestaltists' influence resulted in large part from Nazism and World War II. In 1933, the psychologist Max Wertheimer, one of the movement's founders, fled Germany and took a position at the New School in New York City. Two years later fellow Gestaltist Wolfgang Kohler resigned from the Psychological Institute of the University of Berlin after taking a public stand against the Nazis' abuse and then expulsion of Jewish scientists; he took a job at Pennsylvania's Swarthmore College. The movement's third founder, Kurt Koffka, had already moved to the United States, where he was teaching at Smith College in Northampton, Massachusetts. By the mid-1930s, then, Adolf Hitler had driven the entire Gestaltist establishment to the northeastern United States.

Between their physical presence, then, and a rash of English translations of their work, in the 1940s the Gestaltists' ideas began to penetrate the American psychological establishment. And central to these ideas was an emergent theory of what they called "problem solving." Karl Duncker's *On Problem-Solving*, like Pólya's *How to Solve It*, appeared in English in 1945; it built on research like Pólya's by using insights about how people solve math problems to make claims about how they address higher-order problems in the real world. Max Wertheimer's monograph *Productive Thinking*, also published in 1945, used plain language to distinguish "productive thinking"—solving a problem quickly, without a plan, through insight—from "reproductive thinking," the process of deliberate problem solving via an intentional method. The former was the process of creative revelation; the latter, as would soon become evident, was the mechanism behind the algorithm.

What precipitated the marriage of problem solving with *design*, particularly in the United States, was the Cold War. The Cold War motivated the US government to pour massive funding into the production of basic scientific knowledge that might enable future global dominance in technology and warfare. That government funding enabled Herbert Simon to try to program a computer to solve problems like a person. In the book about that process, Simon described "problem solving" as "design." Soon, that equation—problem solving is design, and design is problem solving—would become an article of faith across academic disciplines.

That story begins in the decade after World War II. Simon described the mid-1950s as "the most important years of [his] life as a scientist." For his whole career, he had been a scholar of politics and economics. Now—because he was obsessed with how human beings solved problems—he became a psychologist. And—because he was obsessed with using computers to simulate that human problem-solving process—he became a computer scientist.[27]

He had relatively little prior experience with computers. He had experimented a bit in the late 1930s and 1940s with early computing machines. He'd read American computer scientist Edmund Berkeley's accessible 1949 book *Giant Brains*, which attempted to "talk about what these machines can do in the future and to judge their significance for us." And he'd played with a programmable do-it-yourself computer—made simply of batteries and adjustable wires—that Berkeley had marketed alongside the book.[28]

But beginning in the early 1950s, Simon had collaborators who would help him learn more. This was due to a strange Cold War institution called RAND. Established as an independent nonprofit in 1948, RAND—the name combines the words "research and development"—was the original Cold War think tank, established by the US Air Force to try to harness the brainpower of the intellectuals who had served the government during World War II and repurpose that brainpower to build US power during peacetime. "Think tank" is a "curious phrase," the historian James Allen Smith has written, suggesting both "the rarefied isolation of those who think about policy" and "their prominent public display, like some rare species of fish or reptile confined behind the glass of an aquarium or zoo." In RAND's case, being a think tank meant doing ostensibly independent research (it had spun off from the Air Force into an independent "corporation") on topics in the formal, natural, and social sciences. The ultimate goal of that research was to design a highly optimized "science of warfare" that could be deployed against the Soviet Union.[29]

RAND was a funny place. Its scientists were mostly academics, and there was a revolving door between its halls and the country's universities. While at RAND, many socialized by playing a game called Kriegspiel. It was something like chess, in that two players tried to beat one another on a chessboard—but also something like poker, in that neither player could see the other player's pieces. (A referee enumerated the available moves.) It was, as one historian has written, "a fitting activity: a mixture of ancient strategy and manly bluffing." Its name meant "war game," which was, of course, RAND's specialty. When not playing Kriegspiel, the scientists elaborated game-theoretical approaches to international diplomacy, weapons acquisition, and, most fundamentally, the prevention of nuclear war.[30]

RAND recruited Herbert Simon in 1952, inviting him to spend summers at its offices in Santa Monica. They were interested in Simon because he was a quantitatively inclined expert—a rationalist—focused on human decision making, which was at the heart of the corporation's war games. RAND tasked Simon with helping establish its new Systems Research Laboratory, which was supposed to organize large studies investigating how human institutional groups, like an Air Force unit, behaved and made decisions. While working on the laboratory's first large-scale study, Simon met an energetic and brilliant twenty-five-year-old mathematician named Allen Newell.[31]

Newell, like Simon, was committed to applying math and quantitative analysis to questions about human behavior. "In our first five minutes of conversation," Simon remembered, "Al and I discovered our ideological affinity." They launched into the first of decades of animated conversation. Soon, on a long drive to the March Air Force Base, the two men began to toy with a set of ideas. One was that human minds were machines that processed information in the form of individual units—ideas—that Simon called "symbols." The second was that a computer, too, might be able to process such "symbols." And the third, arising from the first two, was that one might learn something, specifically something about how human minds solve problems, by trying to model with a computer the processing of symbols to solve a problem.[32]

But computers didn't process symbols at that point; they only processed numbers. To see whether it might be possible to get a computer to process symbols, Simon and Newell set out to build a program that could prove algebraic theorems, which involved not just numbers but nonnumerical symbols like x and y. They used the theorems in Bertrand Russell and Alfred North Whitehead's *Principia Mathematica*: statements like "$2^y > y$." To write the program that proved these theorems, they recruited a genuine computer scientist, Cliff Shaw, from RAND. Shaw invented a new programming language—one that could handle not just numbers but symbols—for the purpose. Then Simon and Newell designed the program's rules. They wrote each rule out on a physical index card; each card held a different piece, in other words, of a hypothetical computer's memory.[33]

Now came the test. On a winter evening in January 1956, the researchers assembled a small group—some graduate students, Herbert's wife, Dorothea Simon, and his three children (ages nine, eleven, and thirteen)—in a classroom on the Carnegie campus. Herbert Simon and Allen Newell gave each person one of the index cards, containing a rule or a simple set of rules; the person holding each card could do nothing but follow its rule or rules. Simon's middle child, Peter, later remembered sitting in a row of chairs and standing up when it was his turn to perform his rule (called "not p"); Katherine, the oldest, remembered writing out a branching process on the chalkboard. Together, by following their assigned rules, they simulated the new computer program. And it worked. They had shown through simulation that a computer program could process symbols—and hence thoughts—rather than just numbers. The children and their mother would remember it vividly as the moment they demonstrated for the first time, together, that a machine could think.[34]

All that was left was to write it down in the new programming language. Called the Logic Theorist, it was the first computer program to solve nonnumerical problems using heuristics: the kinds of procedures laid out in *How to Solve It*, which Newell had learned about, as a Stanford undergraduate in the late 1940s, from George Pólya himself. The Logic Theorist's heuristics enabled the computer to narrow the otherwise enormous field of possible solutions to a relatively manageable set. The computer could then search that narrower set for a solution that worked.[35]

When the spring semester began, as one graduate student remembered it, Simon strode proudly into the class he was teaching. "Over the Christmas holiday," he announced, "Al Newell and I invented a thinking machine." It was a bold statement, but it was true. The Logic Theorist couldn't prove all fifty-two theorems in *Principia Mathematica*, but it proved thirty-eight of them. The program was "proof positive," the historian of technology Pamela McCorduck has written, "that a machine could perform tasks heretofore considered intelligent, creative and uniquely human"—that a machine could process not just numbers but ideas. It has been called the first instance of artificial intelligence.[36]

● ♥

Simon, Newell, and Shaw would become authorities in the new field of artificial intelligence (AI). They kept writing computer programs: one that played mediocre chess, another (the General Problem Solver) that solved symbolic problems by using a humanlike "means-ends analysis." They also published papers on human problem solving and its computer simulation, and they ran seminars on the topic at RAND and at Carnegie Mellon. (In 1975 Simon and Newell would win the A. M. Turing Award, computer science's highest honor, for their contributions to knowledge in both AI and human cognition.)[37]

Simon himself was interested in building better AI programs, but what he really cared about was devising a model or theory of what AI did. He believed such a theory would also explain the workings of the human mind, since AI was just a simulation of those workings. And when he finally did devise his theory, it was indeed a theory of human cognition more than a theory of AI. The theory was that human cognition was very simple: it was just the processing of knowledge in the form of symbols. That symbol processing only *looked* complex because the symbols were always changing in response to their environment. That process of continual change—searching through new symbols and selecting the one that fit best for the situation—was what Simon called "problem solving." Because it took place not just inside the mind but in relationship to the environment, he also called it "design." In a 1968 lecture at the Massachusetts Institute of Technology and then in the 1969 monograph *The Sciences of the Artificial,* Simon described all human and machine problem solving—all processes of devising a solution to a problem by conceptualizing how things *ought* to be and drawing a map from the present state to a preferred future state—as design. "Everyone designs," Simon wrote, "who devises courses of action aimed at changing existing situations into preferred ones."[38]

Almost by accident, then, a computer scientist and political economist became one of the twentieth century's preeminent theorists of design. He made it clear that he meant "design" in a capacious sense: engineering was a form of design, he wrote, but likewise medicine and business and education and law and painting were all "concerned not with the necessary but with the contingent—not with how things are but with how they might be—in short, with design." Engineering and medicine and the other "professions," then—as distinct from the natural sciences—were the "sciences of the artificial" of the book's title. Whereas the natural sciences cared about how things simply *were*, the professions concerned themselves with how things *ought to be* in order to attain a goal.[39]

Simon's treatise was also a manifesto: a call for reason, rigor, and method. One group of historians of science—Paul Erickson, Lorraine Daston, and others—has described a phenomenon they call "Cold War rationality": the midcentury American intellectual project to identify the workings of rationality and then deploy it to head off global catastrophe. Funded mostly by the US government and driven by military-industrial institutions like RAND and the Harvard Council on Foreign Relations, Cold War rationality was often marked, the historians write, by "a near obsession with methods, especially algorithmic and formal ones." *The Sciences of the Artificial* is a kind of object lesson in the phenomenon of Cold War rationality, particularly in its screed against the way design methods were currently taught.[40]

The problem wasn't that there wasn't a method; the method, of course, was problem solving. It was that no one *taught* the method. "Design" education, Simon wrote—meaning formal education toward any problem-solving profession—tended to be veiled in a kind of methodological mysticism. Professionals tended to explain their acts of problem solving as acts of judgment, experience, intuition—what Max Wertheimer would have called "productive thinking"—while failing to describe the methodical "reproductive thinking," the systematic symbolic processing, behind the veil. What professional education programs taught was, resultingly, "intellectually soft, intuitive, informal, and cookbooky." And if America was to win the Cold War, this must change. Students should be given "a body of intellectually tough, analytic, partly formalizable, partly empirical, teachable doctrine about the design process." Such a "science of design" seemed not only possible but emergent. It would be the science of problem solving: of taking rational steps, in pursuit of a goal, in the context of constraints.[41]

The Sciences of the Artificial was a success. Among other impacts, it gave designers and design researchers themselves a theory of what they did. And it did so in a way that felt urgent, important, part of the larger Cold War effort to defeat communism and avoid mutual atomic annihilation. In the minds of the Cold War rationalists, Erickson and his colleagues write, "nothing less than the fate of humanity hinged on the answers to these questions."[42]

It comes as no surprise, then, that when Simon's manifesto was published there was already a larger movement afoot to rationalize design. It consisted of design critics and teachers—"design researchers," they'd begun to call themselves—who sought to render design intelligible, explicable, repeatable, teachable, algorithmic.

"Cold War rationality" is not the only contextual frame that helps make sense of this movement. The design historian Hugh Dubberly suggests that the drive to codify design methods in particular was an earlier—indeed, a modernist—impulse, originating in Europe and the United States around the end of the nineteenth century. As people retrofitted their handcraft-making skills for industry, Dubberly argues, it made sense for them to explain their methods not as idiosyncratic or subjective or intuitive but as rigorous and repeatable. Walter Gropius asked in 1943, in *Scope of Total Architecture*, "Is there a science of design?" He hoped so, he wrote. He wanted to render design "objective" rather than subject to "personal interpretation." He wanted to explain it, in short, as problem solving: a "method of approach which allows one to tackle a problem according to its peculiar conditions."[43]

There were other reasons that the idea of codifying a repeatable, rational design "method" was particularly attractive in the decades after World War II. In wartime, "design" had for the first time become central to national security, in both the Allied and the Axis countries; "designers" had been drafted into the service of the state, their contributions acknowledged, their value ratified. After the war, design simply seemed more important than it had before, and there was more curiosity about exactly what designers did. What counted as design, and what didn't? Were architectural design and industrial design and fashion design all the same thing?

How was design different from any other way of thinking or knowing? Was it simply planning? Planning by professional planners or planning like everyone did every day? The Japanese Society for the Science of Design was founded in 1954. By 1962, a Design Methods Movement was assembling itself in the United States and Great Britain, organizing conferences, publications, and seminars on both sides of the Atlantic. The participants of this and other, similar groups brought together ideas from operations research, information theory, cybernetics, architectural design, and beyond, in the name of describing and cataloging and rationalizing design. Simon, with his belief that the process was so predictable that it could be reproduced as a computer program, perhaps went furthest. But he was in good company.[44]

C. West Churchman, another midcentury systems scientist like Herbert Simon, served as midwife to much of design's new methodological self-consciousness. A Quaker-educated Philadelphia native, Churchman had joined the University of Pennsylvania's philosophy faculty as an assistant professor in 1939 after finishing a dissertation on the branch of logic called propositional calculus. As the United States prepared to enter the war, Churchman took a position doing more concrete, applied work at the US Ordnance Laboratory at Philadelphia's Frankford Arsenal. Frankford Arsenal was an enormous, coordinated, modern place, with a workforce of both soldiers and civilians. Its purpose was to design, manufacture, and test munitions. Churchman became head of the mathematical section, where he solved problems of statistical quality control. He also designed experimental methods for testing the arsenal's small arms ammunition.[45]

When the war ended, Churchman left Frankford Arsenal, but he never returned to "pure" or wholly abstract academic scholarship. Instead, and again like Simon, Churchman veered into the new, largely government-funded, national-security-minded fields of "operations research"—the application of scientific methods to decision making, especially on the institutional level—and then "systems analysis," a closely related field focused on understanding and optimizing high-level systems. Churchman became interested not only in systems' structure and function but in their design. Might better-designed social systems improve the human condition? Like Simon, he also wondered whether everyone designed—everyone *planned*, didn't they, insofar as they thought about the future?—or whether design should be considered a specialized discipline.

In 1958, Churchman became a professor in the School of Business Administration at UC Berkeley. (Like Simon, he maintained strong connections to the military and to industry, consulting for the US Department of Energy, the Texas Energy Council, the US Fish and Wildlife Service, the National Aeronautics and Space Administration, and others, even as he was founding Berkeley's graduate programs in operations research.) At Berkeley, Churchman began a weekly faculty and graduate workshop dedicated to understanding design and design methods. Colleagues called it "West's seminar." Its premise, one participant recalled later, was "that design is a ubiquitous activity practiced by almost everybody, at least some of the time, and that there may be some generalizable observations to be made about how people go about it." Its project, in short, was to observe and codify the processes by which design happened: to rationalize design.[46]

In the name of that project, West's seminar—like Paul Rand had done, and like Gropius's Bauhaus and its descendants had done, and like Simon was doing around the same time—embraced the idea that design was problem solving. By the 1960s, it made all the sense in the world. The language of problem solving was exploding across discourses in English, driven both by the burgeoning psychological discourse of problem solving and now also by the rise of computer science. Of all the "bigrams" (two-word phrases) contained in Google Books's digitized sample of books published in English in 1920, the percentage that are either "problem solving" or "problem-solving" is extremely minimal. Run the same search on publications from the year 1940, though, and you'll see that that same percentage has increased fivefold; by 1960, it has increased fourfold again. The phrase's prevalence keeps multiplying this way through the 1990s, when English-language discourse reaches peak "problem solving." Then the numbers begin to level off.[47]

In West's seminar and at the first Conference on Design Methods, convened in London in 1962, the mood was orderly and optimistic. In 1964, the British engineer and designer Bruce Archer wrote that the growing application of systems analysis to the design process had posed a "fundamental challenge to conventional ideas on design." That same year, the Berkeley architect and design theorist Christopher Alexander published *Notes on the Synthesis of Form*, an elegant little book that argued that, because design problems are complex, they should be approached—systematically, rationally—by simplification. Design is like math, Alexander wrote. Just as a mathematician does when calculating the seventh root of a fifty-digit number, a designer should write down a problem and break it into smaller problems. Then those problems can be reorganized into sets and subsets and patterns, which will point to the right solution.[48]

Thinking of design as problem solving, and of problem solving as design, has some major implications for design practice. The most obvious is that the referent of that phrase, "design practice," expands dramatically. Design becomes a very broad category of human activity. It includes, in Simon's words, all "courses of action aimed at changing existing situations into preferred ones." This does mean, as Simon argued in his section on methodology, that doctors and painters and businesspeople are also designers in their professional lives. But it also means that *everyone* is a designer, since everyone acts purposively, at least some of the time, on the world. Simon's "design" is a universal process, completely untethered from the production of any physical artifact.[49]

This first implication has had an impact on the world insofar as thinking about design this way makes it relevant to a lot more people. If everyone designs, then everyone can participate in even formal design processes. This is one of the premises behind what, in the early 2000s, would come to be called "design thinking."

A second implication is subtler. You'd think that, if design is understood as problem solving, then there should be one right answer: the single, optimal solution to the problem. This was, indeed, how Paul Rand saw things ("I will solve your problem for you. And you will pay me"). But for Herbert Simon, this wasn't the case at all. When a person decided how to deal with a problem, as Simon understood it, that person tended to begin by producing a wild proliferation of *possible* solutions: by imagining, in Simon's words, a set of "possible worlds," each of which might fulfill the goal in the context of the various constraints.

The postwar American philosopher Nelson Goodman would later describe such imagining, across disciplines, as "worldmaking." We "make" worlds, Goodman wrote, by assembling symbolic systems, whether in words or blueprints or numbers or musical scores or any other medium we like. In stroke after stroke, revision after revision, we make yet more possible worlds. And there is no logical limit to the number of possible worlds—nor is there a single right one. We can juxtapose various world-versions, Goodman writes. We can compare them, and we can judge them against one another. But each is, in some sense, "true." In the end, we simply choose the one we want.[50]

That was how Simon saw it, too. Design begins with that proliferation of solutions, and then it proceeds to the process of "judgment." Having dreamed up many possible worlds, the designer must select for the "rightest" world-version, the one that will solve the problem best. Simon thought this judgment tended to take the form of a "heuristic search": a designer uses heuristics, rules of thumb, to identify the most promising subset of the proliferation of worlds, then tests those candidates within the subset to see how well they hold up. In any case, though, the objective of the judgment process isn't to find the one "optimal" solution, "the best of all possible worlds." That's not really possible. It's to find something "satisfactory": a "sustainable" world, an "acceptable" world, a "good-enough" world.[51]

A third implication concerns where all those possible worlds come from in the first place. There's a process in mathematics called "encoding": representing information in a way that makes processing it possible. The same process, Simon asserts, applies to design: it's not about making something new so much as it's about reorganizing existing elements. "Solving a problem," Simon writes, "simply means representing it so as to make the solution transparent." Nelson Goodman, that philosopher of "worldmaking," drew similar conclusions. Asking what worlds are made of, Goodman concluded, "Not from nothing, after all, but *from other worlds*. Worldmaking as we know it always starts from worlds already on hand; the making is a remaking."[52]

This third implication rings true to my own experience of doing design. When I look at some design masterpiece or other—a Paul Rand logo mark, an Isamu Noguchi table, a film by Charles and Ray Eames—it usually appears to me as some miracle of originality: something so novel, so unexpected, that it seems made, in some divine creative act, from nothing. As I learn over and over, though, *creatio ex nihilo* is a fantasy. Design doesn't work that way; new things never come from nothing; the *least* generative possible starting place is the blank page. The Eameses' design process began with the enumeration of constraints. Rand wrote that the designer must "coordinat[e] and integrat[e] his material so that he may restate his problem in terms of ideas, signs, symbols, pictures." Not until there's a specific problem—a goal and a set of constraints, or just a set of materials to be turned over, inverted, manipulated, recombined, reimagined—does imagination begin.[53]

If conceiving of design as problem solving has implications for design practice, it also has a politics. It's idealistic. It casts design as a special but universal process that "chang[es] existing situations into preferred ones." It assumes implicitly that design is objective, impartial, rational—that it exists outside ideology and beyond any worldly system of interests, like capitalism or white supremacy. And it casts design as inherently good. Design, by definition, solves problems. Design advances and improves human life.

Herbert Simon identified as a New Deal Democrat—one of those characters that so maddened Walter Teague—and a civil libertarian. (He'd started out as socialist, but he'd gotten disenchanted with Stalinism after the Moscow show trials of the 1930s. He hadn't understood them, he wrote later—"Why did the victims confess so abjectly? What were they really guilty of?"—until he'd read Arthur Koestler's *Darkness at Noon*, that novel based in part on Eva Zeisel's imprisonment.) "Among the fundamental problems in every society," Simon wrote of his beliefs in his 1996 autobiography, two stood out to him as the problems that a political system must address. One was that people had to be motivated to contribute to society—to "produce"—so that civilization might continue. And the other was that people had to be supported and protected if they were unable to do so themselves. "You can think of it," Simon wrote, "as the balance between incentives and distributive justice. Too much concern with the latter may weaken the former, and vice versa."[54]

Simon remained committed throughout his life, in his writings and other forms of explicit political position taking, to that "balance between incentives and distributive justice." He campaigned for reform candidates, subscribed to left-wing newspapers, canvassed from door to door, and joined progressive political organizations like Americans for Democratic Action. At work, though, Simon suspended his political priorities. His job, indeed his life's calling, was to create new knowledge. Never mind that he was doing it in the service of the Cold War US state, which tended not to prioritize "distributive justice" except as a performatively counter-Communist political project. That Simon's politics and his employer's were misaligned seemed not to strike him as relevant. He believed the human and natural sciences had the capacity to advance humankind.[55]

This was also how he saw what he called "design": as a good in and of itself. Design was good because, being simply another word for problem solving, it was inherently rational. Design was objective, perhaps mathematical; it was separate from any specific interest or position or intent. And, of course, it solved problems. Problems were self-evidently bad, so solution finding must be self-evidently good.

Inherent in the idea of design as problem solving, in short, is the utopian fantasy that sciences of all kinds can be objective and rational—and thereby can arrive at answers that will necessarily advance human life. This fantasy runs through all the "design methods" work and other design-rationalizing projects, and it is implicit in our contemporary idea of design. Simon's own "design" work advanced not the welfare state or the institutions of democracy but the engines of US global economic domination and the US national security state—and indeed much "design" work today is done in the service of global corporations, which ultimately exist, in even the most idealistic of formulations, to "grow [their] value over the long term." But we still regard design as problem solving, and we still see this—regardless of the institution or project on whose behalf it's being done—as a good thing.[56]

●◗

Politics aside, the idea of design as problem solving also doesn't hold up that well as a description of reality—that is, as a theory of how "design" gets done in the real world.

Take Charles and Ray Eames. Members of the same generation as both Paul Rand and Herbert Simon (and members of that same pantheon of great American modernists that Rand occupies), the Eameses were products of Finnish architect Eliel Saarinen's Cranbrook Academy of Art, where Ray was a student and Charles a young teacher. And they learned from Saarinen to regard design as a problem-solving activity. As their work together evolved, they unfailingly described it as problem solving. They began their design processes, as noted above, by outlining the problem to be solved and the constraints. "Create bent-and-molded plywood furniture, with curves rather than corners, cheaply enough for mass production," for instance, led to the creation of the "Lounge Chair Wood" (1945), exhibited in 1946 by the Museum of Modern Art.[57]

Office of Charles and Ray Eames, molded plywood lounge chair with wood base ("Lounge Chair Wood" / "LCW"), 1945. © Eames Office, LLC. All rights reserved.

The Eameses also explicitly *theorized* design as problem solving. In the mid-1950s, as they shifted focus from designing furniture to mounting exhibitions and making films, their interest in problem solving became a kind of meta-interest, the explicit topic of much of their work. Charles was fascinated by the emerging technology of the computer; to try to understand it, he began studying mathematical and computational models—particularly game theory and linear programming—for problem solving. Soon the couple's films began to explore some of the same aspects of problem solving that were also occupying Herbert Simon. How, for instance, did a person judge between potential solutions, selecting the rightest possible "world-version"? How could a person speculate in the context of imperfect information and limited computational ability? It didn't matter if these were called computer problems or philosophical problems or real-world problems or design problems. "The steps in solving each," one Eames exhibition explained, "are essentially the same."[58]

Thus the Eameses, as the critic John Harwood has put it, reduced design—at least in their explicit statements, writings, and theorizations—to "a self-consistent set of rules, a logic, identical to that undergirding the operations of information technology." And yet this neat and tidy homology, this rational theory of design, didn't come close to capturing the Eameses' actual design *practice*. In fact, for the Eameses, design was also something very *unlike* problem solving—something not rational at all. Design was made of luck and spontaneity and intuition and whimsy. Design was *play*.[59]

Look at the Eames's famous toys, their masks, their games, and you'll find that most of them are designed to solve no problem at all. Charles and Ray loved to juxtapose objects for the juxtaposition's own sake; they loved color and texture and detail and decoration. Or consider Ray's early 1940s covers for *California Arts & Architecture* magazine, many made in an explicitly playful, seemingly improvisatory, collage-like (and yet still fully modern) style. Or take the whimsical instrument the couple created in 1957 for the Aluminum Company of America. Called the Solar Do-Nothing Machine, it was an assemblage of colorful moving parts powered by miniature photovoltaic-driven motors. It explicitly evaded functionality; it refused to solve any problem. "It is not supposed to do," Charles explained. "It is supposed to be. Its whole function is in its being." The machine spun, oscillated, shone in the sun, alternated, swung, revolved. It poked implicit fun at everything functional, everything purposive, every solution. It played.[60]

Other design luminaries who have stumped for design as problem solving—or as rational in any way at all—have later

Office of Charles and Ray Eames, Solar Do-Nothing Machine, aluminum, water, photovoltaic cells, 1957. © Eames Office, LLC. All rights reserved.

abandoned that faith. And even scientific evidence seems to come down on the side of design and art being resolutely *irrational* acts. In 1976, Jacob Getzels and Mihaly Csikszentmihalyi published a longitudinal study that traced a group of prospective artists and designers from their early days as art students through to the middle of their creative careers. The study, titled *The Creative Vision*, found that those participants who went on to be successful artists (designers included) were distinguished from their peers by one characteristic: they were less focused on problem solving than on problem *finding*. The "gift" of artistic "genius," Getzels and Csikszentmihalyi concluded, "is not only the possession of technical skills or the facility for solving problems, but also the sensitivity and imagination for finding them."[61]

One of the clearest voices calling out the distance between problem solving and design or art—in this case, poetry—was the writer Gwendolyn Brooks. Every year from 1951 until 2004, designers gathered in Colorado for the International Design Conference in Aspen, and every year the conference had a timely theme; in 1961, that theme was "Man / Problem Solver." George Pólya was invited but could not make it. Also invited that year was Brooks, who by then had won the Guggenheim Fellowship (twice: 1946 and 1947) and the Pulitzer Prize in poetry (1950). The panel on which she was invited to speak, in keeping with the theme, was titled "All Creative People Are Problem Solvers."[62]

Brooks spent most of her conference appearance reading her poems. Before she began reading, though, a moderator asked her what, in this room full of designers, made her different. "I don't believe it's the province of the artist to solve problems," she said. "I feel that he should be an eye, an ear, a mind, a heart—but I think that the solving of problems should

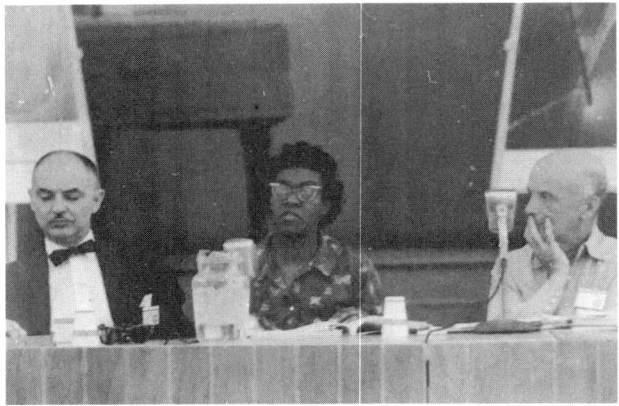

International Design Conference in Aspen (IDCA), publicity photographs, Gwendolyn Brooks and other participants at IDCA, 1961. International Design Conference in Aspen records, 1949–2006, The Getty Research Institute, Los Angeles, Accession no. 2007.M.7.

be left to others who are more active and perhaps more muscular." There was a swell of uneasy laughter from the audience. Brooks continued, "I feel that when [an artist] has given his best and has written as well as he can, about things that he deeply feels—well, that material, there, will provide activity for the true fights and real problem-solvers. And I'm going to read poems that I have written that deal with the materials that the problem-solvers can work with, and you can see just much or how little I can do about the solving of problems."[63]

She went on to read her 1945 poem "kitchenette building," which depicts life within a set of nested social and historical problems: poor housing conditions, the shortage of housing available to Black Americans, housing discrimination, structural racism, the legacies of slavery. The poem's speaker describes the lives of herself and the other occupants of kitchenette worlds: "We are things of dry hours and the involuntary plan, / Grayed in, and gray." The poem doesn't solve anything; "poetry," as W. H. Auden put it, "makes nothing happen"; solving things isn't its job. If art was about problems at all, Brooks continued in her written remarks for the conference, it should provide only "the interpreted photograph of the thing-to-be-solved."[64]

Brooks spoke as an artist—and design, of course, isn't only art. But it isn't only science, either. Speaking in 1952, Charles Eames acknowledged that what he and Ray did was different from pure art: Ray "hasn't done a lot of paintings lately," he acknowledged, "in the sense that you can paint something and put it into a frame." And yet design did have something in common, Eames continued, with a painter's work. An artist's perception, "feeling," "thinking again beyond the surface," he continued—the artist's ability to "anticipate," to make "contact with nature or situations," to draw on "intuitive feeling for what the appropriate form may be"—was as much a part of design as was any consideration of solutions and problems. Efforts to rationalize design might make it seem more professional, more repeatable, more valid. But they missed something real and crucial to the thing at hand.[65]

Chapter 4

HUMAN-CENTEREDNESS

The air changed in 652 Barrows Hall when Horst Rittel walked in in the fall of 1967. West Churchman had been assembling his Berkeley colleagues and students in that room every week for a half decade. They came from all over the university: the music department, the public health program, political science, engineering, art, business administration. Together, this group—they called it "West's seminar"—had chipped away systematically at the project of explaining and rationalizing and documenting "design." The idea was to capture the design process accurately enough that it could be applied systematically to the problems of contemporary life.[1]

They knew their project was idealistic. It involved challenges that were probably, ultimately, insurmountable. Even if design could be fully understood and modeled, for instance, trying to use it to solve major system-level problems might be futile—since trying to improve a system (say, public education in the United States) probably required fully understanding it, and fully understanding a system of that scale was probably impossible. But Churchman and his colleagues were pragmatists. They proceeded on the assumption that things could be improved with design, even if the process could never be wholly understood and the outcomes would never be perfect.[2]

Horst Rittel saw things differently. Born in 1930 and raised in Berlin, Rittel had an open, sad face and a high forehead, and, as of the 1960s, he always wore a suit. Like many of the others in West's seminar room, he had seen World War II—but from the other side: born in 1930, he'd grown up in Nazi Berlin, witnessed the regime's brutalization of Europe as a German high school student, and attended university in postwar Germany at the University of Göttingen. Rittel had come to Berkeley in 1963 from a German college of design, the Hochschule für Gestaltung Ulm, descended from the Bauhaus. It was an internationally admired institution whose faculty had been decimated, before Rittel's departure, by infighting over politics. Like Herbert Simon, Rittel had a rangy interdisciplinary background, spanning mathematics, theoretical physics, sociology, astronomy, and operations research. He also had a cosmopolitan's sense that Western civilization's long march of progress might, as of 1967, be coming to a bitter end.[3]

Rittel was skeptical about rationalizing design, at least the kind of design that mattered. He saw the effort to understand it, to make it scientific, to render it reproducible—including by describing it as simple problem solving—as a fool's errand. When he arrived in the seminar room in 1967, he had come to read out a new paper on that topic. The paper argued that it would be impossible to rationalize anyone's design or planning process. (Rittel sometimes referred to "design" as "planning" and to "designers" as "planners"; the words were, for him, interchangeable.) Rittel *did* think that design was something akin to problem solving, but he thought the problems worth solving—societal problems, like where to put a freeway, how to modernize a school curriculum, how to tax people justly, how to reduce poverty—presented potentially insurmountable roadblocks to designers. In his paper he described this class of problems, historicized it, and gave it a name.[4]

What characterized these problems, Rittel said, was first that they were "indeterminate." It was always hard to tell, in other words, whether you had the problem right, because if you dug deeper—"But *why* is it this way?"—you could always find a more foundational root cause than the one you were addressing. These problems also didn't have true or false answers; they only had better or worse solutions. They were not, contrary to Christopher Alexander's argument in *Notes on the Synthesis of Form* (1964), like math problems; there was no mathematical method that might balance all the forces at play. There was also no definitive test of a solution, no proof. Putting in more effort might always lead to something better.[5]

There were other ways, Rittel continued, that these problems were not like math. They were intrinsically high-stakes, in that any implemented solution would leave "traces" that couldn't be undone. And the designer had no "right to be wrong," because the problems mattered. Human lives were at stake.[6]

Rittel named them "wicked problems." They were "wicked" not because they were unethical or evil but because they were malignant, tricky, hard. Take the problem of poverty. Solving it, Rittel suggested, would mean identifying what stopped certain people from securing adequate income. But where to start—and how far to go? Was that problem the result of macroeconomic failures on the national or regional level—or of skill deficiency within the labor force? If the latter, which parts of the educational system should be reformed? Did the problem of poverty also include poor physical and mental health? Did it include "cultural deprivation? spatial dislocation? problems of ego identity? deficient political and social skills?" Once the root causes were identified, solutions would be, presumably, easy to formulate. But identifying the root causes was very difficult. The roots went further down than any human being could dig.[7]

Not every design problem was a wicked problem, wrote Rittel and his colleague Melvin Webber when they published these ideas in 1969. There were some very simple problems, too. But those had already been answered. (Churchman wrote in the wake of Rittel's seminar presentation, "One was led to conclude from the discussion that the membership in the class of non-wicked problems is restricted to the arena of play: nursery school, academia and the like.") And now that the easier problems had been dealt with, the only problems worth designers' time were the wicked ones. The convoluted problems that contemporary social life had surfaced, as of 1967, called for design's exclusive focus and concentration.[8]

For Rittel, the wickedness of meaningful design problems meant that they could never be subject to a single process of resolution. There could be no one design "method." Textbooks tended to break down, say, engineering work, Rittel and Webber wrote, into "phases," like "gather information," "synthesize information and wait for the creative leap," and the like. But for wicked problems, "this type of scheme does not work." Understanding the problem required understanding its context. Gathering full information wasn't possible before starting to formulate a solution concept. Nothing could be linear or consistent. Indeed, designers just weren't likely to think that way, at least not as part of their work. If there was any describing the design process, it was as an *argument*: a multiplicity of critical voices batting a problem back and forth around a rough terrain until it formed itself, or didn't, into some kind of solution.[9]

Rittel saw design's ineluctable methodlessness as a good thing. It afforded an "awesome epistemic freedom," he would write later, without logical constraints or algorithmic guidance or rules of validity. But for those of his peers who had been committed to identifying and systematizing one single comprehensive design method, Rittel's uncompromising, rigorous, calmly academic voice of refusal helped spell the end of a rationalist era. He changed their minds. John Chris Jones, who had organized the first "design methods" conference in London in 1962, now renounced the whole rationalist project. Christopher Alexander, who in *Notes on the Synthesis of Form* had analogized design to math, repudiated that book and the rest of his own methodological work. "There is so little in what is called 'design methods' that has anything useful to say about how to design buildings," he told an interviewer in 1971. "I would say forget it, forget the whole thing. . . . Most of the difficulties of design are not of the computable sort."[10]

It was not an optimistic time. In the United States, President John F. Kennedy and civil rights activist Medgar Evers had been shot dead in 1963, Malcolm X in 1965, and Dr. Martin Luther King Jr. and Robert F. Kennedy in 1968. Bodies piled up, too, in Vietnam. In April 1969, the total number of Americans dead in the war reached 33,641, surpassing the US death toll from the Korean War. The Vietnamese civilian death toll, by contemporary estimates, surpassed one hundred thousand that same year. Meanwhile, the US government expressed unalloyed contempt for war protestors and other people who dared resist the government or the status quo. "Drugs, crime, campus revolts, racial discord, draft resistance," new US president Richard Nixon incanted to a South Dakota audience in mid-1969. "On every hand, we find old standards violated, old values discarded, old principles ignored. . . . Old and young across the nation shout across a chasm of misunderstanding, and the louder they shout the broader the chasm becomes."[11]

The year 1968 had brought a global surge of energy and solidarity: the growth of social movements, of struggles against dictatorships and authoritarian rule, of resistance even in the face of violent repression. But 1969 saw a massive global letdown. Coalitional hopes sagged nearly worldwide, replaced by feelings of chaos, dread, and hopelessness. A newspaper reported in January 1969 that British citizens, facing seemingly endless economic setbacks and reflecting on widespread social unrest, had adopted a "national mood" of "defiance mixed with despair." In May 1969, in Kuala Lumpur, hundreds of people died in a Sino-Malay race riot in response to the outcome of Malaysia's general election. Later that month, in Los Angeles, a coalition of white liberals, Blacks, and Chicanos rallied behind—but then saw the defeat of—Black liberal mayoral hopeful Tom Bradley, who then conceded to the viciously racist and Red-baiting incumbent Sam Yorty. That election was followed by sinister law-enforcement actions against the Black Panthers, Brown Berets, and other activist groups. In August, bloody clashes broke out between Protestant loyalists and Catholic nationalists in Derry and Belfast. Later called the Northern Ireland Riots, these episodes of violence would be seen retrospectively as the beginning of the thirty-year sectarian political conflict called "the Troubles."[12]

"Design," whatever that might be, no longer looked to anyone like the answer. At the 1969 International Design Conference in Aspen (IDCA)—the same conference that in 1961 had been themed "Man / Problem Solver," that had emphasized the designer's "great social responsibility" to help build "a new society with new institutions," that had celebrated design's capacity to "'blast off' for richer worlds"—the atmosphere had turned somber. The 1969 conference was titled "The Rest of Our Lives." The industrial designer George Nelson bemoaned, in his conference talk, the difficulty of escape from "the perverted offspring of the American dream"—the dream itself having been brought about, Nelson said, in part by blind faith in technology. The conference's overall mood, one commentator observed later, reflected "the despair the participants felt at the crumbling of American ideals."[13]

But the 1970 conference was even darker. Titled "Environment by Design," it opened with the customary celebratory Sunday reception: "Gypsy girls, headbands, body jewelry, old-liners and newcomers," program chairman William Houseman recounted, "all aswirl" in the garden. "But scant hint," Houseman added, "of things to come." By Tuesday morning, the American architect Carl Koch was declaring from the podium, "Our national leadership is unspeakable. The government's sense of priorities is criminally askew.

Our cities are rotting visibly before our eyes." On Wednesday, Rayner Banham threw out his own prepared talk halfway through. He spoke off the cuff, instead, about the pitiful impotence of design.[14]

By Friday morning, the planned conference format had disintegrated. People gathered ad hoc in the conference tent to connect with one another and express ideas about the current crisis. A group of French participants read a screed against design itself, written for the occasion by Jean Baudrillard. Baudrillard's statement lambasted the conference's environmentalist theme as disingenuous ("Nothing better than a touch of ecology and catastrophe to unite the social classes"), even as it acknowledged, "The real problem is far beyond Aspen—it is the entire theory of Design and Environment itself, which constitutes a generalized Utopia; Utopia produced by a Capitalist system." (Utopia, here, seems to imply the most self-delusional kind of fantasy.) Several proposed resolutions, all unsponsored by the IDCA, were read and voted upon by the assembled participants. When one resolution seemed to have passed, there was an uproar: the losing side charged that the vote was illegal, that it had been passed under threat of violence, that conferees had been coerced and misrepresented. "I could suddenly feel all these changes running together in a spasm of bad vibrations," recalled Banham, that session's intended chairman. "An epoch had ended."[15]

The final hours of the conference, IDCA president Eliot Noyes wrote afterward, underlined "the relative irrelevance of the design subject in the minds of many who were attending." At the subsequent board meeting, Noyes resigned as president, and the board resolved to search for a radically new form for the 1971 conference, if the conference were to be held again at all. Both the conferees and the board, Noyes reflected, now harbored "serious doubt as to whether at this moment in our national history and our state of emotional disrepair a conference on design can or should be held at all." Focusing on design seemed irrelevant at best, or else complicit, malign.[16]

The whole concept of design was also under attack from those outside design's professional bounds. In 1971, the German philosopher Wolfgang Fritz Haug published *Kritik der Warenästhetik* (later translated into English as *A Critique of Commodity Aesthetics*), a Marxist-cum-Freudian manifesto that described designers as the "handmaidens" of capitalism. Design, Haug contended, was an engine of the appetite-generating "illusion industry" of media and advertising, as well as of the broader consumer capitalist system behind them, all of which were organized around driving consumption and thereby producing profits. Haug, like the Frankfurt School before him, charged the modern culture industries and the commodities they produced with the manipulation of human beings. But Haug added a meaningful nuance to Theodor Adorno and Max Horkheimer's thesis: he showed that manipulating people was only possible because design and its peer disciplines colluded with those people's pursuit of self-interest, which was continuous, intelligent, and fully intentional. "Commodities can only manipulate people," the critic Stuart Hall wrote in his introduction to Haug's volume, "insofar as those people have reason to believe it will benefit them." Or, as Haug put it elsewhere, even "manipulative phenomena" must "still speak the language of real needs." And that language was design's native tongue.[17]

Where did that leave design? Was it a necessary evil, or a poison to be eradicated? Neither: it was that poison's dangerously sweet taste. Or, to use Haug's own metaphor, design was like the Red Cross in wartime. "It tends some wounds, but not the worst, inflicted by capitalism," Haug wrote. "Its function is cosmetic, and thus prolongs the life of capitalism by making it occasionally somewhat more attractive and by boosting morale, just as the Red Cross prolongs war. Thus design, by its particular artifice, supports the general disfigurement."[18]

In 1971 the Austrian American designer Victor Papanek published *Design for the Real World*. It has since become one of the most widely read design books in history; it has been published all over the world, has been translated into over twenty languages, and (as of 2024) has never fallen out of print. It's a manifesto against what design, as of 1971, had become. And it's a passionate brief for what Papanek believed design *could* be.[19]

Victor von Papanek was born to a bourgeois Jewish family in Vienna, Austria, in 1923. He grew up there, until the age of fifteen, in that same urban hub of intellectual fervor that had earlier nurtured the young Eva Zeisel. In 1939, just after Zeisel's Soviet detainers ejected her from a train back onto Vienna's streets, Victor and his mother left the city. They traveled alongside thousands of other persecuted Austrians who were fleeing following the 1938 Nazi annexation of the country (the Anschluss), the Nazi regime's first act of territorial expansion. The von Papaneks escaped to Holland, where they boarded the SS *Pennland* to Hoboken, New Jersey. From there, they were transported to Ellis Island, where they were processed with thousands of other "Hebrew" refugees seeking entry to the United States.[20]

In New York, Victor Papanek—he and his mother had quickly dropped the "von," which now seemed ostentatious—moved downtown to a Jewish hostel on Manhattan's Lower East Side. In 1943, Victor enlisted in the US Army, identifying his profession as "artist." He served a year as a German-English interpreter in Alaska and the Aleutian Islands, then was granted US citizenship in June 1945. In 1946, returning from service, he opened a design studio, called Design Clinic, run out of an efficiency apartment near Madison Square Park. He also enrolled, despite lacking a high school diploma, in college. He would be a student in the four-year architectural design program at the Cooper Union, a private art school in the East Village dedicated to making arts education free of cost to talented young people.[21]

It can be hard to trace what really happened in the first few decades of Victor Papanek's career. He was prone to creative invention. But certainly he was influenced by the Finnish designer Alvar Aalto, whose own design work mimicked the vernacular and the organic, and by Edgar J. Kaufmann Jr., the director of industrial design at the Museum of Modern Art (MoMA), who promoted democratic access to functional and beautiful objects. Papanek also seems to have worked, around 1947, with the vanguard German American psychoanalyst and psychiatrist Fredric Wertham, ostensibly conducting inkblot tests as a volunteer at the famous Lafargue Clinic in Harlem. He claimed to have undergone psychoanalysis with Wertham himself. And he seems to have apprenticed in 1948 with Frank Lloyd Wright, who ran an experimental collectivist internship program out of his Taliesin Studios in Spring Green, Wisconsin. (Apprenticeship at Taliesin "did not primarily mean that one studied Architecture," Papanek wrote later. "Instead we were called upon to help give birth to baby piglets, milk the cows, build additions to the barns, sow and harvest the crops, cook and work in the kitchen, serve meals and set the table, burn quicklime and lay brick walls, and so on.")[22]

Back in New York City, though, Design Clinic failed to thrive. Papanek had wanted his agency's work to address the needs of people who "suffer design neglect," as he put it: "the rural poor, and the black and white citizens of our inner cities." But he found, unsurprisingly, that most such potential clients had little cash to spare for industrial design consulting. So when Papanek's apprenticeship at Taliesin ended, he returned briefly to New York, then headed west. He landed in 1950 in California.[23]

The West Coast brought Papanek some success—not particularly with his works of industrial or architectural design, but with his writing and teaching *about* design. In August 1950, the magazine *La Mer* published his essay "Why Contemporary?," which denounced the "bewildering array of so-called modern furniture" that faced American consumers, all of it "slavishly" striving for "superficial effect" rather than solving for any real needs. "Why Contemporary?" doesn't promote any particular alternative to modernist dogma, but it does convey a powerful frustration. (It refers to Le Corbusier's celebrated modernist dictum that a house is "a machine for living in," for example, as "a fascist negation of living.") Its publication began to establish Papanek as a critic. Soon, he was teaching at the Art League of California; by the mid-1950s, he had moved to Toronto to teach at the Ontario College of Art. He also began traveling in the summers to Cambridge, Massachusetts, to attend idiosyncratic two-week summer seminars hosted by the Creative Engineering Laboratory at the Massachusetts Institute of Technology (MIT), which was led by the designer-philosopher John E. Arnold.[24]

Through the MIT seminars, Papanek discovered a potential salve for the ills of modernist design: the idea of turning design toward "humanity." In 1955, he sat in the seminar audience and took notes on a talk by Buckminster Fuller. Fuller was a rational empiricist in the vein of Herbert Simon and West Churchman: he thought of design as a "science." But he added a humanist spin, emphasizing that design's purpose should not be to make profit but to "meet the needs of all humanity without disrupting the ecological processes of the planet." Papanek also attended and took careful notes on a talk by the industrial designer (and Walter Teague collaborator) Henry Dreyfuss, who would publish *Designing for People* that same year. The book is still a classic in its advocacy that designers never forget that "what we are working on is going to be ridden in, sat upon, looked at, talked into, activated, operated, or in some way used by people individually or en masse." That was the point of design, Dreyfuss wrote: to make people's lives easier. If the person-product interaction becomes "a point of friction, then the industrial designer has failed. If, on the other hand, people are made safer, more comfortable, more eager to purchase, more efficient—or just plain happier—the designer has succeeded."[25]

Dreyfuss tells a story in *Designing for People* that shows what an uphill battle it was, in the first half of the twentieth century, for a designer to live by these humanistic principles. Back in the 1930s, Dreyfuss writes, the standard Bell telephone was ugly and uncomfortable to use. It wasn't quite the old-timey candlestick with the hanging mouthpiece—it was a handset in a cradle with a rotary dial—but it looked scrawny and awkwardly proportioned, felt hard and sharp against the head, and turned in the hand during conversations. In 1930, Bell Labs ran a competition to redesign it. Bell asked ten designers to sketch "the future appearance" of the "ideal" form of the home telephone. The winner's design, the company promised, would replace the present model.[26]

Dreyfuss was one of the ten designers whose participation Bell Labs solicited. At twenty-six, he had just moved into a new office in Manhattan; he had furnished it with a borrowed card table, folding chairs, and one potted plant, of which he was extremely proud. Like Walter Dorwin Teague, he was the son of a Brooklyn Jewish immigrant family, and he was a newly minted industrial designer at the start of both the profession and what appeared to be a serious economic depression. He could have used the work Bell offered. The fee for sketches of the "ideal" phone, the Bell representative told Dreyfuss, would be $1,000.[27]

One thousand dollars sounded good. But Dreyfuss turned Bell down. He couldn't just sit down and sketch out a new phone, he said; "an honest job of design" didn't start with an aesthetic makeover. Instead, he would need to understand how people would use the phone, as well as how it worked inside. The Bell visitor shrugged: he was looking for sketches, and Dreyfuss's proposal seemed like far too much process and far too little guaranteed beautification. The conversation seemed to be over.[28]

A year later, though, the Bell company returned to Dreyfuss's doorstep, and now the representative's attitude was different. The competitors' designs hadn't worked out; Bell's telephone engineers had dismissed them as "impractical." If Dreyfuss was still interested, he could have his terms.[29]

He took the job. He went on to shadow Bell repairmen in customers' homes, seeking to understand, he wrote later, "what people did with phones." He collaborated with Bell's engineers to refine the phone's technical workings. Together, they developed the new, handsomely square, more comfortable, more ergonomic Bell Model 302 telephone. It let the user talk on the phone hands-free, cradling the receiver between her shoulder and her jawbone. Starting in 1937, the Model 302 became the American standard. In 1949, Dreyfuss's firm—now thriving—refined it as the Model 500, which in various versions dominated the home and office markets for generations.[30]

By the mid-1950s, then, Dreyfuss and a few others had long experience making waves by trying to focus their design efforts not primarily on aesthetics, nor even on function, so much as on how a design would serve its users. But it would take the world-historical changes of the late 1960s and 1970s to tip the scales in their direction—to make designers worldwide avow that serving human beings was the heartbeat of their vocation.

●◡

By 1971, Victor Papanek was dean of the newly formed School of Design at the California Institute of the Arts (CalArts). Through the influence of Fuller, Dreyfuss, and a handful of Scandinavian design activists with whom he had become close during several summer seminars in Finland (1966–1969), Papanek had begun to develop his own methodology for a design practice focused specifically and explicitly on solving for real human beings' real needs. Papanek preached design's "unique capacity for addressing human issues," as he put it in the magazine *Industrial Design*, and its "value beyond the purely commercial imperative." And he had developed his philosophy of "DESIGN FOR THE NEEDS OF MAN"—a set of seven "main areas for creative attack".[31]

1. Design for Backward and Underdeveloped Areas of the World.
2. Design for Poverty Areas such as: Northern Big City Ghettos & Slums, White Southern Appalachia, Indian Reservations in the Southwest and Migratory Farm Workers.
3. Design for Medicine, Surgery, Dentistry, Psychiatry & Hospitals.
4. Design for Scientific Research and Biological Work.
5. Design of Teaching, Training and Exercising Devices for the Disabled, the Retarded, the Handicapped and the Subnormal, the Disadvantaged.
6. Design for Non-Terran and Deep Space Environments, Design for Sub-Oceanic Environments.
7. Design for "Breakthrough," through new concepts.

That designers should organize their work around addressing human beings' real-world needs, however clumsily taxonomized—rather than around aesthetics, or function, or the profit imperative—was the message of Papanek's book *Design for the Real World*. First published in Swedish in 1970, it found global success when published in English in 1971, taking its place among other leftist English-language jeremiads of the time: Jane Jacobs's *The Death and Life of Great American Cities* (1961), Rachel Carson's *Silent Spring* (1962), James Baldwin's *The Fire Next Time* (1963), Kate Millett's *Sexual Politics* (1970), E. F. Schumacher's *Small Is Beautiful: Economics as if People Mattered* (1973). Papanek's book attributes a lot of agency to design: "In an age of mass production when everything must be planned and designed," he writes, "design has become the most powerful tool with which man shapes his tools and environments (and, by extension, society and himself)." But the book doesn't celebrate that agency. Instead, it charges designers, and the broader economies of production within which they operate, with wasting and abusing their power.[32]

Take the process of creating and distributing a new secretarial chair. In a "market-oriented, profit-directed system such as that in the United States," such a new chair almost invariably "is designed because a furniture manufacturer feels that there may be a profit in putting a new chair on the market," rather than because there is any empirical evidence that a particular population's sitting needs are not being met. The design team is simply "told that a new chair is needed, and what particular price structure it should fit into." The team may consult resources in ergonomics or human factors, but inevitably they will find that the information available about their potential "users" is sorely lacking. So they design another generic chair, made neither to fit a specific population nor to solve a new problem. After some perfunctory testing, the chair hits the market, where, invariably, someone other than the secretary decides whether to buy it for her use. Some money is made. No one's life improves. But the manufacturer is satisfied: "If it sells, swell."[33]

What should designers do instead? "A great deal of research," Papanek replied. Designers should ask "big," "transnational" questions: "What is an ideal human social system? . . . What are optimal conditions for human society on earth?" They should inquire into their potential users' "living patterns, sexual mores, world mobility, codes of behavior, primitive and sophisticated religions and philosophies, and much more." And they should learn about other cultures' ways of prioritizing and addressing needs. They should undertake "in-depth study" of such "diverse social organizations" as the "American Plains Indians, the Mundugumor of the Lower Sepik River basin; the priest-cultures of the Inca, Maya, Toltec, and Aztec; the Pueblo cultures of the Hopi; the social structuring surrounding the priest-goddess in Crete; the mountain-dwelling Arapesh; child care in Periclean Greece; Samoa of the late nineteenth century, Nazi Germany, and modern-day Sweden"; et cetera, et cetera.[34]

Papanek was not the only Western designer turning toward non-Western cultures in the 1960s and 1970s. Americans' and Europeans' interest in non-Western societies had been growing since World War II, as they observed postwar decolonization movements—often complicated, of course, by the US-Soviet geopolitical rivalry—and gained access to works like Frantz Fanon's *The Wretched of the Earth* (*Les damnés de la terre*, 1961), which inspired increasing awareness of anticolonial resistance. By the early 1970s, scholars and journalists had begun to describe what would increasingly be called "globalization." The term itself refers both to the late twentieth-century increase in literal connectedness between economies, cultures, and populations—through the exchange of goods, the movement of capital and data, and the migration of peoples—and to the concomitant increase in people's *consciousness* of their interconnectedness, their feeling of shared experiences and problems and interests.[35]

Papanek himself believed that research into non-Western cultures would benefit designers in particular in at least two ways. Contact with cultures other than their own might lead those designers to question the capitalist assumptions—"that we must buy more, consume more, waste more, throw away more, and consequently destroy Life-raft Earth"—on which their own design practices were premised. And through that contact they might stumble upon new problems worth solving.[36]

That last bit sounds familiar: Papanek might be Herbert Simon, or some participant in West Churchman's seminar, using design methodically to "solve problems." And Papanek did think of them as "problems," these incitements to design. ("It is the prime function of the designer to solve problems," he wrote.) But when Papanek talked about "needs" or "problems," he was talking less about something self-evident—as the "problem" was for Simon or the early Churchman seminar participants—and more about something subtler, an unmet need as experienced by a particular person or group of people. In some regions of the world, for instance, people get sick because waste products cannot be efficiently rinsed away in the absence of modern sanitation systems. The designer must be exceptionally able to uncover this kind of need. The designer must "search for, isolate, and identify problems that need solutions." This was the point of all the research.[37]

Papanek's commitment to identifying needs by learning about the lives of specific users—largely those from non-Western cultures—might be called an "ethnographic" impulse: a drive to study groups of people (usually groups other than one's own) and to document their cultures, customs, habits, and differences from an assumed norm. The ethnographic impulse played out not only in Papanek's blockbuster book but also in his self-curation and self-presentation. He built a personal library, his biographer notes, containing hundreds of volumes of anthropological research and writing: volumes with titles like *The Tewa World: Space, Time, Being and Becoming in a Pueblo Society* (by Alfonso Ortiz, 1972), *Eskimo Artifacts: Designed for Use* (by Paul and Mary Thiry, 1977), and *Japanese Spoons and Ladles* (by Masao Usui, 1979). Beginning in the 1960s, Papanek invited reporters into his home to photograph or draw him and his wife (whoever she was at the time) and their decor: Navajo weavings, Buddhist figures, Inuit masks and ritual artifacts, Balinese masks, other objects of vernacular culture. Papanek also endeavored, through this period, to document his alleged ethnographic capital as a set of professional credentials. In the "biographical data" sheet (something like a curriculum vitae) that he presented to CalArts in 1970, Papanek wrote that he had

a. traveled widely throughout Europe, Thailand, Bali, Java, Cambodia, Japan, etc.
b. spent nearly 6 months (with the Governor's permission) living in a Hopi Indian pueblo
c. spent several months with an Alaskan Eskimo tribe and nearly five years in Canada
d. spent part of 5 summers in an art-and-craft centered milieu in the Southern Appalachians
e. received various grants that took me to Lapland, Sweden and Finland during the summer of 1966; Finland and Russia during the summer of 1967; and will take me to Russia, Finland, Sweden, and Norway during the summer of 1968.

His biographer calls several of these items—particularly those suggesting that Papanek had carried out fieldwork with Hopi and Alaskan Eskimo tribes—"fallacious." But that didn't stop Papanek from repeating them across documents and forums. The biographical data sheet also noted that in summer 1968, Papanek had worked as "a UNESCO Technical Expert (Design) with a cross-disciplinary team of other UNESCO experts from 5 African states at Jyvaskyla, Finland," preparing a report "dealing with the basic design needs of the African sub-continent." It also listed his "outside interests": "Eskimo and Indian art," "Oriental art," "Anthropology."[38]

◗◖

Designers should be students of human culture: designers should be anthropologists. The idea came to Papanek, at least in part, from Finland and Sweden. He idealized Nordic thinking in general, and Nordic design practice in particular, for what he saw as their focus on human necessity. "Almost all excellence of Finnish design," he wrote in 1966, "has grown out of honest need." Papanek himself took a pseudo-anthropological approach to explaining Finnish design tropes. "The northern climate is partially responsible for the fact that the dwelling is regarded not only as a place where one eats and sleeps," he wrote, "but as the true frame around family life. In the South one meets friends in bars and inns; in Finland you invite them to your home, hence the house and its furnishings are of social interest."[39]

In addition to demanding a kind of layperson's ethnographic analysis, Finland and its neighbors seemed, to Papanek's mind, to have their own useful design methodology to offer. Papanek had learned from Nordic design activists that designers should do real research into their potential users' ways of life, whether that research was formal ethnography or something else. In July 1968, attending the Scandinavian Design Students' Organization seminars on the island of Suomenlinna (outside Helsinki), Papanek had met the Finnish Swedish designer Henrik Wahlforss, who was just starting a small design agency called ErgonomiDesign. Wahlforss's agency would focus on theorizing and practicing ways to incorporate into the design process some actual knowledge about the people who might use its end products.

The ErgonomiDesign concern was soon joined by another new design collective, DesignGruppen; united as ErgonomiDesignGruppen, they operated out of an old glue factory outside Stockholm. ErgonomiDesignGruppen became famous for championing the idea that designers should seek informed understandings of their designs' potential users. And they believed in gaining this understanding through ergonomic and ethnographic research.[40]

Other designers worldwide were also discovering what they could learn from anthropologists. Beginning in the 1970s, the critic Alison J. Clarke has written, designers and critics in Europe and the United States—from Papanek himself to the sometimes-primitivist Italian design collective Superstudio—were using objects from other, ostensibly primitive cultures, from woodworking tools to canoes, as statements of "counterpoise to inauthentic capitalist product culture." (Charles and Ray Eames, for instance, regularly used objects from foreign cultures to create what one critic has called "extra-cultural surprise.") Both the idea of anthropology itself and the "primitive" cultures it studied—cultures that made things believed to be uncomplicated, precapitalist, untainted—were now positioned as antidotes to late-capitalist design practice's ills.[41]

Particularly to architects, many of whom for the previous decade had been heavily influenced by structuralism, anthropological analysis made sense. Structuralist approaches examine cultural forms and systems in relation to the basic foundational structures they express: structures like "communication route," or "social hierarchy," or, perhaps, "loaf of bread." As another manifestation of the anthropological impulse in design in the 1970s, Clarke and others point to the 1976 exhibition "MAN transFORMS," at New York's Cooper

Unknown photographer, "Variations on a Basic Item: Bread," from Hans Hollein, "MAN transFORMS," Cooper Hewitt, Smithsonian Design Museum, 1976. Smithsonian Institution Archives Record Unit 287, Box 18, Folder 13.

Hewitt design museum. Curated by the Austrian postmodernist architect Hans Hollein, whom the museum selected over other candidates including George Nelson and Charles and Ray Eames, the exhibition figured itself as a kind of opposite of the MoMA's "Good Design" shows of the 1940s. It turned away from the avant-garde, from fine arts, and from the objects most valued by commerce—beautiful utensils, beautiful chairs— and focused instead on vernacular objects the world over.

The effect, to reviewers' eyes, was somewhat strange. An installation called "Variations on a Basic Item: Bread" consisted of baguettes, bagels, pretzels, tortillas, challah, and other specimens, all arranged on a massive breadbox (glass, bronze, anodized aluminum) atop a marble floor. Another installation focused on fabrics; a third, "Variations on a Basic Item: Hammer," began with Neolithic hand axes. The exhibition as a whole, curator Hollein wrote, was meant to be "a statement about what Design is." Hollein wanted "to show that design underlies human activity and creativity, that all our endeavors are governed by 'design'" (the statement resonates with his oft-repeated dictum "Alles ist Architektur," "Everything is architecture"). At least one visiting art critic, though, did not find any answers at the exhibit to "that old sticky wicket of 'design' and its identity: what is it? How should it be defined, how can it be communicated?" These were, she wrote, questions that "everyone" was asking these days. "Rather than resolving them, the exhibition adds to the confusion—and thus the general malaise."[42]

And so design and anthropology remained locked, throughout the 1970s, in a strange and uneasy little dance. Design found itself intrigued by anthropology's exotic aura. As for anthropology, it turned out to be going through something of its own.

Anthropology was founded as an academic discipline in the United States and Europe in the 1800s. From the beginning, it revolved around the study of non-Western peoples. Its practitioners split early on into a "social" camp and a "biological" camp. While biological anthropologists studied human biological variation and evolution, social anthropologists studied culture.

By early in the twentieth century, social anthropologists had adopted some conventions. Their primary output was the ethnographic study (also called, simply, the ethnography): a description of a group of people in their natural environment. To create an ethnography, one engaged in "participant observation": long-term immersion in and documentation of social life within that environment.[43]

Social anthropologists tended to care about their relevance beyond academia. Even before Bronislaw Malinowski had conducted what is often called the first ethnography—before he set out in 1914 for one of the Trobriand Islands in eastern Papua, staying for two years—early social anthropologists were beginning to consider how their discipline and its outputs might matter outside universities. The terms "practical anthropology" and "applied anthropology" came into use between the 1860s and the early 1900s; they described anthropologists' aspiration not only to create abstract or theoretical knowledge but also to contribute to solving the more immediate problems of public life.

Applied anthropology blossomed in the 1920s and 1930s, when an increase in the number of anthropology PhDs awarded coincided with—particularly as the Great Depression deepened—a decrease in the number of academic jobs. Many newly minted anthropologists turned to positions in government. Such positions were proliferating as colonialism began to collapse and the US government sought experts to help with the postcolonial (or neocolonial) administration of former colonial subjects. Anthropologists also entered industry during this time, often studying social and cultural determinants of worker productivity. The most famous result is the 1930s Hawthorne Study, produced by a partnership between the anthropologist Lloyd Warner, the psychiatrist Elton Mayo, some Harvard University staff, and the Western Electric Company. The study seemed to show that various experimental changes (lighting modifications, changes in payment incentives or rest periods) increased how much factory workers got done.[44]

The life of anthropology outside the academy exploded during World War II, when the American pivot from isolationism to involvement in the world created unprecedented demand, in government and beyond, for people who knew something about how culture worked. Anthropologists and other social scientists became involved in training officers for military government and administration, particularly of Pacific and Asian nations. They created new military fields of expertise—like "human factors analysis," a systematic approach to studying human abilities and limitations so as to inform industrial design and thereby reduce risk from human error. They wrote and implemented public policy. They ran public health initiatives and economic development projects. They participated in the reconstruction of Germany. Unsurprisingly, the discipline's turn outward was also a turn toward the contemporary: it shifted overall toward the study of living people, and particularly toward the changes that those people were experiencing with the onset of "modernity."[45]

Anthropology grew rapidly after World War II, when money flowed into academic anthropology departments from governments and foundations. In 1947 and 1948, 139 American anthropology departments granted BAs, 26 granted MAs, and 24 granted PhDs; by the mid-1970s, these numbers had multiplied, respectively, to 6,008, 1,078, and 445. But this flourishing actually helped quash the discipline's practical aspirations, because one of the primary drivers of all that new funding was the postwar influx of students to be taught in universities. The wave of new university students had caused a significant labor shortage in academia, which needed to hire professors again to populate its wealth of new and expanded social science departments. Anthropologists left applied work for increasingly lucrative teaching jobs. Anthropology PhD students were again trained exclusively for college and university teaching roles. Universities became the center of the discipline again.[46]

And then, in the late 1960s and early 1970s, the tide turned back in the other direction. In the United States, the United Kingdom, and beyond, birthrates had dropped again just as anthropology departments had expanded their ranks and reoriented their doctoral training toward academia. Suddenly, there were not enough academic jobs to absorb all the new anthropologists for hire. A generation of early career anthropologists was forced back out of the nest.[47]

One of those who left was Dr. Lucy Suchman. Born around 1950 in Ithaca, New York, to Janet Malkin and the sociologist Edward Suchman, Suchman arrived for college at Berkeley in 1968. Horst Rittel and West Churchman were on campus; so was a generation of politically informed and highly activated college students. "Like all students at Berkeley at the time," Suchman remembered later, "I was quite preoccupied with the major institutions in the United States, and what I felt was problematic about them." The social sciences seemed to offer some hope, given their assumption that, as Suchman put it later, "social structure is not a given, it's ongoingly and actively constituted and reproduced." If things were always being constructed, then there was always the possibility of constructing them differently. That space of contingency was a space of promise.[48]

Suchman stayed on at Berkeley for a doctoral program in anthropology. For a time, she was fascinated—like many anthropologists before her—by American Indian cultures. But as she learned more, she felt that "the last thing that Native Americans needed was another anthropologist studying them." The anthropologist Laura Nader, informed by anthropology's colonial history, had recently published the article "Up the Anthropologist," which advocated for the idea of "studying up": investigating not only the cultures of the powerless but also the cultural forms and institutions of the powerful, the cultures to which most anthropologists themselves belonged. If social scientists wanted to make a difference, Nader argued, they should get a "vertical slice" of society, learning about poverty and exploitation and technology and progress by examining the dominant as well as the dominated.[49]

Suchman decided, upon reflection, to "study up." Ultimately, she settled on the institution of the American corporation, that increasingly potent and inscrutable agent in global political life. She would study the "mundane everyday enactments" of corporate power: how corporate power, like any other aspect of social structure, was continually constituted and reproduced. She would try to open up the black box of the corporation and look inside.[50]

But how to get access? In 1979, Suchman secured an internship with Xerox. Founded in 1906 in Rochester, New York, as a manufacturer of photographic paper—at the time its name was the Haloid Photographic Company—Xerox had achieved fame and prosperity in 1959 with the introduction of the Xerox 914, the world's first machine to make photocopies on plain paper. Suchman would be a research assistant, transcribing interview recordings for another Berkeley anthropology student who was already working at the company. It was the perfect placement. She had positioned herself, as she put it later, not only inside a corporation but in a part of a corporation that was "posited to be a central and superior site of knowledge making."[51]

◆♥

More than other American corporations, Xerox was associated with "knowledge making." The reason was its experimental West Coast division: a research group called Xerox Palo Alto Research Center (PARC). PARC had been born in 1970, when Xerox had taken some of the outsized profits from the Xerox 914—the company's revenue was $500 million by 1965—and used the money to start an experimental research facility focusing on "basic" (as opposed to "applied") research. Also called "pure research," basic research is any scientific activity aimed at increasing general or foundational knowledge: advanced physics, materials science, new computer languages. Such research is standard in universities, but it's less common in companies, which tend to want their research investments to produce new technologies that can be sold for a profit. Xerox had the freedom to make a longer-term investment. PARC was meant to give the company a foothold in the scientific and technological future.

When Lucy Suchman arrived in 1979, PARC was nine years old. People said its founders had deliberately located it as far as possible from Xerox's corporate headquarters in Rochester, New York: the more separation the researchers were afforded, the more intellectual freedom they'd feel. The region soon to be called "Silicon Valley"—opposite coast, hippie values, Northern California sunshine—seemed the ideal spot.[52]

By 1979, PARC had delivered. The freedom to be impractical seemed to have given its scientists and engineers the latitude—somewhat paradoxically—to produce not only new basic knowledge but also new technologies. So far, they'd developed the first computer laser printer (1971), the first personal computer (1973), and the graphical user interface (1975). In the end, PARC's legacy would be a somewhat sad one: Xerox ultimately failed to exploit these inventions, letting other corporations capitalize on them instead. But the 1970s and early 1980s were, for PARC, largely years of possibility.[53]

Suchman was placed as an intern in PARC's short-lived Office Research Group, whose computer scientists were exploring ways to free up workers by automating routine office tasks. They had already automated payroll processing; now they wanted to automate the more complex processes coming to be called "knowledge work." Automating these processes would require modeling them. Each must be represented as a set of programmatic procedural instructions that could then be programmed into a computer. As Suchman observed, the scientists "would take formulations of procedures—whether from manuals, or by talking to people—and they would map them as information flows." These maps became the basis for software.[54]

It all made a kind of sense. It was based on the assumption—the same idea behind Herbert Simon's Logic Theorist—that at the time grounded all attempts to create artificial intelligence (AI): the assumption that all human problem solving could be represented as a diagram or program, then reproduced in that form by a machine. But Lucy Suchman, having studied human interaction and behavior in depth, had a feeling that this assumption might be flawed. Even at the bottom of the corporate hierarchy, the way people got things done seemed discretionary, variant, knowledge intensive, contingent, judgment based. Most work might not really be representable as an "information flow." It might not be programmatic at all.[55]

How to be sure? Suchman set out on a parallel path to that of the rest of the Office Research Group: rather than studying and diagramming complex knowledge work, she would identify the most mindless, most routine kind of office work she could find. She would study it in depth, not by diagramming but by watching and listening. And then she would evaluate the degree to which this work was, or was not, like a diagram: the degree to which it could or couldn't be reproduced, in other words, as a program.[56]

She began in PARC's accounting office. Its employees processed expense reports and accounts payable: they got things paid. She spent months watching them do it. And she came to the conclusion that all the manuals and oral descriptions and diagrams left out a major part of the job. The accounting office was actually tasked not just with getting things paid but with *creating records* that showed that those things had gotten paid. The record making was a tacit expectation—but also in some ways the most important expectation, since at any moment an auditor might walk in, open a file drawer, and inspect a record. The procedures were an important referent, but the primary work was to make a document of an event that took place "according to procedure."[57]

If it was true more generally that procedural descriptions like office manuals tended to leave out or misrepresent key aspects of people's work, then workplace machines must be flawed, because their programs were based on these procedural descriptions. In that case, humans who were led to expect the machines to match their own moment-to-moment courses of action would inevitably be left disappointed and confused. Suchman effectively tested this hypothesis by placing two eminent computer scientists in a room and asking them to use a brand-new, feature-rich Xerox photocopier. The machine was being advertised as easy to use: to unleash its formidable power, the advertisement promised, one must only "press the green button." Surely these PhD scientists—the computational linguist Ron Kaplan, who created the Natural Language Theory and Technology group at PARC, and the computer scientist Allen Newell, Herbert Simon's collaborator in creating AI—would have no trouble operating a photocopier.[58]

But Suchman's hypothesis checked out. She took low-fi video of the computer scientists' encounters with the machine, capturing their remarks to one another as they tried to make copies. These included, within a minute or two, "What?"; "You gotta be kidding"; "Does that relate to that?"; "Oh, shit"; several snorts of laughter; and "So our first batch is SOL"—"What is that?"—"Shit outta luck." The problems were abundant and various. The researchers had one hundred pages to copy, and the machine wanted only fifty. The start button didn't respond, but it wasn't clear why. The machine gave directions about "the paper tray," but the users didn't know which tray "the paper tray" was. The machine demanded that the users reverse the order of all fifty originals. Double-sided printing seemed hopeless. The machine was not at all easy to use.[59]

Suchman refined her arguments in her first book, the 1987 *Plans and Situated Actions*. It shows that "plans," as cognitive science understood them—"prescriptions or instructions for action," akin to the business "procedures" we've been discussing here—are just one of the many resources that people use as they carry out "situated actions" (actual courses of action in actual contexts). The implication is that software that aims to reproduce people's plans of action programmatically or algorithmically, from start to finish, will never be as intelligent as human beings are. It can't be, because it's not taking in new information and redirecting accordingly.[60]

Consider the interaction between Kaplan and Newell and their photocopier nemesis. In spite of all the process diagramming that the machine's engineers had done—and all the programming they'd carried out on the basis of those diagrams—the machine could not anticipate what its users would do from moment to moment. Kaplan and Newell weren't just carrying out a plan; they were responding in real time and space to the specifics of the document to be copied, to the size of the paper, to their understandings of previous instructions, to the machine's instructions, to that "first batch" being "SOL," to one another. "However planned," Suchman wrote, "purposeful actions are inevitably *situated actions*": actions taken in the context of particular circumstances, including bodies and spaces and distractions and scenarios and the other messy contexts of human life. Suchman drew another example from whitewater canoeing:

> In planning to run a series of rapids in a canoe, one is very likely to sit for a while above the falls and plan one's descent. The plan might go something like "I'll get as far over to the left as possible, try to make it between those two large rocks, then backferry hard to the right to make it around that next bunch." A great deal of deliberation, discussion, simulation,

and reconstruction may go into such a plan. But, however detailed, the plan stops short of the actual business of getting your canoe through the falls. When it really comes down to the details of responding to currents and handling a canoe, you effectively abandon the plan and fall back on whatever embodied skills are available to you. The purpose of the plan in this case is not to get your canoe through the rapids, but rather to orient you in such a way that you can obtain the best possible position from which to use those embodied skills on which, in the final analysis, your success depends.

Why, then, do we describe our actions so programmatically, as if we had always been acting "according to plan"? Primarily, Suchman wrote, because of cultural bias: the idea that a human person's activity is plan based and procedural is part of the concept that it is rational, and that concept is itself deeply rooted in Western scientific ways of thinking. Now the idea of plan-based action was being reified in the design of thinking machines. But technologists ignored "situated action" at their peril.[61]

●♥

Suchman's was one of several books published in the mid-1980s that revolutionized how people thought about the relationships between humans and computers. It was a powerful call for a design practice in which representations of work—such as plans and procedures—were taken, as Suchman would put it later, "not as proxies for some independently existing organizational processes but as part of the fabric of meanings within and out of which all working practices—our own and others'—are made."[62]

And it made an impact. The idea of "symbolic action" posed a real challenge to the Herbert Simon school of artificial intelligence, since it seemed to give the lie to the idea that intelligence involved no more than the manipulation of symbols, independent of changing situations, and therefore could be reproduced by a symbol-manipulating machine. The challenge produced a great deal of research and scholarship from partisans on both sides of the divide—including from Herbert Simon himself, who wrote back to Suchman directly, arguing, incorrectly, that her book dismissed the processes of internal cognition—whether called "planning" or "problem solving"—at the heart of his own AI work.[63]

There were other ways, too, that the "situated action" thesis was influential. In the 1980s, designers of technology would begin incorporating insights from ethnographic research—which might reveal the situations of action—rather than just those of behavioral science, which emphasized plans. But Suchman's very presence at PARC was, in some quarters, an even more powerful influence in making this happen than her particular scholarship was. Suchman was one of the first anthropologists that a global corporation like Xerox had ever hired. Rarely before had ethnography been used within and on behalf of a business. Its use now, in a relatively visible way, set a real example.

Suchman stayed at Xerox for twenty years, hiring more anthropologists and establishing the influential Work Practice & Technology research group. Its members never fully assimilated into the PARC milieu; Suchman remembered them being semiregularly "hailed by some of our computer science colleagues at PARC, if we happened to walk down the hall together, with the (only semi-ironic) warning, 'Here come the anthropologists!'" (Ultimately they embraced the Jets reference, "donning satin gang jackets with our group name emblazoned on them.") But whether despite or because of its persistent semi-separateness, the group's collective presence opened space at Xerox for work on human-machine interface and usability, for the collaborative development of "participatory design" methodologies, and for activism on behalf of this and other methods that placed the human "user" at the center of the design process. It also certainly made Xerox technology work better for the people who used it.[64]

The anthropologists' presence at Xerox also set an example for other social scientists who might not otherwise have considered moving into industry. "The idea that the folks at PARC were prodigiously credentialed in their various academic domains, active in professional societies, and yet worked for a copier company was something more than simply eye-opening," write Maria Bezaitis and Rick E. Robinson, both PhDs who entered industry ten to fifteen years after Suchman did. The PARC anthropologists' work—across methods and topics—made new practices and applications of the social sciences seem possible.[65]

Finally, the image of Suchman and her team at Xerox PARC also made a forceful case to the leadership of corporations like Xerox and its peers. Innovation-minded corporations should employ social scientists, this vision image suggested. They should charge those social scientists with helping them learn about their potential users' relationships to technology and to the problems that technology aimed to solve. This was particularly true when it came to making tools to aid the employees of other businesses, since, to cite a remark from sociologist David Wellman that Suchman used to introduce one of her papers, "How people work is one of the best kept secrets in America." In a world in which profit depended on understanding and automating such work, ethnographies that might render it visible suddenly seemed necessary to capitalism.[66]

Anthropologists' impact in industry was represented in the media in a reductionist—sometimes inaccurate—way. One oft-told story was that Suchman's insights had led Xerox to design the big green "start" button that its photocopiers often feature. With a little ethnographic research, then, complex products could become easy enough for a toddler to use. The story was almost the opposite of the truth, as Suchman herself often noted; her research argued strongly *against* the big green button and the marketing of products as self-evidently easy to use. New and unfamiliar machines were never easy to use, for anyone. "The green button," Suchman wrote, "actually masked the labor that was needed to become familiar with the machine and incorporate it effectively into use." (Suchman makes this point repeatedly in her work: she militates against "the systematic erasures of labor," the "trivializations . . . [and] betrayals of labor that are involved in the development of technological systems." Work—whether traditional office work or the work of learning a new machine—is never as simple as technologists want it to be.)[67]

Facts aside, English-language media ate up the stories of anthropologists in corporations. In 1991 the *New York Times* ran a story, "Coping with Cultural Polyglots," on anthropologists in corporate settings. Later that year, *Businessweek* published a piece called "Studying the Natives on the Shop Floor"; in 1996, *Fast Company* reported a similar story under the headline "Anthropologists Go Native in the Corporate Village"; another *Businessweek* piece, "The Science of Desire," appeared in 2006. For corporations, these articles explained, observing current and potential customers using ethnographic methods was allowing access to, as the 2006 *Businessweek* piece put it, "their customers' unarticulated desires."[68]

That was the surface-level thesis of those stories. But they also announced, tacitly, a new era in the discourse of design. That era had long been slouching toward Silicon Valley to be born: it had been ushered in not only by these anthropologists in industry but also by Papanek and the other socially minded designers of the 1960s and 1970s, and before them by Horst Rittel and his colleagues and their turn away from rationalizing design as simple problem solving, and before them by the human-factors engineers of the World War II and postwar periods. But not until the early 1990s did this new era arrive in full. We might call it the era of the "user," or of "human-centered design."

After Xerox hired social scientists, so did Microsoft Research, Bell Labs, IBM, GM, Arthur Andersen, Nissan, Nokia, Nestle, Intel, and the US Centers for Disease Control and Prevention. Consultancies grew up to specialize in ethnography for innovation: E-Lab LLC, the Dublin Group, Sonic-Rim, Sapient Corporation, IDEO. "User research" became a critical step in the design process. "Twenty years ago," the design researcher Jane Fulton Suri wrote in 2010, "it was rare for designers to even talk with human and social scientists, never mind to employ their theories and methods." Now, she continued, "many progressive organizations" had "embraced human-centered design research."[69]

Fulton Suri herself was one of the figures whose work introduced me—around 2012, as I was finishing my own doctoral degree—to the discourse of "human-centered design." As the first design researcher at IDEO, she had fleshed out a user-research-driven design process that had been popularized worldwide. Her process derives from academic anthropology: it consists primarily of simply observing people in their natural habitats. Her writing about that process helped make me a "user researcher."[70]

●♥

"User research" is very different from the ethnographies that the academic discipline of anthropology has produced and refined over time. Given the cost constraints and market pressures under which user researchers labor, their work tends to happen very fast. In 1999, Don Norman noted that research for design and innovation had come to be known as "rapid ethnography." By the time I entered the field in 2013, we sold it to clients as "lean research," a process that could be completed—interviews, analysis, synthesis—in a single week.[71]

And given the demand for "user research" and "user researchers," our training now varies radically. User researchers have responded to the demand for their services, Bezaitis and Robinson write, by "training new researchers from a huge range of backgrounds," meanwhile "trusting that tools and processes would compensate for uneven foundations or variations in skill." I, for one, have no training in anthropology or sociology or psychology or any other social science. My graduate degree is in the humanities: cultural history, from an English department. My prior background is in journalism and communications. But in 2013 I read some books, learned the language of the field from some generous people I found on LinkedIn, and then walked into a consultancy that was desperate to hire a researcher to staff a client contract set to begin that week. Within a few days, I was a "senior user experience associate," conducting weekly cycles of interview-based user research on a digital-product-design project for a global healthcare company.[72]

There are consequences to this kind of dilution. The labels of "ethnography" and even "user research," Bezaitis and Robinson write, have come "to stand for much less than they really should have": sometimes for simple description of people's behavior without any interpretation, sometimes, even, for just a quick "usability test" conducted on a product to make sure the product works as intended before its release. Such processes don't give product developers any deep insights into people's current lives and workflows or their unarticulated needs. Not that academic ethnography is sacred. Anthropologists would be the first to point out that the practice has, as the anthropologists James Clifford and George E. Marcus put it, a complex and often difficult "poetics and politics." Ethnography, like any other representational practice, is shaped by the history (in this case, colonial history) and power (in this case, exploitation) that have helped define the genre's conventions. Still, when we claim to be doing "ethnography" or something derived from it as part of a design process, we should be clear about what it is we're claiming.[73]

There are other ways, too, that early twenty-first-century design falls short of its proclaimed ideology of "human-centeredness"—or else that the phrase itself falls short of any substantive political meaning. Most working designers are embedded in corporate life. We're part of the machine. However compelling the user problems that we and our research partners might uncover, we will be granted the resourcing to try to solve them only insofar as such solving serves our client's or sponsor's bottom line—preferably quickly, on the design-and-development timelines afforded by the exigencies of short-term earnings and quarterly shareholder dividends. Likewise, whatever everyday behaviors we discover, whatever acts of adaptation and imagination, we'll be sponsored in supporting them with technology only insofar as there's a potential sponsor who believes that this support will increase worker productivity or incite consumer desire. Often that sponsor does exist and is willing to pay for our work, both in identifying user needs and in designing for them; even manipulative phenomena, Wolfgang Haug would remind us, must "speak the language of real needs." And yet, as Haug also asks, "Do instincts and needs still have any progressive value under these conditions?"[74]

As for Suchman, her time at Xerox PARC was shaped by these realities. She had arrived in the late 1970s hoping not only to critique but to intervene in corporate life. And intervene she did: in prevailing ideas within information-systems design, in academic discussions about labor and human action, in ideas about what "design" was and could be. It was a good run. But over time, the space for such interventions began to shut down. As Xerox's valuation and finances faltered, its Wall Street performance became "a constant preoccupation," Suchman has written. "Stock prices and business analyses [were] discussed at every lab meeting." For an employee to speak critically or to think systemically—to engage, for instance, in any "critical discussion of the political economies to which our work was increasingly accountable"—came to seem "anachronistically naive" at best, "biting the hand that feeds you" at worst. The work PARC was willing to support also changed. Originally a basic-research laboratory, PARC became focused exclusively on product development, the creation of information systems for which corporate customers would be willing to pay. Needless to say, Suchman and her colleagues began to lose the latitude to do any research not explicitly aimed at maximizing market performance.[75]

One evening in the mid-1990s, Lucy Suchman was listening to National Public Radio while driving her car down Palo Alto's Hillview Avenue when she heard a technologist proclaim, regarding Silicon Valley, "The future arrives sooner here." Suchman felt "a bodily resistance to being hailed into this claim to the vanguard," she wrote later, "with its attendant mandate to enact the future that others will subsequently live." At the beginning of her years at PARC, corporations had seemed like big, inscrutable, monolithic black boxes; now, having been inside one for a decade and a half, she had come to understand them better. But she had also become deeply skeptical that even the best-intentioned and savviest people inside them could use them to enact any meaningful and positive structural change. She had, more than ever before, "a sense of the immovability of these institutions." "Human-centeredness" might be a powerful tool, but it wouldn't improve collective human life when deployed in a corporate framework. The money-making imperative was too powerful. With the invention of the internet, capitalism—having conquered the globe with commerce—was now simply inventing new ways, new financial instruments and techniques, to make money at human beings' expense. It felt like "an expansive time," Suchman wrote, "for certain forms of capitalism." But it didn't feel very expansive otherwise.[76]

Suchman left Xerox PARC in 1999 to return to academia. She joined the faculty of Lancaster University, in England, as a professor of the anthropology of science and technology in the Department of Sociology. The academy, she felt, might be increasingly corporate—increasingly neoliberal—but it still afforded freedoms different from and perhaps broader than those of industry. In January 2002, the Xerox Corporation, having flirted with bankruptcy, turned PARC into an independent subsidiary. It was expected to generate revenue by licensing its intellectual property, hiring itself out to other corporations for sponsored research, and commercializing its findings.[77]

Chapter 5

EXPERIENCE

Nobody thinks they live in simple times. But few have been so obsessed with their era's complexity as were the people of the world's industrialized countries at the end of the twentieth century. Something was changing, and life seemed to be becoming more complicated—in ways that sometimes surpassed human understanding. "The squirming facts exceed the squamous mind," the American poet Wallace Stevens wrote midway through World War II. By the 1970s, it seemed even truer.[1]

Certainly the problems were more wicked. But even the solutions seemed terribly complex. Take the industry now known as "finance." It arose as a major global force in the United States and other developed countries in the 1970s, and—as the historian Greta Krippner has shown—it solved a problem. The problem it solved was that the United States seemed to be heading toward an economic and sociopolitical crisis: over the 1970s, economic conditions were deteriorating. The broad prosperity of the postwar period was being supplanted, in a new neoliberal era, by slower growth and higher unemployment.

The phenomenon now called "financialization" helped head off the fiscal, social, and legitimation crises that these conditions might otherwise have precipitated. Figuring they couldn't afford a crisis, politicians ushered in new policy regimes that deregulated financial markets, drove up interest rates, and made credit freely available. In response, American firms across industries reshaped their strategies: they would focus less on growing by *making things* ("productive" activity) and more on growing by *betting on future gains* ("financial" activity). Between the 1960s and the early 2000s, accordingly, financial-sector profits grew from 10 or 15 percent of the total profits in the US economy to somewhere around triple that number. And as American profit making shifted from productive activities into financial channels, there seemed to be more money to go around. Problem solved: the looming crisis seemed to retreat, fading back again from seeming imminency into the safer realm of mere possibility.[2]

Financialization enabled the US economy to continue growing, in other words, even as the industrial era came to an end. But financialization also made life more complicated and less comprehensible. "Do CEOs of large, complex financial institutions today know everything that's on their balance sheet?" Gary Gensler, himself a former Goldman Sachs partner and former head of the Commodity Futures Trading Commission, wondered aloud to the journalist Rana Foroohar in 2014. "It's not possible to know. There are just too many things going on for their operations now in the markets for them to know."[3]

How does a regular person, for that matter—a *non*-financial-industry CEO—even begin to understand finance? How can anyone without specialized training be expected to estimate a sensible bottom-up price for the equity of an investment bank like Goldman or JPMorgan Chase—or even to understand what it means to own a "tranche of a collateralized debt obligation"? Can any human mind understand the convoluted instruments of financial engineering—instruments enabled only by advanced computing technology—at all? In the work for which Herbert Simon was, in 1978, awarded the Nobel Prize, Simon added some fundamental qualifications to the basic premise of "rational choice theory," the theory of capitalist economics that assumes that people always make decisions that maximize their personal utility. His point was that people making decisions within contemporary market systems *can't* act all that rationally, because they have limited access to and comprehension of the information that they would need to make the best possible rational decisions. Rationality, in other words, is "bounded" by human comprehension and cognition. Given this insight—and given the rise of finance and the seemingly unfathomable complexity that's come with it—can we still think of capitalist economy as animated by any "rationality" at all? And how should a society begin to *regulate* complex securities when even policymakers briefed at length by experts can't begin to understand them?[4]

By the 1980s, finance alone—sheerly by adding complexity to political economy—seemed, to many observers, to be driving substantial economic and political risk. But finance wasn't the only source of complexity in contemporary life.

The ways that human beings organized themselves into groups, sociologists observed—from multinational corporations to alliances to nongovernmental organizations—were also becoming more complicated. And even the hard sciences seemed to be running into complexity at every turn. In the 1960s, scientists and mathematicians had begun to uncover a set of behaviors, observable in fields from physics to climatology to mathematics, that seemed to evade prediction or understanding via traditional scientific means. These behaviors seemed to arise in certain complex systems that were so "dependent on initial conditions," as scientists put it—so radically influenced by even infinitesimal inputs—that the outputs could not be predicted by the instruments available to humanity. Scientists called the phenomenon "chaos."[5]

Weather sometimes exhibited chaotic behavior. So did epidemic disease. You could never predict the weather a year from today, or the next outbreak of measles, because you could never know everything about conditions today in that infinity of relevant states of the atmosphere, or in human social life, or in any other possible realm that might influence the course of events. The facts evaded mathematical formulation, bested the most powerful computer. They existed at a level of complexity that humanity couldn't access—and they revealed the world around them as something as fundamentally alien as it was familiar. This world was very different from Sir Isaac Newton's perfect and predictable clockwork universe. It was anarchy all the way down.[6]

The scientific discovery of chaos had something in common with the explosion of financial complexity, and even with the expansion of social complexity: all three discoveries, and some of the phenomena themselves, were enabled in part by the growth of computing. Computers had "fundamentally changed the world's investment patterns," the *New York Times* marveled in 1986: they'd enabled the creation of heavily traded new financial instruments, inundated investors with data, and facilitated round-the-clock trading involving instantaneous transactions. A computer had enabled the initial experiments that revealed the existence of chaos. Earlier technologies like the telescope and microscope had let people see what was otherwise too large or too small for the human eye; now, a new technology, the computer, was allowing people to begin to grasp what otherwise would be too complex for the human mind.[7]

Scientific discovery tends to be seen as a social good. But computers were also causing forms of complexity that were clearly undesirable. To take an extreme example, networks of computers could themselves be subject to chaos. In 1988, the *New York Times* reported that a large computer network in Europe—run by the major global weapons manufacturer TRW—had been found to be exhibiting "strange, unpredictable behavior"; after investigating, TRW's engineers "now suspect[ed] that they were confronted with the mathematical concept called chaos." (Their conclusion was correct, apparently.) And even everyday computers were making regular people's lives more complex. Increasingly, nonexperts were expected to use them, at work and potentially at home. But the "personal computers" of the time—intended for both home and small-scale office use—were literally black boxes, with inner workings that almost no one could understand.[8]

And computers' user-facing elements were almost as bewildering. One commentator recounted in 1988 in the *New York Times* that he'd gone to a store with an interest in purchasing a computer; he wanted to use it, he told the clerk, "for writing articles, letters and books." The clerk responded by exclaiming something about "'word processing!'"—not, at the time, a familiar phrase—and then vocalizing "a garble of 'PC-megahertz-megabytes-floppy disc-dot matrix-MEG RAM-modem-cursormouse.'" Once the writer got his computer home, it required a learning process he described as "mechanized masochism: trial, error, error, error." Its user interface (UI), a black screen marked with green characters that spelled out indecipherable fragments, did little to decrypt the complexity inside. And when the writer paused to stretch and his foot knocked the plug out of the wall, his work was lost.[9]

●♥

Even computer people were beginning to worry about computers' complexity. In 1981, there appeared on the ARPANET—the Advanced Research Projects Agency Network, a public computer network that was a forerunner of the modern internet—an unpublished essay titled "The Trouble with Unix." Written by Donald A. Norman, a professor at the University of California, San Diego (UCSD), the essay contained both a powerful critique of Unix's complexity and some powerful ideas about how to solve for it. "The Trouble with Unix" had made its way over the network to MIT, and from there to AT&T's Bell Labs, where Unix, the operating system named in the title, had been developed in the late 1960s. The Bell Labs engineers found the essay provocative; eventually, it would help define the direction of software design as a field.[10]

Unix itself was both beloved and loathed. Its inventors at Bell Labs had designed it specifically for software engineers; its intended users, in other words, were technically savvy people. By the early 1980s, though, various versions of Unix were in relatively wide use not just among engineers but in universities and laboratories. Norman's UCSD colleagues used it, he wrote—albeit not without some Sturm und Drang—as a word processor and an experimental tool. Unix was powerful. It was modular, it was stable, and it made it easier to create highly customized and capable systems. There was even talk of it becoming the standard operating system for home and office computers.[11]

And yet there was indeed a problem with Unix. Norman's secretarial colleagues loathed using it; they persisted, he wrote, "only because we insist." And even Norman himself—who after twenty years of computer experience was a relatively knowledgeable Unix user—still made regular errors in the system. He would find himself inadvertently copying an old version of a file over a newer one, or accidentally "transferring a file into itself until the system collapsed." Or he would end up removing all the files in a directory just by typing an extra space into the argument string. Unix made it almost impossible not to make such mistakes.[12]

The trouble with Unix, in other words, was that it seemed to have been developed without the human mind in mind. The mind was error prone, but Unix made it difficult or impossible to recover after an error. The mind was distractible, but Unix punished it for inadequate concentration ("Get distracted at the wrong time and you lose your place—and maybe your file"). The mind was forgetful, but Unix demanded that it remember arbitrary command names and long strings of interactions. Unix was "a disaster for the casual user." Its designers' motto, Norman quipped, seemed to have been "Let the user beware."[13]

The Unix engineers at Bell Labs did not particularly appreciate "The Trouble with Unix." Norman recalled receiving thirty pages of messages, also over the ARPANET, "about how I didn't understand and how incompetent I was." When the computer magazine *Datamation* published the essay in November 1981, it included a rebuttal by the Unix engineer Michael Lesk, who noted that the Unix operating system worked the way it worked for a reason. Unix had "grown more than it ha[d] been built," Lesk wrote. Much of its appeal lay in its "hospitality to new commands and features." This openness had also meant a diversity of names, styles, and behaviors. To some, Lesk wrote, this diversity was a great strength; to others, it was frustrating. "But to hope for the hospitality without the diversity is unrealistic."[14]

But Norman's goal in "The Trouble with Unix" hadn't been to lambaste Unix for its heterogeneity or to criticize the openness from which the heterogeneity arose. His point hadn't even been to attack Unix in particular. Norman's point was that *of course* Unix had a terrible user interface; almost all software programs, even this profoundly powerful one, had terrible user interfaces. Almost all software programs forced their users to grapple with the software's underlying technical complexity. Because almost all software programs ignored the workings of the human mind.

What was to be done about complexity? Norman had some ideas, at least when it came to fixing Unix and systems like it. When we read a text or watch a play or see a movie, "we do not think of ourselves as interpreting light images," Norman wrote soon after. Instead, "we become a part of the action: We imagine ourselves in the scenes being depicted. We have a 'first person experience.'" It was the same with a good video game, he wrote. So why not with a computer? Why not strive to give the user "the feeling that the computer is invisible, not even there"—and that what is present, instead, is "the world we are exploring" through the computer, "be that world music, art, words, business, mathematics, literature, or whatever your imagination and task provide you"?[15]

Designing the right "first-person experience" would mean thinking not technology-first but experience-first, Norman figured. It would mean taking a phenomenologically oriented approach to design: assuming that design was not about making a technology available to a user but instead about shaping their subjective experience. And this would mean embracing two major design principles. The first was that the designer must design *all* of the experience of interacting with the device or program—not just the traditional user interface but every element from marketing language to hardware, software, and customer support. Take, for example, the experience of acquiring a computer. "When you first discover it, when you see it in the store, when you buy it, when you can't fit it into the car," in Norman's later description, "Ooh, it's in this great big box, it doesn't fit into the car!—when you do finally get it home, opening the box up, and—ooh, it looks scary. . . !—all of that is user experience. It's everything that touches upon your experience with the product. . . . It's everything."[16]

We might call this first rule the "everything principle": the idea that designing an experience is designing not just a product or program or service but everything associated with it.

The other principle is less intuitive, but it would turn out to be equally important. A well-designed thing, Norman believed—whether it was a product or a software program or a service or an object—would prioritize providing the user with a *specific vision of how it worked*. Norman called this vision a "conceptual model" or "mental model." The user relied on this model to be able to learn and interact with a system whose internal technical complexity might actually lie beyond the user's comprehension. The model allowed the user to cognize the otherwise incognizable and to "derive possible courses of action and possible system responses."[17]

To understand this second rule—call it the "mental-model principle"—think of a contemporary e-commerce experience: Amazon, eBay, Etsy. The web app with which the user interacts is built on top of a database that contains relevant information about customers, products, and orders in progress. Users can send changes to the database in real time, constructing and refining their orders before conducting transactions. The database might include static data (data a user retrieves, e.g., about products and discounts); session data (data enabling the system to remember live interactions, e.g., the user's selection of an item to add to an order); and processed data (data the system will keep, e.g., order and payment details). When a transaction is completed, data sets will be moved, for instance, from the shopping_session table to the order_details table and from the cart_item table to the order_item table.

It's a lot to wrap one's mind around. But one doesn't have to wrap one's mind around any of it in order to buy, say, a foraged crabapple twig wreath on Etsy. Instead, one simply selects the wreath ($160.65), adds it to the shopping cart, adds shipping and payment details, and checks out. The shopping cart is a kind of metaphor that evokes—with a simple icon and a few labels on screen—a mental model. Because we know how a shopping cart works, we don't have to think about any of those sessions or data tables or queries in the background. The mental model provides a memorable metaphoric representation that enables us to understand and remember the system, at least on some simple level, and to predict how it will behave.

The idea of the mental model had a history in psychology, and Don Norman, although trained originally as an engineer, was a psychologist. Born in 1935 in New York and raised around the United States and El Salvador (his father was in the civil service), he'd gone to college at MIT, where he majored in electrical engineering. After college he obtained a PhD in psychology from the University of Pennsylvania, then took a postdoc up the road at Harvard. As a member of Harvard's psychology department in the early 1960s, Norman questioned the behaviorist orthodoxy—the idea that only human behavior, not human cognition, could be studied reliably—still dominant in psychology at that time. That orthodoxy held particular authority at Harvard, where the behaviorist B. F. Skinner was a tenured star. But Norman wanted to understand what *led* human beings to perform the behaviors in which Skinner and the other behaviorists were interested. He wanted to access exactly what Skinner had said was inaccessible: the mechanisms behind, rather than the surface manifestations of, human behavior.[18]

One of those mechanisms—one of the ways human beings determined how to behave—was the creation and processing of mental models. The phrase originated with the Scottish philosopher Kenneth Craik, who in 1943 had proposed that the human mind deals with unknown or complex real-world phenomena by producing "a convenient small-scale model" that it can use to anticipate events relevant to those phenomena, test actions against them, and form explanations of them. The function of this "symbolisation," Craik wrote, was to enable the person to experiment with and predict reality: "If the organism carries a 'small-scale model' of external reality and of its own possible actions within its head, it is able to try out various alternatives, conclude which is the best of them, react to future situations before they arise, utilize the knowledge of past events in dealing with the present and future, and in every way to react in a much fuller, safer, and more competent manner to the emergencies which face it."[19]

Craik stopped there. Two years after publishing his theory, while cycling to his college in Cambridge through crowds celebrating Adolf Hitler's surrender—it was May 1945—he was knocked off his bicycle by a car door and thrown beneath a passing lorry. He died the next day, VE Day, at thirty-one. But the concept of the "small-scale model" lived on, despite behaviorism's continued dominance through the 1950s. And in the late 1970s and early 1980s, as behaviorism faded, the concept was revived. The cognitive psychologist Philip Johnson-Laird published a book arguing that the mechanism enabling human beings to think rationally was not logic—that frequently cited abstraction—but the ability to create mental representations of real life. To Johnson-Laird, mental models were something like analogies: internal tableaus made up of elements that stood in as "structural analogues" for the real-world phenomena they represented. Soon others joined the discourse, and the mental model became a widely accepted concept within the new cognitive psychology.[20]

Norman thought designers should take hold of the mind's tendency to create mental models and make use of it. In fact, the designers of technically complex new tools, like computer text editors and new digital watches and the interfaces for piloting aircraft, could intentionally shape the models that their users would develop to make sense of how the underlying technologies worked. Designing and conveying an intentional model would make the user's own mental model less likely to be, as Norman put it, "contradictory," "erroneous," "messy," "sloppy," "incomplete," and/or "indistinct." It would make the user more likely, he wrote a few years later in his breakout book *The Psychology of Everyday Things* (1988), to develop a model that facilitated genuine learning: "The operation of any device—whether it be a can opener, a power generating plant, or a computer system—is learned more readily, and the problems are tracked down more accurately and easily," if the user has a good model. "The designer must develop a conceptual model that is appropriate for the user, that captures the important parts of the operation of the device, and that is understandable by the user."[21]

Mental models represented those elements that were important for operating the system—and only those elements—in a way that the user could understand. And that, Norman believed, was the answer to complexity. If the design could convey a good model, it could render complexity comprehensible. That was how to design with the human mind in mind.

Over at the Xerox Palo Alto Research Center (PARC), researchers were experimenting with some of the same ideas. Xerox was worried about computers' complexity for the company's own reason: it believed that this complexity would prevent the computing industry from growing into the office and consumer markets, where users were less technically savvy and more impatient than in more technical domains. So the Xerox researchers wanted to test ways to vanquish that complexity. They set out to test the hypothesis that intentionally designing a "mental model" into a computer's interface might make the computer feel less complex and more comprehensible.

PARC's experiment came in the form of a new product line called Xerox Star. Under development at PARC since around 1978, Star was a package of well-integrated hardware and software—servers, laser printers, Ethernet, a computer with a graphical user interface (GUI)—aimed at nontechnical professionals. One of the first instances of what would come to be called a professional "workstation," the package was meant to provide office professionals with everything they needed to do their jobs.

Before the Star group began its work, its lead developer, David Liddle, had commissioned a study from PARC's own internal experts on the question of how to do software design. Published inside Xerox, the study's report—"A Methodology for User Interface Design" (1977), referred to as "the Irby study" after its lead author, Charles Irby—laid out a complete design methodology where none had existed in writing before. And one of its key findings was that a good user interface, in addition to displaying information and enabling the user to communicate with the system, must communicate a coherent mental model.[22]

Prioritizing the mental model was by far the most important part of the design process, Liddle emphasized later on. "Everything else should be subordinated to making that model clear, obvious, and substantial." And Liddle's team took that mandate to heart. When the Star system was released, the publishing industry analyst Jonathan Seybold described the foregrounding of the mental model as the Star's main differentiator. "Most system design efforts start with hardware specifications, follow this with a set of functional specifications for the software, then try to figure out a logical user interface and command structure," Seybold wrote. "The Star project started the other way around: the paramount concern was to define a conceptual model of how the user would relate to the system. Hardware and software followed from this."[23]

Star communicated its model through a graphical user interface. First developed in the 1970s, GUIs weren't yet in wide use; Star aimed to bring them to office workers. Star's GUI featured the first "desktop," a visual representation guiding users to a particular understanding of how their files and programs were organized. It had resizable "windows" that overlapped one another, and "icons" and a "pointer" that could be manipulated with a "mouse." "Moving a document," the designers explained, "is the electronic equivalent of picking up a piece of paper and walking somewhere with it." Users would no longer be asked to decipher cascades of green characters on black screens. Instead, they would interact with representations of real-world objects. "To print a document, you move it to a picture of a printer," the designers wrote, "just as you take a piece of paper to a copy machine."[24]

Star, in short, used graphical representation to communicate a conceptual model that analogized the system and its objects to the scenarios and objects involved in analog office work. Of course, Star overlaid the mental model of the office workstation onto a technology that worked very differently from an analog desktop. But what mattered was that the model was recognizable, intuitive, and useful. It attempted, as some of its architects would put it later, "to apply users' existing knowledge," specifically their knowledge and mental models of their own existing office environments, "to the new situation of the computer."[25]

Star didn't sell. Because the team had sought to design the *ideal* functionality—ignoring all questions of technical feasibility—the system was extremely slow; it simply did not have the computing power to do everything it aimed to do.

(One of its designers attested that it ran "like molasses." An industry analyst called it "a jack-of-all-trades that does none really well.") Also, it was expensive. And it was a closed and insular system, programmed in a language not released to the public, incompatible with other such tools. Ultimately only thirty thousand Star workstations were sold, whereas Xerox had hoped to sell hundreds of thousands.[26]

Yet Star's impact was enormous. For the computer industry, it helped establish the process of designing a user's interaction with a piece of software as an accepted step in the ideal software-development process. It centered prototyping and user testing as key steps in that design process. And it made communicating a meaningful mental model into that process's primary goal.[27]

Xerox achieved this impact largely by giving away Star's insights to Apple Computer. Since Steve Wozniak and Steve Jobs had started Apple in Jobs's garage in 1976, they had released two personal computers, the Apple I and the Apple II, the latter featuring a plastic case and a video display with color graphics. By the end of the 1970s, the Apple II was selling briskly—on its way to becoming, as the historian Laine Nooney has written, "one of the most iconic personal computing systems in the United States, defining the cutting edge of what one could *do* with a computer of one's own." But around 1979, Steve Jobs got word of Xerox PARC's nascent Star project. Immediately, he had a sense that what came next would come not just from Apple but from Xerox PARC.[28]

Xerox was, of course, a competitor. But Jobs negotiated an agreement with its executives: Apple would let Xerox purchase one hundred thousand private shares of coveted Apple stock before the Apple IPO, and in return, Xerox would let

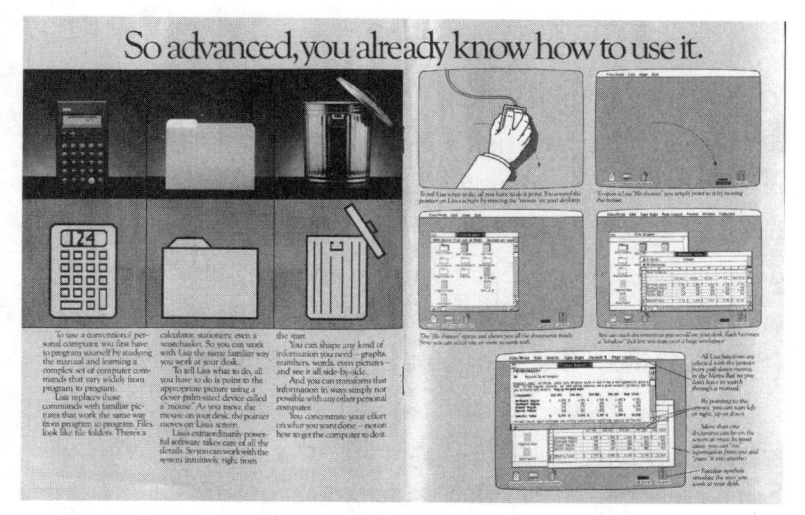

Print advertisement for the Lisa ("You control the pointer on Lisa's screen by moving the 'mouse' on your desktop"), ca. 1983. Apple Computer.

Jobs bring a team of Apple researchers into PARC to observe and take notes on the Star technology and its predecessors. The Apple team visited in 1979 and was entranced. Jobs himself was "blinded," he said later, by the Star's graphical user interface: "I thought it was the best thing I'd ever seen in my life. . . . Within, you know, ten minutes, it was obvious to me that all computers would work like this someday."[29]

Hence the Mac. Apple's team first implemented the new concepts in the largely unsuccessful Apple Lisa, but those concepts found their apotheosis in the project that came after that: the leaner, cheaper, more streamlined, ultimately revolutionary Macintosh. Introduced in 1984, the Mac was the first successful mass-market personal computer with a GUI. Like the Star, it was beautiful, usable, and intuitive; like the Apple II, it was priced within reach for (some) individual consumers. And so it was the Mac that became the first widely used computer to communicate a mental model via a graphic interface. Apple had ridden Xerox PARC's wave into the future.[30]

These days "mental model" (and "conceptual model," used near-interchangeably with it) are inside-baseball terms, not part of the broad public discourse of design. This is because, over the course of the 1980s and 1990s, the model-driven design process became known as something else: user experience (UX) design.

"Experience" first became a buzzword in business schools. In the early 1980s, business school professors had begun to argue that traditional ways of understanding consumer behavior—approaches that understood consumers as rational actors who consumed goods and services to solve problems—had neglected aspects of consumption that weren't driven by reason at all. Consumption, the researchers Morris Holbrook and Elizabeth Hirschman wrote in 1982, was also driven by aesthetics, sensory pleasure, fantasy, emotion, release. It involved aspects that a researcher could get at only by asking people questions like "What makes you happy?" or "Which tastes better?" or "Which painting is the most beautiful?" Consumer researchers, Holbrook and Hirschman argued, ought to ask more of these questions. They ought to embrace the "experiential view." It would afford them a deeper understanding of—and better ways to incite—people's urge to buy things.[31]

Before long, researchers were seeing "experience" as something even bigger: not just one face of consumer behavior but a whole era in human development. As the twentieth century drew to a close and not only goods but services were becoming commoditized—widely available, interchangeable, distinguishable only by cost (and therefore only minimally profitable to sell)—companies were surviving by offering consumers "experiences," wrote the business school professors

Joseph Pine and James Gilmore in 1998. Experience was a differentiator. Creating experiences was a way for companies to stand out and to charge more. Experience, then, had emerged as the "next step" in "the progression of economic value." Pine and Gilmore's article was titled "Welcome to the Experience Economy."[32]

They made their point by tracing the evolution of the birthday cake. It was an object lesson, they claimed, in the history of "economic progress." The first birthday cakes, the authors wrote, were made from scratch. Then, as industrial economies replaced agrarian ones, people began to pay for premixed ingredients in the form of boxed cakes. With the late twentieth-century emergence of the service economy, "busy parents ordered cakes from the bakery or grocery store," paying more for the service of the cake's preparation. Now, the authors wrote, "in the time-starved 1990s, parents neither make the birthday cake nor even throw the party. Instead, they spend $100 or more to 'outsource' the entire event to Chuck E. Cheese's, the Discovery Zone, the Mining Company, or some other business that stages a memorable event for the kids—and often throws in the cake for free."[33]

What *was* an experience, though, other than a day at the Discovery Zone or Chuck E. Cheese? One could argue—following Supreme Court justice Potter Stewart, who in 1964 described his test for obscenity as "I know it when I see it"—that we know an experience when we *feel* it. But Pine and Gilmore offered their own definition. An experience occurred, they wrote, "when a company intentionally use[d] services as the stage, and goods as props, to engage individual customers in a way that create[d] a memorable event." Experiences combined goods and services into events or processes that took place over a duration of time.

Experiences produced memories. And experiences were personal, "existing only in the mind of an individual who ha[d] been engaged on an emotional, physical, intellectual, or even spiritual level." No two people could have the same experience, because the experience arose only from the *interaction* between the staged event and the individual mind.[34]

Over the decade leading up to the publication of "Welcome to the Experience Economy," "experience" had already begun to seep into the world of digital design, thanks in large part to Don Norman. In 1993, Norman had left academia for Apple, where he was hired as an "Apple Fellow"—which, he wrote later, "gave me absolute freedom to do anything I wished." Within a few months, he'd renamed himself: he would be Apple's first "user experience architect."[35]

Norman chose this role to try to solve the most urgent problem he'd observed in the course of those first months. As he had wandered Apple's halls and met with its employees, from software developers up through senior executives, he'd begun to realize that all was not well at the tech company. Specifically, Apple's "great reputation for ease of use and understanding," he wrote later, "was slowly eroding." In the decade since the Macintosh had launched, the world had come to know Apple as the company that built the usable computer: the PC with the first integral GUI, with the first mouse, with the interface that almost anyone could use. But since 1985, when Steve Jobs had left Apple after a power struggle with the company's CEO and board, the company had struggled.[36]

What ailed Apple? One answer was market confusion: the company was offering too many versions of its products, and customers didn't know how to choose. Another problem was that the Macintosh operating system, on which Apple had continued to build, was falling down on the job. It was outdated and clunky and unable to support the company's aspirations, and it would take a herculean effort to modernize. A third problem was that several new Apple consumer products—a CD player, a video game platform, a digital camera—had simply never found their markets.[37]

But all these issues derived, Norman believed, from the same deeper problem: complexity. Particularly, they arose from the "increasingly and seemingly never-ending" complexity of the personal computer and related technology. Personal computers, no matter who made them, were becoming bogged down in their own size, expense, and involution. The operating systems for these ostensibly basic machines were now so complex, Norman wrote, as to "defy description or understanding." The software sitting on top of the operating systems added an additional layer of increasing complexity. "The squirming facts," in Wallace Stevens's phrase, "exceeded the squamous mind."[38]

Norman began by assembling a team to populate the Office of the User Experience Architect. He brought together visual designers, cognitive psychologists, prototypers, researchers who tested prototypes. Next he defined the office's work: optimizing "the experience of working with a particular technology, how the experience feels," with particular attention to "high-level structure and functionality" rather than the detailed design to come later. Finally, Norman designed "user experience design" itself. He devised a set of four principles to guide his office in designing effective experiences. First, they should solve the right problems; second, they should focus on people; third, they should take a "systems view," focusing on understanding and optimizing the whole system rather than just individual parts; and, fourth, they should continually test and refine their ideas to ensure that they would truly meet users' needs. It should all be done in the service of helping users understand the product or service with which they were interacting. And that, Norman emphasized, required a good mental model.[39]

That mental models mattered to digital design, of course, was one of the major revelations of Norman's career to this point. Now it was being enshrined as law within the influential superpower that was Apple. Soon, though, something unexpected happened: Steve Jobs returned. Apple's 1996 acquisition of Jobs's company NeXT had brought home the company's prodigal son. Jobs was charged with reinventing the company and repositioning it to lead the personal computer industry.[40]

Steve Jobs's approach to design differed from Donald Norman's. Jobs's approach can be described in a single word: simplification. He simplified Apple's menu of product offerings. ("I couldn't figure out the damn product line after a few weeks," he told an audience in 1997, so he "got rid of 70% of the stuff on the product roadmap.") He simplified the company's manufacturing, distribution, and marketing. And he promoted and empowered product designers who would simplify the products themselves. The industrial designer Jonathan Ive, whom Jobs now promoted to senior vice president of industrial design, had one idol: Dieter Rams, the German designer who advocated a philosophy of "less but better" (*Weniger aber besser*).[41]

In the immediate term, Jobs's drive to simplify everything spelled the end of Apple's Office of the User Experience Architect. Jobs shut it down, and he fired Don Norman.

(Norman went to work at Hewlett-Packard, then left that company to go into business with usability-focused engineer Jakob Nielsen in 1998 as the still-extant Nielsen Norman Group.) But the term "experience design" survived. It just came to mean something slightly different from what Norman had hoped.[42]

Apple's version of "experience design" is documented, to this day, in the company's "Human Interface Guidelines" (HIG). Now a bible of experience-design principles—emulated by every other major modern tech company (today they all have HIGs) and followed to the letter by product-development teams all over the world (including at various times myself)—the Apple HIG was first drafted by a design-minded software engineer named Bruce Tognazzini, in 1978, for the purposes of training new developers of software for Apple products. For that first edition, Tognazzini, who went by "Tog," drew on the Macintosh interface, which of course was based in large part on Xerox Star. He also drew heavily on the work of Don Norman, then still at UCSD. The result was, unsurprisingly, a document focused on making products as easy as possible to learn, understand, and use. It focused on principles like the "metaphor" (a variety of conceptual or mental model), "consistency," "user control," "feedback and dialog," and "forgiveness."[43]

After Jobs returned to Apple, though, the HIG's principles began to shift. As Apple introduced the iPhone and then the iPad—both based on a new operating system, iOS, and designed to be manipulated not with a mouse but with taps, presses, swipes, scrolls, pinches, pushes, and drags—the HIG reduced the space it gave to principles of learnability and discoverability and become more focused, instead, on simplification. Visual communication, it emphasized, should be simple and subtle. Designers should reduce the number of onscreen controls. As Don Norman and Bruce Tognazzini wrote from outside Apple in 2015, the guidelines' emphasis was "clearly on appearance, in particular the appearance of simplicity, along with user pleasure and enjoyment." The fonts were smaller, with thinner stroke widths and reduced visual contrast, and thus less readable. There was no explicit way to discover the new touch-based interactions—pinching, double-tapping, stretching—except through luck. There was no longer an "undo" button; you could violently shake the phone to undo an action, but there was no way to discover that except by accident. Visual simplicity and elegance, it seemed, were now more important to design at Apple than was the communication of coherent mental models through clear, easily learnable, easily navigable user interfaces.[44]

It seems to have worked for Apple. (As of 2023–2024, the company was neck and neck with Samsung in the competition for leader of the global smartphone market.) But some observers—not least Norman and Tognazzini—say the changes have left Apple users worse off. The products *look* beautifully simple, Norman and Tog assert, but they are difficult to learn and, for many people, difficult to use: "Today's iPhones and iPads are a study in visual simplicity. Beautiful fonts. A clean appearance, uncluttered by extraneous words, symbols, or menus. So what if many people can't read the text? It's beautiful."[45]

These same users blame themselves when their devices fail them, Norman and Tog write: "If I weren't so stupid . . . !" But it's not their fault. They are victims of the tyranny of simplification.[46]

Addressing complexity with simplification is not, of course, an idiosyncratic approach. A lot of people seem to have had the same idea. Design practitioners often cite the German industrial designer Dieter Rams—specifically his statement "Good design is as little design as possible"—to argue for simplicity. The principle that things should be as simple as possible is one of the foundational ideas of modernism, traceable back to the earliest thinkers—Heinrich Hubsch, Eugène-Emmanuel Viollet-le-Duc, Louis Sullivan, Adolf Loos, the Bauhaus group—who argued that architecture should move away from the ornamental complexity of the past. As for Rams, he seems to have held on to it long after modernism's midcentury apex. ("The only plausible way forward is the less-but-better way," he told a journalist in 2017. "Back to purity, back to simplicity. Simplicity is the key to excellence.") So has much of the rest of the design field.[47]

But simplification isn't always the answer to complexity. Sometimes, in fact, it makes things worse. Take the common user interface pattern of using a hamburger menu to hide critical navigation. Originally developed for mobile interfaces but now common across the web, the hamburger menu is itself elegant—three discrete and clean straight lines—and reduces clutter on a page by hiding the website's navigation. A user must touch or click the hamburger in order to reveal the navigation, one layer at a time. By removing the messy menus from the top of the page, the hamburger pattern simplifies interfaces.

Unfortunately, though, the hamburger menu doesn't work. A decade ago, rigorous usability research showed that hidden navigation like the hamburger menu was significantly less discoverable—read: harder to notice, grok, and use—than nonhidden navigation. Charged with carrying out a task via a website, test participants using a desktop device to navigate a site with a hidden menu discovered and used that menu in *only 27 percent of cases*, while participants discovered and used nonhidden navigation almost twice as often.[48]

One might assume that findings would look different now, a decade later, when the hamburger menu is so ubiquitous that most users are very familiar with it. Surely the hamburger's discoverability problem is now solved. And yet people still have trouble—of another kind now—with hidden navigation menus. A 2021 study showed, once again, that the use of a hamburger menu dramatically impacted users' satisfaction with a website, because the user has to navigate back and forward to find a specific menu item. In contrast, a menu providing access to the whole navigation at once—a markedly unsimple, inelegant "mega-menu"—had a strong positive impact on user satisfaction.[49]

In the early 1980s, Don Norman himself—by his own account "a fierce opponent" of complexity, at least at the time—argued vigorously for simplifying tools and systems. Simplification in this context meant reduction: fewer controls, fewer displays, fewer features. Norman made a particularly memorable case for such simplification in his landmark book *The Design of Everyday Things* (originally *The Psychology of Everyday Things*), published in 1988 to best-selling success.[50]

Since then, though, Norman has reconsidered. In 2010, he published the monograph *Living with Complexity*, which argued that in fact complexity isn't the enemy at all. Complexity in digital products is often unavoidable, Norman writes here, because it reflects the real complexity of the world on which those products seek to operate. "Whether it is the international banking scene, the management of trade, the scheduling of freight and passengers, or even the fare systems of airlines," Norman wrote, "the rules are so complex that no single person can hope to master them. The operating system of a home computer may contain over 50 million separate lines of commands."[51]

The complexity could be overwhelming. And yet a world without complexity, Norman wrote, was not to be desired: "The real problem is that we truly need to have complexity in our lives. We seek rich, satisfying lives, and richness goes along with complexity. Our favorite songs, stories, games, and books are rich, satisfying, and complex. We need complexity even while we crave simplicity." The enemy was not complexity but *confusion*: the psychological distress that results from poor design, from design that fails to provide its users with ways to handle that complexity. Complexity itself was ineluctable.[52]

Moreover, the solution to confusion wasn't necessarily simplicity, Norman argued—at least not simplicity as most people understood the term. Reducing the number of controls or displays a product offered would likely make it *more* confusing, not less:

> Simplicity is *not* the goal. We do not wish to give up the power and flexibility of our technologies. My single-button garage door opener may be simple, but it hardly does anything. If my cell phone only had one button it certainly would be simple, but all I could do would be turn it on or off: I wouldn't be able to make a phone call. Is the piano too complex because it has eighty-eight keys and three pedals? Surely no piece of music uses all of those keys. So should we simplify it? The cry for simplicity misses the point.

Instead, the solution to confusing digital products—and here Norman returned to his own first principles—was to go back to the basics of model-driven design. Designers should ease the processes of learning, understanding, and using a product by providing a coherent mental model for that product. The more complex the topic or process, Norman wrote, the more important the conceptual model. What made something feel confusing or easy, in short, wasn't how many dials, controls, or features it provided; it was "whether the person using the device ha[d] a good conceptual model of how it operate[d]."[53]

Norman's own design-research firm, the Nielsen Norman Group, went on to substantiate these claims, including by conducting much of the hamburger-menu research cited above. As Apple goes, though, so goes the industry, and "user experience design" today is still focused on mediating complexity through simplification. Indeed, the term "user experience" refers, in its widest use, to a kind of overlay that renders a product's complexity navigable for a user by simplifying it. This overlay—we could call it the "simplification layer"—*may* convey a memorable and clarifying conceptual model, but its main job is to provide a simple-looking skin on top of the rest of the technology. Where UI text might have specified an affordance's function, this layer offers an icon instead; it works, at least for those people who know how to interpret the picture. Where form fields once had labels, replace them with placeholder text; people will see it, at least so long as they haven't typed anything yet. Where configuration was once possible, hide it behind an accordion menu; just hope the user knows to click the caret if they want to find it.

The dissemination of the idea of experience-design-as-simplification, from Apple through the rest of the computer

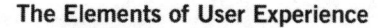

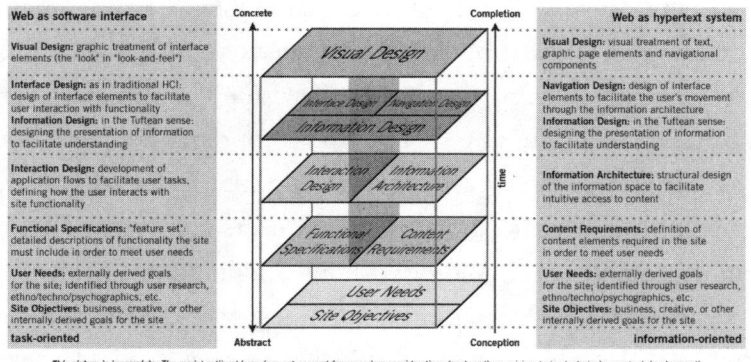

Jesse James Garrett, "Elements" digital image (diagram), March 2000.

industry, happened quickly. In 2000 the web designer Jesse James Garrett created a matrix-like diagram to make sense of the different terms and concepts in use in the emerging field of "user experience." His diagram looks something like an epidermis in cross section. There's a surface stratum labeled "visual design," a stratum below that for interface and navigation and information design, and more strata for interaction design and information architecture, requirements, and user and business goals. There is no chronology to it; it isn't a diagram of a design *process*. It's the anatomical diagram for the "experience" stratum. What began as a method had become a part, a component, a layer, that could be added on, often—although Garrett wasn't endorsing this, or even saying it explicitly—with minimal communication between the UX designer and the engineering and product teams. Garrett published his diagram on the web in March 2000, and in the year after its release it was downloaded more than twenty thousand times.[54]

Since the early 2010s, when I became a full-time "user experience designer," I've felt a tension between these two different ways of defining the term and the field. Many of us want user experience design to go deep: to involve learning about potential users' existing habits and needs and ways of thinking, to mean working hand in hand with engineers to design a fundamental structure that will be comprehensible to users, to mean designing an architecture and interface that convey a useful conceptual model by which users can interact with highly complex technology without undue pain. But there's a version of UX that requires much less work. This version involves just adding a simplifying layer to a product that's otherwise complete. UX designers are constantly asked to come in at the end of the product-development process, take a glance at what's been built already, and then design some interface elements that will make things simpler and easier for the user. Never mind that we're being asked to do the impossible: to vanquish real-world complexity with a pixelated veneer.

Elizabeth Tunstall was a newly minted PhD in anthropology when she moved to Chicago in 1999. The dot-com bubble was at its peak; in the four years since 1995, when Norman had institutionalized the term "user experience" at Apple, the Nasdaq Composite Index had tripled. Tunstall, who goes by "Dori," arrived in Chicago with a Doberman pinscher named Jerry and an offer to join a digital design consultancy called Sapient as a "user experience strategist." Chicago, she recalled later, was "a city like I've never known": both gleaming and gritty, arranged on the grid, with high-rises trumpeting the promise of "better living through technology." Tunstall took the Red Line to work each day, riding into the city center and around the Loop, watching other riders get on and off the train in Chicago's various ethnic neighborhoods. Sapient's studios were in an old warehouse converted into lofts. Tunstall made six figures there, and the strike price of her shares in the company was $150.[55]

Sapient had been founded in Cambridge, Massachusetts, in 1990. It called itself an "e-services consulting group"; today we might call it a digital agency focused on product design and technology. In 1999, Sapient had acquired E-Lab, a market and user research firm, with the intention of strengthening the research dimension of its new "user experience modeling" practice. In the Bauhaus tradition, Tunstall remembered later, Sapient valued interdisciplinary collaboration, teaching through workshops, and using technology to improve people's lives. Tunstall had high hopes for her time there. Within four years, she believed, she would become a millionaire. And her work would matter: she would get to make technology that truly benefitted her community of origin.[56]

Tunstall is a Black woman. As a person of color, she was in the minority at Sapient. But as demand for "user experience design" grew and the company hired more "experience strategists," Tunstall found herself contributing to UX teams that included increasing—albeit still small—numbers of Black and Latinx members. As so many design firms and other institutions would do again during and after the summer of 2020, the American tech firms of the late 1990s were making loud public declarations of their commitments to diversity and inclusion. In fact, Tunstall has written, "my presence was often used as a tangible proof of their commitment." But Tunstall and her colleagues of color felt genuinely optimistic about the impact they could make. "We believed that by being in tech and bringing our communities with us," Tunstall writes, "we could make technology work for us because it was at least influenced by us."[57]

Tunstall comes from South Carolina by way of Indiana. She was born in 1972 in Columbia—on the lands, she notes, of the Catawba, Pee Dee, Chicora, Edisto, Santee, Yamassee, and Chicora-Waccamaw nations—and raised in Indianapolis. From early on, she loved to read, write, and draw; her favorite place, she recalls, was "inside the ideas in my own head." And from the time she began school, she was "bicultural," she writes. "I was in the advanced programme in many of my classes, the only black person in the classroom, so I had to learn about white culture, and then I would go home to a predominantly black community and had to culturally adapt to being there." She became an astute observer of culture's role in human experience. As a college student at Bryn Mawr, she studied anthropology, then earned master's and doctoral degrees in the same subject from Stanford.[58]

From the first, Tunstall saw her specific subjectivity, and the background that informed it—her family, her upbringing, her identity, her ancestry, the places she'd lived, her vocations, her career—as crucial to her work as an experience strategist. Being a petite Black woman, she writes, positioned her to see problems that the modernist design tradition had failed to address. She had encountered "commercial eyeglasses that don't fit my flat nose bridge, seats and shelves too high for my 5'3" stature, medical adhesives not in my flesh color, hats that don't accommodate my afro." Every such encounter communicated to her "that I don't belong there, whether it is a shop, a café, or my home, a clinic, or my own undergraduate graduation." Part of her role at Sapient was to bring these experiences to the table. With her help, teams might see the gaps in the products they hoped to bring into the world.[59]

It was brutal. Tunstall and her colleagues of color—Black, Latinx, Asian, Middle Eastern, and Indigenous—were charged with "taking the blows of the institution, showing them the blood and how much it hurts, and then helping the institution to heal and change the systems causing pain." This was an extraordinary amount of labor—material labor, emotional labor, spiritual labor—to demand from a group of workers to whom the firm provided no extra compensation, no particular guidance, and no protection against the "workforce reductions" that tended to target those recently hired employees of color first. And the "diversity" that their hires were meant to generate was rarely allowed to inform the company's norms or strategy. Instead, Tunstall writes, Sapient expected the reverse: "My inclusion required me to culturally assimilate to the dominant norms, often working against my own values." Tunstall's own writing on this topic says it best: "No one tells you how painful this work is."[60]

And yet she made an impact, both at Sapient and beyond. At Arc Worldwide, the agency she joined in 2003 after leaving that first job, Tunstall volunteered to work on a project with the US Army. The team's mandate was to help the Army drive recruitment by providing more relevant and useful information to the people who influenced recruits' decision making: parents and caregivers who were helping young people decide whether to join the service. Having watched the Black men in her own family enter the military as a pathway to social and economic mobility, Tunstall writes, she felt that her perspective could help inform better decisions by families like her own. Yes, she felt ambivalent about driving recruitment for the Army. In this case, though, there was enough "moral ambiguity," Tunstall said later, for her to "see if I can find that space where my presence can help make the situation better." One had to "engage with those systems that exist," she continued, "so that you understand them enough to be able to hack or find the vulnerabilities in them, to make other decisions, to create other possibilities."[61]

Likewise, in 2005, when Tunstall became managing director of the American Institute of Graphic Arts's Design for Democracy program (as well as a professor at the University of Illinois Chicago), she very deliberately used her specific subjective knowledge to facilitate better design outcomes. Design for Democracy aimed to increase civic participation by using design methods to make elections more understandable and accessible to potentially disenfranchised citizens. During Tunstall's period as director, it was charged specifically with using "information design principles of clarity and simplicity to make voting easier and more accurate for the US voter." But Tunstall didn't take the bait by proposing a single "simplifying" change to vanquish the complexity of the voting system. Instead, informed by both her own intersectional experience and her anthropological insight into the importance of what Lucy Suchman would call "situatedness," Tunstall led the project to create not one set of designs but a set of design *guidelines*. These specifications and patterns enabled local election officials to design their districts' own ballots and polling places according to the needs of their specific citizens. They empowered election officials to make design decisions informed by the full social complexity of their contexts.[62]

●▼

Dori Tunstall has become a leader in guiding the institutions that sponsor design—from design firms to universities and community organizations—to "cede space and power" to

Indigenous, Black, Asian, Latinx, and Middle Eastern people, as well as to others who have been structurally excluded from those institutions over their previous histories. After Tunstall returned to academia in 2005, first as a professor of design anthropology at the University of Illinois Chicago and then at Melbourne's Swinburne University of Technology, she took a position in 2016 as the dean of the Faculty of Design at Ontario College of Art and Design (OCAD) University. She was the first Black dean of design at any college or university worldwide. As dean at OCAD University, she facilitated a "cluster hire" of Black design faculty, raising $7 million to fund three new tenure-track Faculty of Design positions specifically designated for Black candidates. "In recognition of the UN Declaration of the International Decade for Peoples of African Descent," the call for applications read, "OCAD University invites applicants to three (3) tenure-track positions within all

Dr. Dori Tunstall discussing her book *Decolonizing Design: A Cultural Justice Guidebook* with Holly Harriel and Alvin Donel Harvey, MIT Morningside Academy for Design, March 2023. Photo by Afy Deborah Lauren Tsogbe for MIT Architecture and MIT Morningside Academy for Design.

disciplines of the Faculty of Design as well as design-related Graduate Studies to address our 144 years of Black underrepresentation." The opportunity was open, the call continued, only to qualified individuals who self-identified as Black and of African descent.[63]

The response was extraordinary. On Facebook, Black Twitter, and beyond, Black designers shared the call for applications at lightning pace. (Within an hour of its release, Tunstall recalls, one of her former students had received it directly from five different people, all telling him to apply. "I never knew that it was possible for a job description to go viral," Tunstall marveled.) In June 2020, OCAD announced the hiring of not three but five new Black tenure-track design faculty: Angela Bains, Kestin Cornwall, Dr. Kathy Moscou, Michael Lee Poy, and Marton Robinson. Their areas of specialization range from visual art that confronts colonialist discourse (Robinson) to innovative user experience design for community health (Bains). Equally importantly, OCAD University's leadership has demonstrated a commitment to retaining these faculty, providing them with specific support in onboarding to their roles, opportunities for dialogue and feedback, and some degree of shelter from the constant requests for administrative service under which faculty of color usually labor.[64]

It's worth pausing for a moment to consider the language that Tunstall's OCAD University hiring committee used to identify the value they hoped new Black faculty in particular would bring to the university. Their call for applicants stated that the design faculty was seeking Black candidates whose *lived experiences* informed deep professional commitments to intersectional Black communities. That phrase, "lived experience," was repeated throughout. Tunstall herself comments on it explicitly. In earlier searches, she writes, we had learned how the phrase "lived experience" reframed the expectations of all our job candidates such that they gave a fuller picture of who they are. . . . It also set up a system that would eliminate diverse candidates who might tick off a diversity box, but who were not connected to diverse communities and/or did not express the relationship to their identities through their work. [Using the phrase "lived experience"] has helped make sure that we were seeking deep-level diversity, which management psychologists . . . defined in 1998 as the characteristics that go beyond the surface-level differences in race, gender, age, ethnicity to recognize differences in what [Hui] Liao, [Aichia] Chuang, and [Aparna] Joshi label as "personality, attitudes, beliefs, values, and lifestyle."[65]

"Lived experience" has become a watchword among people committed to dismantling the structures that have rendered the design field inaccessible and inhospitable to all but the most privileged. These advocates—I count myself among them—urge institutions to seek out designers who bring the broadest possible set of lived experiences to the design process, thereby enabling the products of that process to cater to users with an equally broad range of experiences. The designer-researcher Sasha Costanza-Chock frames her 2020 book *Design Justice*—which aims to provoke conversation about the promises and risks of trying to use design as a tool for social transformation—by describing her own lived experience and the way it informs her storytelling and her theory of design:[66]

> I materially benefit from, and in some ways am harmed by, my location within systems including whiteness, educational inequality, capitalism, ableism, and settler

colonialism. Simultaneously, I experience oppression based on patriarchy (although in the past I experienced both benefits and harms from this system), transphobia, transmisogyny, and cis-normativity. My standpoint and lived experience shape my understanding of design as a tool for both oppression and liberation, and throughout this text I will occasionally return to my lived experience to ground and illustrate key points.[67]

Costanza-Chock does draw explicitly on her lived experience—as a white nonbinary trans* femme queer person, with substantial education and cultural capital, from Ithaca, New York—over the course of *Design Justice*. She begins the book, for instance, with a story of her own embodied experience, which she shares in the hope that it might inform her readers' design practice. She shows the reader some of the history of the strategy of drawing on lived experience, locating its origins in feminist "standpoint theory," which, she writes, "recognizes that all knowledge is situated in the particular embodied experiences of the knower." Black feminist thought in particular, Costanza-Chock writes, "emphasizes the value of situated knowledge over universalist knowledge. In other words, particular insights about the nature of power, oppression, and resistance come from those who occupy subjugated standpoints." Without understanding people's subjective experiences—particularly the subjective experiences of people who have experienced and resisted oppression—anyone who's trying to make something will be making it without a full box of tools.

Her insights about experience drive Costanza-Chock to define the ideal of "design justice" in a refreshingly concrete way: "trying to ensure that community members are actually included in meaningful ways throughout the design process." The most valuable part of the concept, she writes, is that it fully includes and is fully accountable to the specific people who have lived with the specific conditions that the designers are trying to change. The idea draws on the adage "If you're not at the table, you're on the menu," and on the disability justice movement's famous call for "nothing about us without us."[68]

The phrase "lived experience," of course, uses the same word—"experience"—that Norman used to talk about model-driven design and that a whole generation of designers adopted, beginning in the 1990s, to refer to that simplifying layer sitting atop a complex technology. But the discourse of "lived experience" (as opposed to "experience design" or "user experience design") militates not in the direction of simplification but in the opposite direction: toward acknowledging complexity, specifically the welter of lived experiences that potential users might bring to designed products and services. Concurrently with the rise of "experience design" as a field, and often speaking from within the same agencies and universities (think of Sapient) that have institutionalized user experience design, Tunstall, Costanza-Chock, and others have demanded that design not reduce itself to naive simplification but instead expand to incorporate the real social complexity of the present.

And yet it's probably no coincidence that Tunstall, Costanza-Chock, and their allies have found and raised their voices from within the moment of user experience design's ascent—indeed, in Tunstall's case, from within the field of UX itself. To conceive of the output of "design" as an "experience"—to imply that a product or service isn't working as intended until a user has a specific experience of it—is to acknowledge that that user's specific subjectivity matters. (In the words of the designer Matt Kahn, "Design is the art form that is incomplete until it is engaged.") And so the "experience" lens has helped open the way for design leaders to demand that design serve more of us, more of the time. For that, at least, it deserves our thanks.[69]

Chapter 6

THINKING

At first, David Kelley was an engineer—but not a great one. As a high school student in the late 1960s, in Barberton, Ohio, Kelley had been good at math; in fact, he'd "lettered" in it, receiving a felt varsity letter like the ones the football players were given. But college was different. Enrolled in Carnegie Mellon University's undergraduate electrical-engineering program, which tended toward theory and analysis—surrounded, in his classes, by dedicated math heads—Kelley felt mediocre and adrift. It was clear, he mused, that he hadn't been put on earth to think in a purely analytical way.[1]

Kelley took some art classes for fun, and he slogged through the rest of his engineering degree. He resigned himself to an undistinguished career. But before graduation, he made a discovery. He was hand-sawing lumber one day outside his apartment—part of a larger project to build custom cabinetry for his Dodge van (it was 1973)—when a friend passed by and suggested a better tool: "They got a table saw in the design department." "Design?" Kelley thought. "What's that?" He followed the tip, though, and ventured down into the basement of a nearby building to find Carnegie Mellon's Department of Industrial Design. There, he recalls, "I thought, boy, I'd died and gone to heaven."[2]

Part of the appeal was that, in the design department, people were making things with their hands. Kelley had spent his childhood taking apart the car and the washing machine and putting them back together. Part of it was that it felt safe here to embrace art and aesthetics. And part of it was the chance to use another section of the brain: to exercise the "intuitive mind," as Kelley thought of it, rather than the "analytical mind" alone. By the "intuitive mind," Kelley seems to have meant the mental function that Daniel Kahneman would later call "System 1": the "fast-thinking" operations that produce impressions, perceptions, and intuitions. Kelley's "analytical mind," by contrast, maps roughly to Kahneman's "System 2," the part of the mind that engages in slow, deliberate, effortful thinking or problem solving.[3]

Once he graduated, Kelley did indeed head out west, to Seattle, to join the Boeing Company. ("I was out there in the real world being a bad engineer," he remembers.) He worked on the interior of the Boeing 747. But he didn't stay long. He'd fallen in love with System 1, fast thinking, the "intuitive mind." He'd fallen in love with design.[4]

From Seattle, Kelley applied to Stanford University's graduate program in product design. He arrived there in 1975, and nearly instantly he felt that he had found his "fit" in life. He struck up a friendship with the professor and industrial designer Bob McKim, a "visual thinker"—McKim's term—who had helped shape the product-design program from its beginning. And he started making things. Over the three years he spent at Stanford University, he says, he never once visited the Stanford Shopping Center: "I was in the machine shop the whole time."[5]

Among the Stanford product-design program's axioms was that it was as important to find the *right problem to solve* as it was to solve that problem the right way. Kelley began his final project in the master's program, accordingly, by visiting Stanford's medical school on a problem-finding mission. A doctor there showed him the filing cabinets where they stored medical records. The cabinets looked, Kelley thought, like something out of *Raiders of the Lost Ark*. Pointing to a file folder, the doctor asked Kelley, "You know what happens if we misfile this medical record? . . . *We never find it.*"[6]

That was a good problem to solve. Kelley began work to design a solution that would give patients control over their own medical histories, so that they could safeguard those histories and voluntarily share them with the medical institutions of their choosing rather than trusting them to those filing cabinets. His solution was a system called "medical passport": a machine that a doctor could use to write medical records to a portable microfiche, so that the patient could carry them around and control them. It was, of course, superseded by the arrival, soon after, of digital medical records. But the *problem* was the right one: to this day, the challenge of securing and providing patient control over medical records animates a whole industry adjacent to healthcare itself.[7]

As of the mid-1970s, as Kelley saw it, there were two kinds of people in product design: industrial designers, who had been trained in art schools, and engineers, who had gone to engineering school and were technical experts. The Stanford product-design program had been organized in reaction to this disciplinary segregation. Founded in the early 1960s, it was now co-run by professors from Stanford's art department and professors from its engineering school. Still, the program didn't have much to say about what lay at the intersection of the two. "You really did kind of walk back and forth between the art department and the engineering school," Kelley told an interviewer later. "You didn't have your own identity. When you went to art class you were thought of by the art people as a nerd, and when you went with the engineering people, they thought you were wildly artistic compared to them, but you didn't fit in any group. There was no center, in my mind, anyway, called 'design.'"[8]

In this way, the Stanford program reflected the silos in which Europeans and Americans still understood the making of things. Industrial designers, engineers, and other types of design practitioners had *begun* to talk more about a unified entity called, simply, "design." Institutions like the International Design Conference in Aspen, for example—founded in 1951—brought together practitioners from various design disciplines (industrial design, fashion design, graphic design, architecture) to talk about "design" as a more general entity. Likewise, the Design Methods Movement of the 1960s, discussed earlier in this book, was broadly ecumenical. In practice, though, and in popular English-language discourse, there was no unified idea of "design." There was architecture, a profession all its own; there were graphic design and fashion design, whose practitioners were often artists by training; there was industrial design, a relatively new and separate discipline; and there was engineering, a close neighbor of design but not a recognized part of it. "Design" was, discursively, a collection of fragments, not a cohesive entity in and of itself.

The mandate to design "experiences" would soon begin to change this. Recall Don Norman's "everything principle": experience includes all kinds of phenomena, from buildings to things to words to digital interactions. The design researchers Jane Fulton Suri and Marion Buchenau make the same point by describing the experience of snowboarding down a mountain. "It depends upon the weight and material qualities of the board, the bindings and your boots, the snow conditions, the weather, the terrain, the temperature of air in your hair, your skill level, your current state of mind, the mood and expression of your companions," Fulton Suri and Buchenau write. "The experience of even simple artifacts exists not in a vacuum but, rather, in dynamic relationship with other people, places, and objects." Hence designing for "experience," the authors explain, meant designing for a range of different sensory phenomena using a broad range of design skills. "More and more we find ourselves designing complex and dynamic interactions with converging hardware and software, spaces and services," they write—for example, "systems of connected interactions such as those which occur on a train journey or an Internet shopping spree."[9]

By definition, in short, designing a person's entire experience of interacting with something ought to mean designing both the object and the physical space it occupies, both the hardware and the software, both the shapes and the text, both the movement and the sounds. In practice, of course, "experience design" projects have often been much less holistic than all that. But the 1990s-and-beyond *ideal* of the "experience designer" was, in Bill Moggridge's phrase, the vision of the designer as disciplinary "integrator": someone who brought together practitioners across disciplinary silos, from engineering and architecture to interaction design, to enable a unified design practice and a cohesive final result.[10]

David Kelley saw that change coming, helped catalyze it, and capitalized on it. He saw that people might come to understand "design" as one unified idea. In so doing, he led design discourse and design practice to places of which the design practitioners of the early twentieth century could not have dreamed. That story began when Kelley left Stanford and started out into Silicon Valley on his own.[11]

◼◖

Palo Alto, the town around Stanford University, might today be called the epicenter of Silicon Valley. As of the late 1970s, though, Silicon Valley was new. The high-tech sector was beginning to swell, buoyed by the Cold War–driven demand for integrated circuits—to create smaller, lighter technology that could guide weapons and satellites—and the rise of the microprocessor industry. While most cities around the United States suffered, flirting with collapse under the weight of deindustrialization and of racial and economic inequality—and while global energy costs skyrocketed, global inflation soared, the percentage of American workers who were union members dropped, and the percentage unemployed nearly doubled—Silicon Valley boomed.[12]

It was enough to make the British businessman Bill Moggridge contemplate going west. Moggridge, an industrial designer, had already had a major career: he ran a respected London-based design agency that worked across at least ten European countries. Over the course of the 1970s, though—as postindustrial Britain, like most of the rest of Europe and the United States, faced "stagflation" and unemployment—the work had slowed down. And so, in 1978, Moggridge and his family flew to the United States. They rented a Ford wagon, embarked on a camping trip around the country, and scouted US cities for the right place for Moggridge to open a US-based design studio. After traveling the East Coast and Midwest, Moggridge had nearly concluded that he should open up an office in the Boston area. But then someone suggested he check out California.[13]

"I had an image in my head of Silicon Valley as an industrial wasteland in the desert," Moggridge remembers, "with enormous machines gouging raw material from burnt sandy rock." He was surprised to find forests and marshes, orchards and fields, low office complexes and university buildings and suburban neighborhoods. All that was solid was, indeed, melting into air—new technologies were sweeping away the stability of the industrial era in the United States—but it was all happening in virtual, not physical, space. Moggridge observed the strong relationships between Stanford and the surrounding industry. He noticed proliferations of venture capital firms and start-up companies. He rented an Eichler home in Palo Alto—a flat-roofed, glass-walled wooden house designed after World War II by the social visionary Joseph Eichler—and in the summer of 1979 he moved his family into it and converted the garage into a studio.[14]

The Scottish engineer John Ellenby, a recent alumnus of Xerox's Palo Alto Research Center (PARC), was among Moggridge's first US clients. Ellenby had a start-up called GRiD Systems. It was planning to develop a computer with a display small enough for professionals on the move to carry it around like a briefcase. Moggridge designed the physical object, including a flat graphics display, a slim keyboard, a die-cast magnesium enclosure, and a hinge that allowed the screen to fold down over the keyboard. It is sometimes called the first laptop.[15]

Meanwhile, David Kelley was finishing his degree, plus an extra year, at Stanford. This time, rather than rejoining a corporate behemoth like Boeing, Kelley sought out a business partner. He found Dean Hovey, another recent Stanford graduate, and talked him into joining Kelley in standing up a new design and engineering agency. In July 1978, Kelley and Hovey rented space on Palo Alto's University Avenue above a dress shop. It was "a little dump," in the words of the design researcher Barry Katz. Hovey and Kelley paid $90/month. But the opportunity felt huge. "Being in Silicon Valley in the late '70s, early '80s, was a wonderful time," Kelley remembers, "because everything you were given to design was new to the world." For the new Hovey-Kelley agency, it was "a kind of dumb luck."[16]

The luck manifested early. In 1979, around a year into the company's life, Kelley walked a few blocks southwest on University Avenue to the office of Jerry Manock, another Stanford-educated engineer who, since graduating a decade earlier, had been making a name for himself doing engineering and design work for the Valley's new and expanding high-tech companies. Kelley found Manock in his office, alone, drawing. He introduced himself and described the Hovey-Kelley company's aspirations. To Kelley's delight, Manock replied that he could use Kelley's help: Manock was consulting for Apple, and he had more work than he could handle. Hovey and Kelley knew little about Apple at the time, but they could use all the work they could get, and they came aboard as partners to Manock on his projects. Kelley received a badge that said "T1": Apple's first-ever temporary employee.[17]

One of their first collaborations for Apple derived from Steve Jobs's 1979 visit to Xerox PARC. David Kelley was among the group of Apple associates who accompanied Jobs on that visit, and Kelley watched as Jobs had his realization that the future of personal computing lay in the Xerox Star's graphical user interface. The Apple-Xerox deal that Jobs proceeded to broker gave Apple the right to use not only aspects of that Star UI but also PARC's concept for a pointing device with which to manipulate that UI. The pointing device had been devised by PARC engineer Doug Engelbart and since refined, and PARC called it a "mouse." This mouse was fairly complex—it used many ball bearings—and unreliable, susceptible to wearing out quickly and to clogging with eraser fragments. It also cost around $400 to produce. This worked fine in a lab, but Apple needed the mouse to be viable as a relatively inexpensive consumer product. So it charged Hovey-Kelley with redesigning the mouse to make it "realizable": affordable, reliable, low maintenance, manufacturable, suitable for sale.[18]

Hovey-Kelley's designers, all Stanford graduates, worked according to the Stanford product-design method: they prototyped, they tested their prototypes, they prototyped again, they tested again, ad nauseam. Among their first prototypes for the Apple mouse was a plastic butter dish from Walgreens that covered a rolling ball held in place by glued-in parts. Over nine months, they refined their prototypes, resolving key questions—how big the mouse should be, how to keep the ball from making noise on the table, whether people would rest their hands on the table while using it or hold their wrists up, what shape would feel good in the hand—until the mouse was reliable and mass-manufacturable for around $25. That first Apple mouse, sold with the Lisa and then with the Macintosh, became the archetypal personal-computer pointing device, setting a precedent that remained unmatched in the computer industry for almost a decade.[19]

As more Apple projects followed, and as David Kelley Design grew (Hovey departed three years into the company's life), Kelley started to worry that the firm needed greater industrial-design expertise. He had met the British émigré Moggridge through his Stanford mentor Bob McKim, and now he reached out to Moggridge's thriving US agency, called ID Two. The two firms began a partnership that provided Kelley with the European industrial-design sophistication he felt he lacked. Kelley saw Moggridge as a visionary, with both a more finely tuned "sensitivity to form" and a sharper macro-level "sense of the future of design" than his own. Moggridge found in Kelley's firm both valuable engineering expertise and a rich roster of Silicon Valley clients. In 1991, the two agencies—and that of a third partner, Mike Nuttall, who earlier had spun off from Moggridge's firm as a separate company—merged into a single entity. To name the new agency, Moggridge picked the prefix "ideo-" out of the dictionary. It was the first half of "ideology," derived from the Greek ιδέα.[20]

IDEO was set to launch—as an international design-and-engineering consultancy of around 120 people—in the spring of 1991. But first, Kelley thought, it needed a new brand identity. The reigning emperor of identity design was still Paul Rand, who by then had developed logo systems for IBM, Westinghouse, UPS, ABC, Atlas Crankshaft, the US Bureau of Indian Affairs, Yale University, and Steve Jobs's own NeXT Computers. So Kelley took a trip to visit Rand in his home studio in Weston, Connecticut. He hoped the great master might recommend one of his many talented trainees to take on the job. To Kelley's surprise, Rand volunteered himself.[21]

It didn't take long for Paul Rand to "solve," as he himself might have put it, David Kelley's "problem." Rand assembled a logo of four building blocks—an *I*, a *D*, an *E*, and an *O*—rendered in stark black and white. It has defined IDEO ever since.[22]

▗▐

Shift gears, for a moment, from this swarm of ambitious interconnected California-dwelling cisgender white men—Kelley, McKim, Hovey, Moggridge, Manock—to meet another ambitious cisgender white man, this one on the other US coast. Anthony Lyons was a little younger than the others: born in 1969, in the former mill town of Manchester, New Hampshire. Soon enough, though, he'd become a businessman, a civil servant, a kind of doula for postindustrial urban development, and one of IDEO's clients.[23]

Lyons stumbled his way into his career fields. Raised middle-class, he went to college at Indiana University, where he majored in art history, intending to get into the auction business. After college he went to Greece and then the Netherlands, where he lived in a camper and made a living by buying and selling phone cards. When he moved back to the United States, he began to produce phone cards himself.[24]

By 2000, Lyons was living in Brattleboro, Vermont, working from a downtown office above a storefront, developing and selling phone cards—retail, promotional, collectible—as well as gift cards for retail stores. Like David Kelley at Boeing, though, Lyons was bored. He hated running a phone-and-gift-card company; it was not, as he put it, "soulful." So around 2000, when his wife left the country to teach abroad for three months, Lyons decided to leave for-profit business. "I wasn't sure what to do next," he remembers. "I was still trying to figure out my place."[25]

By chance, Lyons saw a job ad seeking an executive director for a "Main Street" program—a downtown-revitalization effort—for the postindustrial town of Claremont, New Hampshire. Kelley had never thought of doing work like this. Growing up, he realized, he hadn't known anyone in the public sector. And Claremont was "a small, rural New Hampshire town," as he put it later—"no kind of place that we would live." But he applied, and sometime around the spring of 2000 he was offered the job.[26]

* * *

Anthony Lyons wasn't the only American trying, at the beginning of the new century, to figure out what to do next. In Silicon Valley, the year 2000 marked the beginning of the end of what would come to be called the "dot-com bubble." In February of that year, the tech-heavy NASDAQ Composite Index spiked to above five thousand. Then it dropped precipitously, seemed to bounce back over the summer, and by September 2001 had plummeted to below fifteen hundred. Seasoned investors saw their gains vanish. Venture capital dried up. Confident e-commerce start-ups barreled to the ends of their runways and collapsed. Markets were glutted with office furniture from tech firms that had gone belly-up. Chip-manufacturing companies and other makers of hardware laid off tens of thousands of workers. By the end of 2001, between the dot-com crash and the immediate economic response to the terrorist attacks of September 11, US job losses were nearing two million.[27]

IDEO had to reimagine its business. In its first decade, the firm's expertise in industrial and interaction design and engineering had positioned it to win jobs designing all kinds of things that Silicon Valley and its customers were just discovering they needed. It now had offices in Palo Alto, San Francisco, Chicago, Grand Rapids, Boston, Boulder, Tokyo, Munich, and Tel Aviv. Its revenues were in the high tens of millions. And it had earned a global reputation. By 2001, the firm had worked on thousands of products, most of which bridged the physical and digital worlds: a user-friendly portable defibrillator, a revamped PalmPilot, a fast-acting mealtime insulin pen, the three-and-a-half-ton mechanical orca for *Free Willy*. ABC news anchor Ted Koppel, in a thirty-minute *Nightline* episode focused on IDEO's product-development process, had described IDEO as "probably the most innovative product design firm in the world."[28]

But now change came fast. Start-ups—internet related and otherwise—had been providing more than a third of IDEO's revenues. Between 2002 and 2003, the firm's revenues fell from $72 million to $62 million. There were layoffs. David Kelley stepped down as CEO—he remained chairman of the company—and the British designer Tim Brown, who had run IDEO's London and San Francisco offices, stepped up to replace him.[29]

What happened next was an acceleration of a change already underway. By 2001, IDEO was regularly conducting an extensive course in human-centered innovation, called "IDEO U" (for University), aimed at senior executives of corporations like Acer, Nestlé, and BMW. And whereas "in the old days," as Kelley put it, "a toaster company would come to us and ask us to design a new toaster," now companies were approaching IDEO for advice about how to do it themselves: "How can we make our company more innovative," in Kelley's paraphrase, "on a routine basis?"[30]

When the crash hit, IDEO went after that business. By mid-2002, Tim Brown was telling the *Wall Street Journal* that the company's "innovation" business had become a much greater portion of its revenue relative to its design-and-build work. "Just like a fish doesn't know he's wet," as David Kelley put it later, IDEO was only now beginning to realize "that our real contribution was that the companies we worked for didn't think like us. And when they did, it really had a lot of advantages for them."[31]

And so it was that, in a meeting with Tim Brown in 2003, David Kelley had an epiphany. Brown and Kelley were "struggling," as Brown remembers it, "to figure out how to keep [IDEO] meaningful and useful in the world." What the world seemed to want from IDEO was its methodology for producing innovation. So why not start packaging and selling exactly that? Why not rebrand what the firm already did? Why be "a guy who designs a new chair or car," Kelley later recalled to *Fast Company*—or, indeed, a software interface—when he could be "an expert at methodology"? Suddenly, Kelley said, "it all made sense." They would stop referring to IDEO's approach as "design." Instead, they would call it "design thinking."[32]

"I'm not a words person," Kelley said later. "But in my life, it's the most powerful moment that words or labeling ever made."[33]

I've been told, both by academic mentors and by corporate bosses, that if you want to win big in life you should coin a memorable phrase. "Design thinking" turned out to be a memorable phrase. It was design thinking—not the Apple mouse, not the lifesaving portable defibrillator, not *Free Willy*—that would make IDEO the world's most famous design firm. It was design thinking that would drive hundreds of thousands of people worldwide to participate in the "OpenIDEO community," running volunteer chapters in thirty cities to organize events around IDEO-conceived "design-thinking challenges." And it is design thinking that has cast the weird spell under which IDEO still seems to hold the design world. "I've been a professional designer for almost twenty years," the former Google Ventures designer Jake Knapp (who is somewhat famous himself) wrote in 2017, "and the entire time, I've been obsessed with IDEO. What goes on inside? How does it work?" Design thinking has been so phenomenally successful as to seem like some kind of sorcery.[34]

It wasn't the first time anyone had suggested that designers thought a particular way or that that way was useful. The design researcher Bruce Archer wrote in 1979, nearly twenty-five years before Kelley's revelation in his meeting with Brown, that his own "present belief" was that "there exists a designerly way of thinking and communicating that is both different from scientific and scholarly ways of thinking and communicating, and as powerful as scientific and scholarly methods of enquiry, when applied to its own kinds of problems." (Archer argued that this way of thinking was a "commutative" one, wherein the designer's attention oscillated between the emerging requirements and her emergent ideas for meeting them.) In 1991, the Harvard design professor Peter Rowe published a book called, presciently, *Design Thinking*, which looked at "some actual examples of designers at work" to argue that the processes of architecture and urban planning were organized by their own general structure of thought (like Archer, Rowe saw an oscillation between what he called "the problem as given" and "the tentative proposals . . . in mind"). But none of these earlier efforts had offered a holistic, shareable, broadly accessible *prescription* for design thinking—and none had been backed by the marketing and communications power of IDEO.[35]

It did take some time for IDEO to package design thinking for public dissemination and consumption and use. "Put simply," Brown wrote in the *Harvard Business Review* in 2008, design thinking "is a discipline that uses the designer's sensibility and methods to match people's needs with what is technologically feasible and what a viable business strategy can convert into customer value and market opportunity." This was, to be sure, not put as "simply" as one might hope.[36]

But other, simpler definitions followed. The easiest one for me to remember is that design thinking is the use of a particular set of design methods to solve problems that traditionally have fallen outside the purview of design. Design thinking also aims to be accessible to individuals without design training: in Tim Brown's words, it "reaches beyond the hard skills of the professional trained designer and should be available to anyone who wishes to master its mindsets and methods."[37]

When I teach design to people new to the field, I show them what's sometimes called the "hexagon diagram," a ubiquitous image that came out of the Stanford "d.school" in the mid-2000s and purports to represent the five steps of design thinking. It consists of five hexagons that read, "Empathize," "Define," "Ideate," "Prototype," and "Test." The idea is that design thinking involves listening to and empathizing with some group of people, then using what you've heard to define the problem you want to solve. Then you come up with ideas, prototype those ideas, and test the prototypes to see if they work.[38]

Thinking

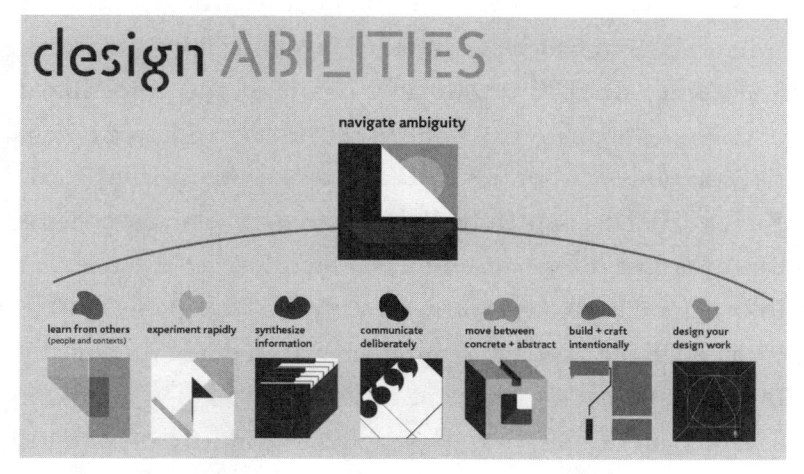

At top, the hexagon "process spaces" diagram (showing the steps or spaces traversed in "design thinking") created at the Stanford d.school in the mid- to late 2000s. The d.school provided permission to reprint this diagram on the condition that it be shown with the one below, an updated diagram titled "design ABILITIES," created more recently at the d.school.

It's a simple, comprehensible diagram. My students come away seeing design thinking as a digestible problem-solving method. They also come away optimistic. Design thinking, they read, has been applied in realms as diverse as education, health, government, and the transformation of corporate culture. Design thinkers are more employable, more useful, more valuable. Suddenly everything is a design-thinking problem: postpartum depression, racial injustice in sentencing, unsustainable growth.

There are other definitions, too—enough that defining "design thinking" can feel confusing. But the stories of design thinking in practice are clear enough. The healthcare consortium Kaiser Permanente hired IDEO to address the fact that, when one Kaiser nursing shift ended and another began, important information tended to get lost, despite the fact that departing nurses spent extensive time briefing arriving nurses about the statuses of their patients. Through a series of workshops—in which participants (including nurses, doctors, and administrators) presumably observed and empathized with nurses' experiences, defined the problem, ideated potential solutions, and prototyped and tested them—IDEO and Kaiser defined a new shift-change process: to prevent the loss of important information, nurses would relay the relevant information *in front of patients themselves*, so that patients were included in the information exchange and could bring up any information that seemed to be missing.[39]

Another example: In 2006, Colombia's Ministry of National Defense approached a Bogotá-based advertising agency, Lowe SSP3, seeking a campaign to convince the guerrilla fighters of the Revolutionary Armed Forces of Colombia, or FARC, to demobilize. The agency followed the hexagons. They conducted in-depth empathy-building interviews with former guerrilla combatants. They found that what the combatants missed most while mobilized were their families. Then the agency prototyped, and in 2010 it launched a campaign called "Operation Christmas." Ten giant jungle trees, each near a guerrilla stronghold, were strung with two thousand motion-activated Christmas lights and banners reading, "Si la navidad pudo llegar hasta la selva, usted también puede llegar hasta su casa. Desmovilícese. En navidad todo es posible." ("If Christmas can come to the jungle, you can come home.

Demobilize. At Christmas everything is possible.") The campaign, and additional iterations launched over the next three years, were credited with motivating many guerrillas to demobilize. (Other factors certainly also drove this trend.)[40]

To be a "design thinker," then, was to see a hospital-shift change and a guerrilla war as design problems. It was to see "design," whatever the word might mean, as applicable to just about anything. But even as "design thinking" rendered "design" yet more capacious, it also jettisoned the self-conscious suspicion of "methodology" at which designers had arrived in the 1960s. IDEO itself has insisted (despite the hexagon diagram) that it's a flexible, multidirectional, iterative approach, not a linear process: Tim Brown has called it "a system of spaces rather than a predefined series of orderly steps," the spaces "demarcat[ing] different sorts of related activities that together form the continuum of innovation." But that nuance has sometimes gotten lost. As popularized beyond IDEO, design thinking is unambiguously a recipe, a five-step program, a jaunt from one colored hexagon to the next.

●◡

Imagine the viewfinder of a camcorder. Anthony Lyons holds it out a car window as the car turns onto Southeast 7th Street in Gainesville, Florida. Lyons is taking footage to show his wife, Wendy, who's stayed home in New Hampshire while Lyons visits this city for the first time. As the car begins to accelerate along Southeast 7th, a verdant tree canopy—live oak, Natchez crape myrtle, flowering dogwood, southern magnolia—envelops the road. One Victorian home enters the frame after another, with elegant black iron gates and white picket fences surrounding rich green lawns. Some homes seem to house single families; others have been converted into bed and breakfasts. Lyons is bowled over by the beauty he's encountering. "I just didn't expect it!," he'll remember later. "Then I got to the rest of the city."[41]

Now the camcorder footage changes. Short, flat stucco buildings enter the viewfinder; so do graffitied fences, barbwire, wide vacant lots, concrete-block homes. The view is bumpier, because the roads are bad. "In the rest of the city, the architecture is terrible," Lyons says. Gainesville contains multitudes.[42]

The video is from 2006. Lyons and his wife were considering a move to Gainesville, where Lyons was being recruited to take over a small redevelopment agency with a million-dollar budget. The agency was known for "having lights put up, having banners put up, planning parties, cleaning sidewalks, putting homeless people away," Lyons remembered later. This didn't impress Lyons much; he'd always thought that "most of that stuff" was "bunk." But over the past half decade, he had done all he could for Claremont, New Hampshire. He'd seen the town from down-and-out status—$4,000 in the bank, 80 percent vacant downtown—through a rich revivification. He'd gotten the mill buildings redeveloped. He'd recruited a tech start-up, Red River Solutions, which by 2021 would grow to a "contract portfolio valuation" of over $120 billion. There was a new pedestrian bridge. Lyons felt proud, and he felt ready to move on. He was interested in Gainesville. He was falling in love with it.[43]

Gainesville was a medium-sized city in the middle of northern Florida. It was subtropical, as Lyons experienced, and often beautiful: its streets were lined with trees, and its buildings crawled with Spanish moss. It was also, in the aggregate, poor. Whatever those well-kept Victorians on Southeast 7th Street might suggest, nearly 34 percent of the city's 134,000 residents lived below the federal poverty line—more than double the national average—and 57 percent struggled to meet basic needs. Gainesville's academically excellent University of Florida enrolled more than fifty thousand students annually, but graduates tended to skip town after finishing their degrees. They went elsewhere in Florida, or to other states, where the opportunity seemed greater.[44]

Lyons and his wife did move to Gainesville in 2006. Between 2006 and 2013, Lyons's Gainesville Community Redevelopment Agency spent $17.2 million revitalizing the city's downtown, from the traditional "having lights put up, having banners put up" to helping build a Hampton Inn, developing new apartment buildings, and turning a former service station into a café. As in Claremont, Lyons recruited tech start-ups to Gainesville. He attracted art galleries. He helped the Cade family, whose patriarch had invented Gatorade, to plan a twenty-one-thousand-square-foot "museum of creativity" in Gainesville's Depot Park. Aggregate downtown property values rose 50 percent, from $128.7 million to $193.4 million.[45]

In 2011, Lyons left briefly for a similar job in Idaho, but in early 2013 he returned. That year the city elected a new mayor, Ed Braddy, a conservative Republican who promised to continue to change the economic outlook. What Gainesville needed, Braddy said, was to become "a more competitive place for new businesses and talent." Greater "competitiveness," he believed, would spur economic activity, keep graduates in town, and build what Richard Florida has called a "creative class." In pursuit of this vision, Braddy and Gainesville's City Commission appointed a Blue Ribbon Committee on Economic Competitiveness. Its director would be Anthony Lyons.[46]

At first, Lyons says, he wasn't sure what to do with Braddy's mandate to make the city more competitive. He analyzed twenty cities around the country to try to understand how they were accomplishing "competitiveness"—but they all seemed to be doing the same things, none of which would give Gainesville an edge. Then, in a conversation with *Fast Company* cofounder Alan Webber, Lyons had a revelation: "*Companies*, not cities, were doing something to make themselves more competitive, and that was to *focus on experience*." Modern companies like Nike were designing intentional, human-centered customer experiences from end to end. Nike in particular had built a distinct brand that informed not only its marketing but its packaging, retail, and try-on experiences. It was experimenting with multichannel digital product innovations like its 2006 Nike+iPod Sport Kit, which introduced a small electronic chip into the shoe to measure the distance and speed of a run and transmit that data to an iPod or sport band, and building smartphone apps, beginning with its 2010 Nike+ running app, which used the iPhone's accelerometer and GPS to measure the same data without a separate transmitter. These investments had given Nike a reputation for making technology the center of its strategy, and they had drawn interest and partnership from other future-oriented enterprises like Apple. "So why couldn't you do that," Lyons thought, "for a city?"[47]

With that mandate in mind, Lyons's new Blue Ribbon Committee on Economic Competitiveness took a trip out to Silicon Valley. Its members visited the legendary global design consultancy IDEO in its San Francisco office. IDEO had worked with governments before, Lyons discovered:

redesigning Singapore's system for issuing work visas, overhauling business licensing in Dubai. Now Lyons presented the firm with a challenge: "Why don't we take this idea of user-centered government and apply it to one city department? . . . What does a user-centered department look like?" It was a match. IDEO, Lyons says, was "pretty jazzed about working with us." Lyons hired the firm to design Gainesville's metamorphosis.[48]

By the time Anthony Lyons walked into IDEO San Francisco, "design thinking" was a spiritual movement all its own—one with a holy land (Silicon Valley), a Temple Mount (the Stanford design school), a bible (Tim Brown's 2009 *Change by Design: How Design Thinking Transforms Organizations and Inspires Innovation*), and a vast diaspora of followers. Indeed, at the Stanford "d.school," as cofounder Robert Sutton put it in 2009, design thinking was being treated "more like a religion than a set of practices for sparking creativity." Anyone could become a design thinker, whether via a self-paced video course—a modest-ish $699 for five weeks online—or via Stanford's executive-education "Design Thinking Bootcamp," priced at $14,000 for four days in person.[49]

It was a hopeful time for stylish, creative, well-heeled technocrats. Barack Obama was president, and America and much of the rest of the world were, as the writer Rebecca Ackermann has put it, "riding high on the potential of a bunch of smart people in a hope-filled room to bend history's arc toward progress." By the early 2010s, you could read about design thinking in a range of popular media around the world. Media in the United States, Europe, and Asia had come to recognize it as a major player in business, education, government, and beyond. "The idea that the design process can be usefully applied outside its conventional context," a *New York Times* columnist observed not long after Lyons's visit to IDEO, "has triggered an explosion of activity that ranges from using design as a medium of intellectual inquiry to devising ingenious solutions to acute social problems like homelessness and unemployment." Meanwhile, a *Chronicle of Higher Education* headline asked, "Is 'Design Thinking' the New Liberal Arts?"[50]

It's easy to poke fun—to marvel at the creepy-sounding case studies, smirk at the overblown rhetoric, mock the vacuous headlines. But the truth is that, a lot of the time, design thinking worked. It pulled people into the design process who might not otherwise have participated. It gave them the confidence to be creative and a structure within which to deploy that creativity. It broke them out of established business processes and helped them come up with new ideas.

And a lot of those ideas are good. The Kaiser "Nurse Knowledge Exchange" was a good idea. It's been implemented at all thirty-three Kaiser Permanente hospitals and beyond, and independent researchers who have studied it have noted that it has significantly improved nurse satisfaction (this was the "first time I've ever made it out of here at the end of my shift," one nurse remarked in a survey). It has also reduced the time it takes for a nurse to see the first patient of their shift, and it has significantly improved the satisfaction of those nurses' patients. I benefited from the practice myself recently, twice, when being treated for severe preeclampsia after the births of each of my two children. That I got to listen to the night nurses hand off information to and answer questions from the day nurses, at my hospital bedside, gave me more trust in the coordination between the people making decisions about my care. It also meant I got more informed care, since I could add information myself if something important—say, a change in medication dosage that hadn't yet made it to my chart—seemed to be left out.[51]

There's a reason design thinking so often works: it draws on a lot of other things that themselves work. It pulls together many of what, in this book, I have called the "ideas of design"—elements of global design discourse and, by now, global design practice—that came before it. The mixed method that results from this fusion marshals, among other values, *beauty*, or aesthetics more broadly: design thinkers pay special attention to aesthetic sensibilities like delight. It also concerns itself with how things work—their *function*. It's a form of *problem solving*, its practitioners often beginning by defining the "problem" or "challenge" to be "solved" (e.g., "1.1 billion people in developing countries do not have access to clean drinking water"). It's innately *human-centered*, involving both initial anthropological observation and user testing, and *experience-oriented*, aiming to bring people from various disciplines to imagine holistic, surface-agnostic solutions that tackle complexity in relatively simple ways. In short, "design thinking" takes all the concepts of design that became dominant in English-language discourse over the century that came before it; packages them with punchy editorial copy and great graphic design; and deploys them to empower everyday people to try to kickstart organizational change.[52]

There's a way of seeing design thinking, then, as the endpoint in a teleology, the culmination of a grand narrative. Tim Brown tells the story of design's development over the course of the twentieth century in exactly this way: "The arc of design, over its hundred-year history," he writes, "has been the story not of (with apologies to the historian Arnold

Toynbee) 'one damn thing after another,' but of an expanding perimeter. Whereas designers were once called upon to apply their skills to alarm clocks and shop interiors and book covers, today we are learning to reframe our questions and to think more expansively: Is it an automobile we want, or transportation? An improved voting machine, or a rich democratic experience?" Elsewhere, Brown describes this development as "the classic path of intellectual progress": "Each design process is more complicated and sophisticated than the one before it. Each was enabled by learning from the preceding stage. . . . As design has moved further from the world of products, its tools have been adapted and extended into a distinct new discipline: design thinking." From this vantage, the "natural evolution from design doing to design thinking" arises organically with the shift from industrial manufacturing to a service and knowledge economy. It's an arrival, a revelation, an enlightenment.[53]

And none of this is wrong. There are a lot of good ideas and useful practices wrapped up in the contemporary concept of "design," and expanding design's scope means those ideas can have greater reach. The problem is that ideas *alone*—without institutional commitment to and resources for implementation—are just, well, ideas.

●▼

Before IDEO came to Gainesville, Anthony Lyons would have to find the money to pay them. The firm's two-month engagement would cost over $200,000. "No way could I go to the city government and say, 'I want to spend a quarter-million dollars just to think about the structure of city government,'" Lyons says. So he went to his contacts around the city—hospitals, universities, realtors' associations, builders' associations, other city government agencies—to ask them to pledge dollars or other resources to help. It worked, he says. The institutions of Gainesville bought into the results they hoped to see.[54]

Among the resources donated was the use of a vacant retail storefront downtown, which the IDEO team converted to a temporary walk-in design studio. Over eight weeks in late 2015, the team interviewed hundreds of city residents at the storefront. They held open design meetings and open houses, and they listened to Gainesville citizens' frustrations. They worked to sharpen the problem they were trying to solve: Was it an absence of "competitiveness" for new business and talent, as Mayor Braddy had suggested? Or was it an absence of human-centeredness, or user-friendliness, or navigability by newcomers? They prototyped and tested solutions. Finally, in collaboration with Lyons, they published a report.[55]

IDEO's Gainesville Blue Ribbon Report is an optimistic document. Its opening pages use desaturated colors: gray-yellow, dull orange, soft brown. But as it reveals its solution, its palette literally bursts into vibrancy. "Today the world runs on ideas," a header announces, its white typeface set off by a neon-bright cyan background. "We have one. And we think it's a very good one." That idea is for Gainesville to become "the most citizen-centered city in the world."[56]

How do you make a city "citizen-centered"? IDEO's report prescribes nine changes for Gainesville. One is to rebrand: adopt a new logo, tagline, and visual style. Several others aim to make the city more design minded. Gainesville should train city employees in "design thinking": the use of design methods to solve problems. It should replace City Commission subcommittees with design-thinking workshops and frame policy questions as design questions. ("Instead of assuming," for instance, "that the right answer to dealing with trees cut as a result of development is a policy to limit the amount of trees that can be cut, why not ask the question, 'How can we maintain a desirable degree of shade and tree coverage as part of Gainesville's overall design?'")[57]

As for the original challenge—*What does a user-centered city department look like?*—the report proposed replacing the current Department of Planning and Development with a new Department of Doing. This new department would consolidate the work of existing business-related government units—so that the many different steps involved in starting or growing a business in Gainesville could all be carried out in one place.[58]

Gainesville's City Commission embraced the Blue Ribbon Report. So did the press. The *Gainesville Sun* endorsed the Department of Doing. In 2016, *Fast Company* published a long feature titled "How One Florida City Is Reinventing Itself with UX Design."[59]

It was a triumph for Anthony Lyons, and he was rewarded. Just before the report came out, Gainesville's city manager had resigned. (The city manager is the administrative head of Gainesville's government; it is an appointed, rather than elected, position.) Now, the city commissioners selected Lyons to replace him.

As city manager, Lyons became responsible, first on an interim and then a long-term basis, for more than a thousand city employees and a general-fund budget of hundreds of thousands of dollars. And he gained the resources he would need to realize IDEO's recommendations. In spring 2017, the *Gainesville Sun* ran an admiring profile of Lyons under the headline "Revolutionary-in-Chief." In a photo, Lyons perches on a play structure in a local park, wearing a suit jacket, black

Gainesville city manager Anthony Lyons, photographed for the *Gainesville Sun*, at Depot Park, which he helped develop, in August 2017. © Rob C. Witzel—USA TODAY NETWORK.

Nikes, and black jeans. He states his mission in simple terms: "How do we make Gainesville better," he asks, "by design?"[60]

◖◗

Lyons pursued Gainesville's design-driven transformation for three years. From the moment he'd been named city manager, he'd become responsible himself for not just sponsoring and cowriting the IDEO report but actually executing on it. Now he did his best to make its recommendations real. Fifty city employees received training in design thinking.

The Department of Planning and Development became the Department of Doing. The Gainesville website received an overhaul. With the help of a local branding agency, the city replaced its logo and branding.[61]

There were other successes. Lyons's initiatives strengthened the city's relationship with the University of Florida, which in 2017 joined Lyons formally in a partnership to make Gainesville "the New American City." The joint initiative, and many of Lyons's other projects, received endorsements from the *Gainesville Sun*.[62]

But there was also opposition. In June 2017, Paul Folkers, one of Gainesville's two assistant city managers, resigned without warning or explanation. Within the week, Lyons replaced him with Dan Hoffman, the former chief innovation officer for Montgomery County, Maryland. That same month, the local National Association for the Advancement of Colored People (NAACP) filed a complaint against Lyons on behalf of city employees, alleging that Lyons had fired qualified employees, forced resignations, passed over qualified city employees for promotions, and hired people—many of them, allegedly, "Millennials"—who were from outside the city and less experienced than internal Gainesville applicants. Human resources director Cheryl McBride, who also resigned, filed an overlapping complaint with the city's Equal Opportunity Office. The claimants settled, and a city investigation into Gainesville's hiring practices did not find that Lyons had created a hostile work environment. It did find, however, that Lyons's team had skirted Gainesville policies in various hiring activities.[63]

More departures followed. In August 2018, both the city's finance director and a longtime city spokesman resigned. (In 2017 the previous finance director had also resigned, after a twelve-year tenure.) The second assistant city manager, Fred Murry, who had focused on affordable housing, resigned as well. By early winter, three of the six city commissioners other than the mayor were advocating for a public hearing regarding alleged forced resignations, low employee morale, and high employee turnover, among other issues. The hearing took place; its real purpose, as one *Sun* editorialist put it, was "so everybody and his brother can weigh in about whether City Manager Anthony Lyons ought to be fired." In December 2018, the City Commission passed the motion to conduct the hearing. Preempting them, Lyons resigned.[64]

Gainesville is among the poorest cities in America—again, 34 percent of its residents, more than double the national average, live below the federal poverty line—and one of the least racially equitable in its distribution of income and resources. Black residents, who make up 22 percent of the city population, live largely in East Gainesville, where residents report severely limited grocery options, inadequate transportation, few places to eat, and poor street lighting. The median household income for Black residents of Gainesville's county is $26,561—just over 50 percent of the median household income for non-Hispanic whites. High school graduation rates for Black residents of the county are 18 percent lower than those of white residents. Black residents are almost 2.5 times as likely as white residents to be unemployed.[65]

Lyons and IDEO's design-driven project aimed to solve the alleged problem of insufficient "competitiveness." That problem, as stated—and the changes Gainesville instituted to address it, including beautiful graphic design, better web resources, and that friendly new office called the Department of Doing—had at best a tenuous relationship to the experiences of many of Gainesville's poor and Black residents.

Although the plans were intended to boost Gainesville's economy on the whole, they did not create affordable housing, eradicate food deserts, or raise high school graduation rates. They didn't address those for whom "competitiveness" seemed a distant concern. They seemed to leave much of Gainesville behind.

Meanwhile, the city was losing visible Black staff, including staff whose jobs did attempt to address these problems. And Lyons's high-profile hires—including assistant city manager Dan Hoffman and Department of Doing director Wendy Thomas—were, like Lyons himself, white people recruited from out of state. Lyons, the *Gainesville Sun* editorial board wrote, "didn't help his cause by pushing through changes, however laudable, without working more to build consensus with staff and community stakeholders."[66]

Lyons himself remembered it somewhat differently than did the people around him:

> It got to a point where I just realized . . . that I no longer had the juice to want to fight to do great things for the city anymore in that capacity. I just no longer cared about this in the way that I needed to in order to implement it. I obviously deeply care about it, but on a day to day basis, . . . I didn't give a shit. That's not a great place to be. So I pulled the ripcord.
>
> . . . I don't feel like, in general, great design is compatible with local politics. . . . It's really, really, really hard. People have to put everything on the line. . . . The work's not hard, the people are hard.[67]

Whether or not "great design" is "compatible with local politics," Lyons's resignation signaled the end of Gainesville's design experiment. The mayor choked up as he said his public goodbye to Lyons; the director of the Gainesville Community Redevelopment Agency praised Lyons's "hairy and audacious" ideas. Others were less convinced. "Gainesville is not a Silicon Valley startup," one resident told the *Alligator*, the newspaper of the University of Florida. "Looking good in a magazine is not a marker of true success."[68]

In 2025, David Kelley and his colleagues at Stanford University will celebrate the twenty-year birthday of Stanford's Hasso Plattner Institute of Design. Kelley cofounded it—with the financial support of the German businessman who founded the multinational enterprise software company SAP—in 2005. Commonly known as the "d.school," it has become, according to the *New York Times*, one of the most desirable programs at Stanford.[69]

Notably, the d.school itself has begun to move on from "design thinking" as such. The design-thinking moment shaped everything about the school, from its remit to apply "design" to massive business problems and questions of civic life—at least one of its several websites still touts projects that, for instance, aim to "put design thinking in the hands of K-12 teachers and bring innovation practices to secondary school leaders"—to its approachable DIY aesthetic (Post-its, Sharpies, whiteboards, the invitation to "Sign up for our [kinda] regular newsletter"). But as Rebecca Ackermann notes, the phrase "design thinking" has disappeared from the materials for its undergrad and graduate programs. The words "make" and "care" have largely replaced "empathize," and the curriculum has begun to ask how to shift "who is centered in these processes" and what its outcomes will leave to future generations. The school's creative director, Scott Doorley, told Ackermann that these shifts had come in large part from the demands of students themselves. "They're entering the programs saying, 'I want to make something that not only changes things, but changes things without screwing everything else up.'"[70]

In Gainesville, design thinking's legacy remains mixed. The Department of Doing has been renamed again: it is now the Department of Sustainable Development. In 2019 it lost the director that Anthony Lyons had hired for it. As for Lyons himself, he continues to pursue development for Gainesville, but from the for-profit side. He is vice president of AMJ, a local development company that, according to local Gainesville news sources, recently received $2 million in city subsidies for a downtown hotel and high-rise.[71]

Gainesville's design experiment doesn't seem to have done any major harm to the city. But it did promise much more than it could have delivered. One reason is that "design thinking" initiatives are very rarely authorized to solve the most fundamental problems at hand. Beneath most problems ("competitiveness"), Horst Rittel would remind us, lie wickeder problems. But a $250,000 "design thinking" project couldn't solve the wicked problems that organize Gainesville's inequality: poverty, income disparity, structural racism, environmental injustice, unregulated capitalism. You face wicked problems by struggling with them, not by taking eight weeks to "solution" them. You argue, you iterate, you lobby, you go door-to-door, you get out the vote, you fail, you grieve, you rebuild, you fight.

Rittel believed that design itself could entail all of that: it could mean fighting one's way to an honest and collaborative approach to a problem of genuine complexity. "The designer's reasoning," he wrote, was much more "disorderly" than classic problem solving—not because designers were intellectually sloppy, but because of the nature of design problems. The designer's reasoning tended to present as a process of argumentation, of debate. It involved navigating a field of competing positions, all of which likely had some merit. The intricate complexity that characterized such argumentative fields in the real world—and the absence of any map—were the sources of that "awesome epistemic freedom" Rittel ascribed to people engaged in the process of design. "Nothing has to be or to remain as it is," he wrote, "or it appears to be." But that complexity and that maplessness were also the sources of design's inherent difficulty. There was no one method to get to the right answer, and no guarantee that it would work out.[72]

And of course you'd need real stakeholder buy-in and massive resources. Which brings us to the second reason that Gainesville's design-thinking project failed: *execution*, not design, is the really hard part of creating something new. And the more complex and abstract the designed artifact, the harder the implementation.[73]

Anthony Lyons remembers his experience writing the IDEO project report as a kind of "Secret Life of Walter Mitty" period in his life: a heroic dream, in Lyons's words a "journey to unshackle himself from himself," that Lyons experienced over four feverish overnight stretches of straight writing and editing. But then, of course, came the real challenge: implementing it. That was a whole different story. "You can imagine the city government seeing this thing," Lyons told me, "and saying 'What is this shit?'" These weren't small changes being proposed. "This was about people's hearts, people's souls, changing people's stuff. . . . This was a whole different matter."[74]

What worries me most about design thinking—not just in Gainesville, but in general—is its colossal and seductive promise. This book has told stories of several earlier American and European vogues for design—beginning with the 1920s and 1930s love affairs with "industrial art," then proceeding in waves through the rest of the twentieth century—that were relatively benign in their claims. If products could look more graceful, people would desire them more; if a machine could be organized "for its maximum of efficiency," it might work better; if an experience could convey a familiar mental model, users might better control complex technology. But this more recent vogue for design thinking seems more insidious because it promises so much more.

Design thinking promises a creative and cooperative escape from difficulty, a caper through the Post-it notes to solutions never imagined before. It promises change quickly, as a service—a kind of paratrooper unit that can drop in and turn things around overnight—at what is often great cost, not just to IBM and Intuit and Starbucks but to villages and nonprofit organizations and cities like Gainesville without enormous resources to spare. And it promises to address even the wickedest problems. Design thinking has "begun to chart some promising directions," Tim Brown writes, from "the redesign of outmoded societal systems" to "the revival of participatory democracy," "the design of cities as the automobile age draws to a close," and "converting from a linear to a circular economy."[75]

These are important problems. And to be sure, design thinking does "chart some promising directions." But none of them is worth much unless it's implemented, and implementing big changes to an established structure or institution or system is difficult and slow. Once a design agency (or an internal department) delivers its proposed solution, someone has to hire a team to develop it. Someone has to project-manage that process, and to resolve dependencies on other systems, and to remove roadblocks that arise along the way. Inevitably the materials won't behave as expected, or the new and old data models won't match up. The foundation will turn out to be full of termites or riddled with technical debt that no one remembered was there. The staff will have been inadequately trained or promised something impossible. Even once the new thing is completed or the old thing transformed—likely into something a little different from what the designers imagined—people will have to change their ways to begin using or patronizing it, and they may need first to be convinced that that's worth the effort. By then the designers are long gone, their glossy deliverables an artifact of a bygone moment of optimism.

There are other problems with "design thinking" as a stand-alone process or method. By embracing "design thinking," we attribute to "design" a kind of superior epistemology: a way of knowing, of "solving," that is better than the old and local and blue-collar and municipal and unionized and customary ways. We bring in "design thinkers"—some of them designers by trade, many of them members of adjacent knowledge fields—to "empathize" with Kaiser hospital nurses, Gainesville city workers, church leaders, young mothers, and guerrilla fighters the world over. We position the designer, as Rebecca Ackermann has put it, as "a kind of spiritual medium who [doesn't] just construct spaces, physical products, or experiences on screen but [is] uniquely able to reinvent systems to better meet the desires of the people within them." Often, as in Gainesville, the implicit goal is to elevate the class bases of the institutions that organize people's lives. Only within this new epistemology can such achievements be considered unambiguously good.[76]

In the end, it's the optimistic energy associated with design thinking that is its greatest strength. The design leader and civic technologist Cyd Harrell has remarked that the method has brought some dearly needed light to some dark places, including public-sector work in a private-sector era. For committed US public servants, "who have had to go through times where things seem really bleak," Harrell told Ackermann, "the infusion of optimism—whether it comes in the guise of some of these techniques that are a little bit shady or not—is really valuable." That's not nothing.[77]

But design isn't magic. Design-as-function isn't magic; neither is design-as-human-centeredness, or design-as-beauty, or design-as-thinking. To address a wicked problem is to go to its roots—and there's no hexagon map for getting there. Stop at "insufficient competitiveness" and what you get is a solution that can be tidy exactly because it doesn't touch the deep causes of Gainesville's economic stagnation. You get a solution that's indifferent to the legacies of slavery and segregation, to the highway projects that systematically cut off and blighted East Gainesville, to East Gainesville's miserable public transportation, and to Florida's $8.46 minimum wage. Stop at that top turtle and you miss that it's turtles all the way down.

Better to acknowledge, as Horst Rittel wrote in 1988, that the top turtle often obscures real and substantial and inconvenient difference. Designers make plans for the commitment of resources, Rittel wrote, and so design decisions materially affect people's lives: "Designers are actors in the application of power." There is no consensus as to how power should be applied, resources distributed, social life arranged, justice done.

To design, Rittel maintained—really design—is to acknowledge divergence, and then to listen and consider and wrestle one's way toward somewhere new. Design is a battleground. He had a point. It's better to fight than to obscure irresolution with optimism. Design thinking may come in an elegant package, but it doesn't always make things right.[78]

Afterword

We love design most when we're afraid.

The nineteenth-century Industrial Revolution and the turn to market fundamentalism extorted painful human costs on both sides of the Atlantic. They disrupted agrarian societies, they polluted the air, and they alienated people who made things from the things that they'd made. Designers and consumers alike responded by embracing industrialists' idea of design as beautification. Our fantasy was that this new capability, design, might mend some of that social fabric that industrialization and capitalism had shredded.

And then it happened again. In the throes of the Great Depression, our terror of New Deal government intervention helped transform design from an idea about aesthetics into a promise to use nongovernmental means to optimize function. And again: amid the uncertainty of the Cold War, we embraced the idea of design as problem solving: rational, objective, repeatable, and inherently good.

This pattern continued through the twentieth century. In the social and political crises of the late 1960s and early 1970s, we turned to the humanistic or "human-centric" idea of design as a kind of protection from capitalism's almost unlivable precariousness. And again: in the 1980s and 1990s, reeling from revelations of complexity and chaos, we embraced design as "experience." And again: in the wake of the millennial dot-com crash and 2008 recession, we welcomed a dramatic broadening, through "design thinking," of design's imagined jurisdiction.

This most recent time, the terror came as we watched the ascension of the knowledge economy—so dazzlingly promising, so broadly inaccessible—even as regular workers and businesses struggled with stagnant growth and economic crisis, from Japan's deflationary slowdown in the 1990s, to the economic shock of the September 11, 2001, attacks on New York and Washington, DC, to the global financial crisis of 2008. Bewildered and anxious leaders, public and private, responded by throwing in their lots with the seemingly magical knowledge work that is design.[1]

But this time wasn't so different from the earlier ones. Each time, life under capitalism has felt newly unlivable, newly estranging, newly strange. Each time, design—that ever-expanding discourse of discourses, that crowded megachurch—has promised salvation, a way for people to maintain their dignity and help fix market society's broken parts, at least imaginatively, from within.

One work persists in my mind as an emblem of design's seductive promise. In 2010, the clothing manufacturer Levi's erected a billboard on the corner of Manhattan's Lafayette and East Houston Streets. It was designed by friends and collaborators Timothy Goodman and Jessica Walsh, who worked for the elite creative agency Sagmeister Inc. Goodman is a graphic designer, illustrator, and muralist who makes—among other things—posters with phrases like "Do you ever think of the lonely people, the ones who bend over at night holding themselves alive wondering why they don't have someone to love?" and "Caring about people is dope as hell." Walsh is a graphic designer and brand strategist from Connecticut who has run an elite creative agency, &Walsh, since leaving her position as partner at Sagmeister & Walsh (2010–2019).[2]

Their billboard was genuinely beautiful. It used elegant, modern sans serif typography, printed on a pure-white set of twenty-four moving gears, to spell out the words "WE ARE ALL WORKERS." The cogwheels really turned; they broke down the typography and then rebuilt it; "WE" spun into chaos, then converged in perfect coherence, then spun again. "I just like that when you first see it, it looks like this abstract spinning design thing," remarked a thin, bald white man who talked with his hands, "and then it all kind of comes into form." "'We are all workers,'" reflected a roundish, brown-skinned man wearing aviators. "Ain't that the truth?" Added a dapper young Black man, flanked by two taxis and a preteen on a razor scooter: "It's hot."[3]

Are we all workers? And what exactly does that mean? With its language and its imagery, Walsh and Goodman's work analogized the designers themselves both to the archetypal working-class industrial laborer—someone who works with machinery, a near-literal cog in the machine—and to the Soho shoppers at whom the installation was aimed, imaginatively uniting them in a mechanically produced and reproduced speech act. It both imagined and tried to actualize a better way of living under capitalism: one that resolved complexity into uncomplicated solidarity; one that spoke with one voice; one that began and ended on an immaculate white canvas on which a clean white machine turned its perfectly synchronized human gears.[4]

Jessica Walsh and Timothy Goodman, "We Are All Workers" billboard (for Levi's), 2010. Copyright Sagmeister Inc.

●◡

You would think that now, more than ever, we would *need* things that make life under capitalism a little easier and more beautiful. The twenty-first century makes the twentieth, barbaric though it was, look almost kind. The twentieth century, after all, saw unprecedented progress toward vanquishing global inequality. As the economist Thomas

Piketty has written, the near century between the assassination of Archduke Ferdinand in 1914 and the terrorist attack on New York and Washington, DC, in 2001 was one of "hope for a more just world and more egalitarian societies"—one "marked by projects that aimed at radical transformation of inequality regimes inherited from the past." And as Piketty himself has shown, those projects—at least for a time—largely worked.[5]

Their success, short-lived though it was, is one of the most genuinely breathtaking twentieth-century stories. Between 1914 and 1945, private property ceased to exist in the Soviet Union, China, and eastern Europe, and it decreased meaningfully in importance in European countries that became social democratic and in the United States. Income and wealth inequality fell precipitously in Europe and the States. As of 1900 to 1910, Piketty notes, the wealthiest 1 percent owned 55 percent of the private property in France, 60 percent of it in Sweden, and 70 percent of it in the United Kingdom; by the 1980s, that same centile owned no more than 20 percent of the private property in any of those countries. Meanwhile, colonial regimes fell, and the societies previously subjugated to them "emerged," in Piketty's terms, as "actors on the world stage."[6]

Now inequality has come roaring back. Since around 1980, in places from social democratic Europe to India to China to the United States, the top centile's share of income and wealth has risen sharply, while the share of the bottom 50 percent has fallen off. Inequality among nation-states has also resurged. The poorest states, particularly in sub-Saharan Africa and South and Southeast Asia, have become poorer relative to the rest of the world, while Europe, North America, and Japan have become richer. Along with the related phenomenon of climate change, Piketty writes, today's global "neo-proprietarian inequality regime" has become one of the world's greatest hindrances: "Whereas the twentieth century witnessed a historic decline in inequality, its revival since the 1980s has posed a profound challenge to the very idea of progress."[7]

So the imaginative project we call "design" would seem more urgent now than ever. But not so fast: if you look carefully at the twentieth century, you'll note that the changes that made it such an extraordinary time were not imaginative but concretely political. They weren't about making market society *feel* less violent; they were about taking steps to actually dismantle market society, steps to subordinate markets materially to human life. These changes were decisions by nation-states to expropriate foreign assets, nationalize firms, apply rent and price controls, reduce public debt through inflation, and impose progressive taxes, which hit the largest incomes and estates with tax rates—70 percent, 80 percent—that today are almost impossible to conceive. These changes did things not just in the mind but in the world.[8]

Yes, political revolutions *begin* in revolutions of hearts and minds. In the twentieth century, the people who achieved the political changes I'm describing *began* by changing the way people understood and judged the systems of private property and unregulated markets, in particular those systems' capacity to bring justice and widespread prosperity and peace. ("Every rebellion," the poet Martín Espada wrote in 1997, "begins with the idea / that conquerors on horseback / are not many-legged gods, that they too drown / if plunged in the river.") But they achieved real transformation because they didn't stop at the mind's edge. They kept going.[9]

So design is a good medium for imagining: imagining redistribution, imagining that conquerors on horseback are not many-legged gods. But imagining can't be the end game.

To get anywhere beyond where we began, we have to look beyond design's utopias and build what the sociologist Erik Olin Wright calls "real utopias." Utopias are, Wright acknowledges, fantasies by definition: "morally inspired" stories that imagine "a humane world of peace and harmony unconstrained by realistic considerations of human psychology and social feasibility." Realists reject such fantasies. But Wright's concept of the "real utopias" pushes beyond utopia's limits by embracing the "tension between dreams and practice." The idea, in Wright's terms, is that "what is pragmatically possible is not fixed independently of our imaginations"—not determined in some completely separate realm of the real—"but is itself shaped by our visions."[10]

One real utopia is Wikipedia. The internet encyclopedia is remarkable for the fact that it's mostly organic, mostly self-organizing—mostly *undesigned*. Wright notes that its ongoing production is characterized by "nonmarket relations," "egalitarian participation," "deliberative interactions among contributors," and "democratic governance and adjudication." These are all norms of radical democratic egalitarianism. None of them seems likely to show up on a colored hexagon. Wikipedia didn't have to be dreamed up by any one person; accretively, autarchically, it built itself.[11]

But most real utopias don't spring up independently of our imaginations. Think of participatory city budgeting, or universal basic income (UBI), or community land trusts, or United Students Against Sweatshops, or the worker-owned coffee cooperative Equal Exchange. These are all designed things. Someone planned them out, made them work, iterated on their form and function, even made them aesthetically and experientially appealing so that people would engage with them. And they are what we need: they are institutional forms that enable people in civil society to seize and utilize collective power over the production and distribution of goods.

Projects like participatory budgeting and UBI are different, Wright notes, from many other projects that would also enhance people's lives and combat real and urgent problems. They're different from programs combating climate change, for instance, or even most antipoverty programs, or most policies of taxation and redistribution. These projects, by contrast, are about *building and strengthening the institutions of economic democracy* and thereby enabling voluntary associations of people in civil society to control the economy. They're what Karl Polanyi imagined when he emphasized that markets must be "embedded": enmeshed in human community, regulated by laws and norms, constrained by institutions of social solidarity.[12]

Another way to say this is that we need more design work like what the graphic designer Sylvia Harris did. Harris was born in 1953 in Richmond, Virginia. When she died at fifty-seven, in 2011, the design community erupted with grief. Harris "inspired those of us on the fringes to be more active in mainstream America," wrote the design leader Bennett Peji. Added design historian Steven Heller, "I looked to her as a beacon." Harris's agency, Citizen Research & Design, had conducted research and participatory design processes with broad publics. It had used the findings from those processes to plan and shape information programs for federal services. It was the kind of work Karl Polanyi might have had in mind.[13]

Take Harris's creative direction of the 2000 US Census. Her friendly, legible, empathic overhaul of the census's graphic and information design helped drive higher participation rates—particularly among Black and Latinx and Native Americans—relative to the 1990 census and to the Census Bureau's expectations. The US Census determines whom US government funding serves. The federal government relies on census data to determine the distribution of about $1.5 trillion across hundreds of federal programs. Think tanks place the value of every completed census form at over $4,000 in federal-funding dollars. Undercounts not only siphon away funding in immediate terms but also deny political representation to undercounted geographical areas, including communities with high Black or Latinx populations. Reducing undercounts strengthens the institutions of economic democracy.[14]

Harris "loved to talk to real people," as the designer Jessica Helfand put it: "to understand what they wanted and needed, to understand how their perceptions impacted or framed something—wayfinding in a hospital lobby, for example, or census forms, or postage stamps." Her firm made information design that was radically participatory. The results were lucid and human and brilliant.[15]

But they weren't unique. Look at Dori Tunstall's work, or the civic technologist Cyd Harrell's, or the design-research leader Dana Chisnell's. They make design that makes material progress toward building the world we want to live in. "I'm at my happiest when I'm working on audacious goals," Chisnell writes, "to chip away at wicked problems." Chipping away at wicked problems—using broadly participatory methods—is how communities build social power, and building social power is how communities make structural change. Design can contribute to that project, and it should.[16]

ACKNOWLEDGMENTS

I want to thank the community of friends that enabled me to write a book while working a full-time job and having children. Thanks to Grace Mennell, Laura Hagadone, and Will Ngo; to Jenny Wu Donahue, Kevin Donahue, Lilach Shafir, Paco Abraham, Jennie Goldstein, Nick Lerangis, Laura Kern, Phil Hennessey; and to Kate Hammond, Lauren Zettler, Meg McGowan, Erin Mazursky, Grey Brooks, and Mike Barry. Thanks to Iris Lapas, and to Lucy Kathleen Gram.

Thanks to Hazel Douglas, whose daily work caring for my children made this book possible.

The "Phil Spector Documentary" group chat made me want to take myself less seriously, write a book, and be a good person. Thanks for nothing, Pete L'Official, Nick Donofrio, Brian McCammack, Laura McCammack, Brian "World's Greatest Booster" Hochman, Jack Hamilton, Tim McGrath, Tenley Archer, Derek Etkin, Eva Payne, Evan Kingsley, and George Blaustein. Thanks also to Memory Peebles Risinger, Jake Risinger, Liz Munsell, Jayna Maleri, Jon Pack, and Verena Von Pfetten. And thanks always to Megan Greenwell.

Thanks to my teachers, Bruce Robbins, Farah Griffin, Amanda Claybaugh, Larry Buell, Werner Sollors, and Luke

Acknowledgments

Menand. Thanks, too, to my design mentors, Andre Mohr, Mike Scopino, Rebecca Lord, Steph Hay, Mohenna Sarkar, and Sara Korba.

Thanks to the Chronophage hang, particularly Eva Payne, Brian Goodman, and Daniel Immerwahr. Particular thanks to those who read this book early on and made it better: Eva, Daniel, Grace Mennell, Brian Hochman, Jack Hamilton, and Nick Donofrio.

My first editor on this project was Nikil Saval. His edits were patient, encouraging, generous, and luminously smart. Many of the best ideas here are his. Thanks, Nikil. Thanks also to my editors at Basic Books—the kind and skillful Kristen Kim, Brian Distelberg, Annie Chatham, Emma Berry, and Claire Potter—and attorney Elisa Rivlin. Thanks to research assistant Scott Hwang. And thanks to my literary agent, Allison Devereux; it's a gift to work with someone so much smarter than myself.

I'm indebted to archivists and librarians at the Getty Research Institute, Los Angeles; the Library Archives of the Museum of Modern Art, Manhattan; the Library of the Cooper Hewitt, Smithsonian Design Museum; the Special Collections Research Center of Syracuse University; the Patent Archive of the US Patent and Trademark Office; the Stanford University Libraries Special Collections; Harvard University's Houghton Library; Yale University's Beinecke Rare Book and Manuscript Library; the Special Collections and University Archives, Richard J. Daley Library, University of Illinois Chicago; and the archives of the *New York Times*. Thanks also to Harvard University's Department of English; the metaLAB at Harvard's Berkman Klein Center for Internet and Society; the American Academy of Arts and Sciences; and the magazine

Acknowledgments

n+1. These institutions gave me the time and space to begin thinking about this book.

Thank you to my sisters, Lucy Kathleen Gram and Nell Chapin Gram; my dad, Dewey Gram; and my mom, Nancy Hunt. And thanks most of all to Jen Tuohy, my person and my partner in all things.

NOTES

Preface

1. Thomas Piketty, *Capital and Ideology*, trans. Arthur Goldhammer (Cambridge, MA: Belknap Press of Harvard University Press, 2020); Mark Blyth, *Great Transformations: Economic Ideas and Institutional Change in the Twentieth Century* (Cambridge: Cambridge University Press, 2002); Howard Brick, *Transcending Capitalism: Visions of a New Society in Modern American Thought* (Ithaca, NY: Cornell University Press, 2016). Among Brick's keen insights is this simple terminological one: "The term *capitalism* had barely come into widespread use before the beginning of the twentieth century, and it flourished from the 1910s onward—precisely as socialist and communist movements, wars, and depressions cast some doubt on the survival of the social order it described" (3).

2. Joseph A. Schumpeter, *Capitalism, Socialism and Democracy* (London: Routledge, 1994 [1942]), 139.

3. Andreas Dorschel, "Diskurs," in *Zeitschrift für Ideengeschichte XV/4: Falschmünzer*, ed. M. Mulsow and A. U. Sommer (Munich: C. H. Beck, 2021), 110–114; Sarah Williams Goldhagen, "Something to Talk About: Modernism, Discourse, Style," *Journal of the Society of Architectural Historians* 64, no. 2 (2005): 154.

4. For Foucault on "discourse" broadly, see primarily Michel Foucault, *The Archaeology of Knowledge and the Discourse on Language*, trans. A. M. Sheridan Smith (New York: Vintage Books, 2010 [1972]), and Michel Foucault, *The History of Sexuality*, vol. 1: *An Introduction* ("The Will to Knowledge"), trans. Robert Hurley (New York: Vintage, 1990 [1978]).

Notes to Preface

5. Victor Margolin, "Design History and Design Studies," in *Design Studies: A Reader*, ed. Hazel Clark and David Brody (Oxford: Bloomsbury Academic, 2009), 34–41, excerpted from Victor Margolin, *The Politics of the Artificial: Essays on Design and Design Studies* (Chicago: University of Chicago Press, 2002), 218–221, 224–230.

Introduction

1. Jeff Chu, "The Rise and Fall of Design Within Reach," *Fast Company*, December 1, 2009; Erika Brown Ekiel, "Rob Forbes: The Power of Simplicity," Stanford Graduate School of Business, October 17, 2012; Fred A. Bernstein, "Is a Solution Within Reach?," *New York Times*, December 30, 2009; CIBC World Markets, William Blair & Company, and SG Cowen & Co., "Prospectus: Initial Public Offering of Common Stock of Design Within Reach, Inc.," US Securities and Exchange Commission, June 29, 2004.

2. For the provenance interpretation, see Chu, "The Rise and Fall of Design Within Reach." On provenance, see John M. T. Balmer and Stephen A. Greyser, "Corporate Marketing: Integrating Corporate Identity, Corporate Branding, Corporate Communications, Corporate Image and Corporate Reputation," *European Journal of Marketing* 40, nos. 7 and 8 (2006): 630–641; John M. T. Balmer, Stephen A. Greyser, and Mats Urde, "Corporate Brands with a Heritage," Bradford University School of Management Working Paper Series 07 (July 2007); Marnie Collins and Marcia Weiss, "The Role of Provenance in Luxury Textile Brands," *International Journal of Retail and Distribution Management* 43, nos. 10/11 (2015): 1030–1050; Lama Halwani and Abeer Cherry, "A Consumer Perspective on Brand Authenticity: Insight into Drivers and Barriers," *International Journal of Business and Management* 19 (December 2023): 21.

3. Roman Mars, "'99% Invisible' Podcast Host Roman Mars Looks Back at 10 Years of Uncovering Design," interview by Joshua Dudley, *Datebook | San Francisco Arts & Entertainment Guide*, September 2, 2020.

4. Aileen Kwun, "'See, Touch, . . . Smell': The Next Generation of Design Gallerists Invites You Inside," *New York Times*, November 12, 2022.

5. Bob Sutton, "Rave Review for Change by Design in *New York Times*," *Bob Sutton: Work Matters*, September 28, 2009; Rob Walker, "Makeover Mania: Inside the 21st-Century Craze for Redesigning Everything," *New York Times Magazine*, November 10, 2016.

6. Bruno Latour, "A Cautious Prometheus? A Few Steps Toward a Philosophy of Design (with Special Attention to Peter Sloterdijk)," in

Notes to Introduction

Networks of Design: Proceedings of the 2008 Annual International Conference of the Design History Society (UK), Falmouth 3–6, ed. Fiona Hackney, Jonathan Glynne, and Viv Minton (Boca Raton, FL: BrownWalker Press, 2009), 3.

7. Le Corbusier, *Towards a New Architecture* (*Vers une architecture*), trans. Frederick Etchells (New York: Dover Publications, 1986 [orig. 1923; trans. orig. 1927]), 289; Felicity D. Scott, *Architecture or Techno-Utopia: Politics After Modernism* (Cambridge, MA: MIT Press, 2010), 18; Colin Rowe, "Introduction," in Museum of Modern Art, *Five Architects: Eisenman, Graves, Gwathmey, Hejduk, Meier* (New York: Oxford University Press, 1975), 3. On design and utopia, see also Manfredo Tafuri, *Architecture and Utopia: Design and Capitalist Development* (Cambridge, MA: MIT Press, 1976).

8. CIBC World Markets, William Blair & Company, and SG Cowen & Co., "Prospectus."

9. Julie Sloane, "Designing Men: In This Economy, Can an Upstart Furniture Store Really Persuade People to Spend $2,000 on a Single Chair? You'd be Surprised," *CNN Money*, November 1, 2003; Devin Gordon, "Meet the Titans of Taste," *Newsweek*, October 26, 2003; CIBC World Markets, William Blair & Company, and SG Cowen & Co., "Prospectus."

10. Bernstein, "Is a Solution Within Reach?"

11. Chu, "The Rise and Fall of Design Within Reach"; Bernstein, "Is a Solution Within Reach?"

12. Belinda Lanks, "Herman Miller Buys DWR for $154 Million. What Does That Mean for Chairs?," *Bloomberg*, July 22, 2014.

13. Kim Dabbs, "Design Thinking and Its Role in the Creative Process," Steelcase, n.d.

14. David Sokol, "Design Within Reach Turned a San Francisco Warehouse into a Certified-Cool Flagship—and AD PRO Directory Members Got a First Look Inside," *Architectural Digest*, March 1, 2024.

15. Sokol, "Design Within Reach Turned a San Francisco Warehouse into a Certified-Cool Flagship."

16. Meyer Schapiro writing under pseudonym John Kwait, "The New Architecture," *New Masses*, May 1932, cited in Scott, *Architecture or Techno-Utopia*, 17; Thomas Germain, "'Magic Intelligence in the Sky': Sam Altman Has a Cute New Name for the Singularity," *Gizmodo*, November 13, 2023.

17. Fredric Jameson, *Archaeologies of the Future: The Desire Called Utopia and Other Science Fictions* (London: Verso, 2007), xi; Nikil Saval, "Design for the Future When the Future Is Bleak," *New York Times*, September 28, 2020.

18. Jameson, *Archaeologies of the Future*, xii.

19. Margaret Cavendish, Duchess of Newcastle, *The Description of a New World, Called the Blazing-World* (London: Printed by A. Maxwell, 1668).

Chapter 1: Beauty

1. All early-life biographical details for Zeisel are from William L. Hamilton, "Eva Zeisel, Ceramic Artist and Designer, Dies at 105," *New York Times*, December 30, 2011; Jyll Johnstone, dir., *Throwing Curves | Eva Zeisel* (Tiburon, CA: Canobie Films, 2014); Martin P. Eidelberg with Derek Ostergard and Jennifer Toher, "Eva Zeisel: Ceramist in an Industrial Age," in *Eva Zeisel: Designer for Industry*, ed. Martin P. Eidelberg (Chicago: University of Chicago Press with Château Dufresne, Musée des arts décoratifs de Montréal, and the Smithsonian Institution Traveling Exhibition Service, 1984), 13–71; Pat Kirkham, "Eva Zeisel: Design Legend 1906–2011," in Pat Moore et al., *Eva Zeisel: Life, Design, and Beauty*, ed. Pat Kirkham (San Francisco: Chronicle Books, 2013), 9–43; Eva Zeisel, *On Design: The Magic Language of Things* (London: Harry N. Abrams, 2011); Judith Szapor, *The Hungarian Pocahontas: The Life and Times of Laura Polanyi Striker, 1882–1959* (New York: Columbia University Press / East European Monographs, 2005); Suzannah Lessard, "The Present Moment," *New Yorker*, April 13, 1987, 36–59.

2. Miklós Molnár, *A Concise History of Hungary* (Cambridge: Cambridge University Press, 2001), 218, 229; Zeisel on the "modern doll" quoted in Kirkham, "Eva Zeisel," 10–11.

3. Kirkham, "Eva Zeisel," 13; Eidelberg et al., "Eva Zeisel," 13, 67n.

4. Molnár, *A Concise History of Hungary*, 208, 218, 226.

5. Molnár, *A Concise History of Hungary*, 233, 235; Eidelberg et al., "Eva Zeisel," 13.

6. Szapor, *The Hungarian Pocahontas*, 61–73.

7. Molnár, *A Concise History of Hungary*, 212, 242–243; Lessard, "The Present Moment," 37; Johnstone, *Throwing Curves | Eva Zeisel*.

8. Judit Szapor, "Laura Polanyi 1882–1957: Narratives of a Life," *Polanyiana* 6, no. 2, 1997; Lessard, "The Present Moment," 37; Sheilagh Ogilvie, *The European Guilds: An Economic Analysis* (Princeton, NJ: Princeton University Press, 2021); András Gerő, *Modern Hungarian Society in the Making: The Unfinished Experience*, trans. James Patterson and Enikő Koncz (Budapest: Central European University Press, 1995 [1993]), 36–38; Gábor Vermes, *Hungarian Culture and Politics in the Habsburg Monarchy, 1711–1848* (Budapest: Central European University Press, 2014).

Notes to Chapter 1

9. Gerő, *Modern Hungarian Society*, 36–38; Vermes, *Hungarian Culture and Politics*, 317ff; Kirkham, "Eva Zeizel," 19; Eidelberg et al., "Eva Zeisel," 13–14.

10. Eidelberg et al., "Eva Zeisel," 13–14; Kirkham, "Eva Zeisel," 19; Eva Zeisel, "The Playful Search for Beauty," TED2001, February 2001.

11. Eidelberg et al., "Eva Zeisel," 13–14; Kirkham, "Eva Zeisel," 19; Zeisel, "The Playful Search for Beauty."

12. Henry Ford and Samuel Crowther, *My Life and Work* (Garden City, NY: Doubleday, Page & Co., 1922), 72; Julian Street, "Detroit the Dynamic," *Colliers*, July 4, 1914, 8–10, 23–27; E. E. Bartlett, "The Utility of Beauty," *Linotype Bulletin* 11, no. 4 (November 1914): 75–77, 76; Arthur W. Einstein Jr., *"Ask the Man Who Owns One": An Illustrated History of Packard Advertising* (Jefferson, NC: McFarland Press, 2014), 97–124; Arthur J. Kuhn, *GM Passes Ford, 1918–1938: Designing the General Motors Performance-Control System* (University Park: Pennsylvania State University Press, 1986).

13. For a synopsis of this transition in the United States, see Jeffrey L. Meikle, *Design in the USA* (Oxford: Oxford University Press, 2005), 109; Earnest Elmo Calkins, "Beauty: The New Business Tool," *Atlantic Monthly*, August 1927.

14. Kirkham, "Eva Zeisel," 20, 12, 22; "Eva Zeisel: Timeline," Eva Zeisel, accessed November 20, 2021.

15. Kirkham, "Eva Zeisel," 22, 25.

16. On early influences, see Kirkham, "Eva Zeisel," 20, citing Leslie Hayward, *Poole Pottery: Carter & Company and Their Successors, 1873–1995* (Somerset, UK: Richard Dennis, 1995).

17. Kirkham, "Eva Zeisel," 23.

18. Pat Moore, "Schramberger Majolikafabrik: 1928," in Moore et al., *Eva Zeisel: Life, Design, and Beauty*, 46–51, 49; Rolf Achilles and Pat Moore, "Christian Carstens KG, Steingutfabrik," in Moore et al., *Eva Zeisel: Life, Design, and Beauty*, 52–55, 55.

19. Gropius, *The New Architecture and the Bauhaus* (Cambridge, MA: MIT Press, 1965 [1935]), 23; Eva Zeisel, "Die Künstlerin hat das Wort," *Die Schaulade* 8 (February 1932), 173–174. (The Bauhaus didn't reject the idea of beauty; Gropius wrote that "the aesthetic satisfaction of the human soul" [23] was just as important as any other goal of architecture. Still, the school became known for its emphasis on values other than aesthetics.)

20. Michael Scammell, *Koestler: The Literary and Political Odyssey of a Twentieth-Century Skeptic* (New York: Random House, 2009), 78; Kirkham, "Eva Zeisel," 25; Lessard, "The Present Moment," 40; Eva Zeisel, "Appendix F: Weimar Berlin," in *Eva Zeisel: A Soviet Prison*

Memoir, ed. Jean Richards and Brent C. Bolin (self-published with Apple Books, 2012), 223.

21. Kirkham, "Eva Zeisel," 25–26.

22. Zeisel, *A Soviet Prison Memoir*, 107–109; Kirkham, "Eva Zeisel," 24, 26.

23. Eva Zeisel, interview with Ronald T. Labaco, published as "'The Playful Search for Beauty': Eva Zeisel's Life in Design," *Studies in the Decorative Arts* 8, no. 1 (2000): 125–138, 133–134; Kirkham, "Eva Zeisel," 26–28, 58–63.

24. Lessard, "The Present Moment," 44; Kirkham, "Eva Zeisel," 26–28, 58–63.

25. Zeisel, *A Soviet Prison Memoir*, 11.

26. Zeisel, *A Soviet Prison Memoir*, 11.

27. Johnstone, *Throwing Curves | Eva Zeisel*; Eidelberg et al., "Eva Zeisel," 28; Zeisel, *A Soviet Prison Memoir*, 11, 15.

28. Zeisel, *A Soviet Prison Memoir*, 43, 35.

29. Zeisel, *A Soviet Prison Memoir*, 63–64, 56.

30. Zeisel, *A Soviet Prison Memoir*, 56, 18.

31. Zeisel, *A Soviet Prison Memoir*, 29, 31–32, 69.

32. Scammell, *Koestler*, 67–69, 78.

33. Scammel, *Koestler*, 78–79, 88–90, 97–99, 158–162; Arthur Koestler, *Dialogue with Death* (as part of *Spanish Testament*: London: Victor Gollancz and Left Book Club, 1937; as free-standing text: New York: Macmillan, 1942).

34. Cf. Kingsley Martin, "Bourgeois Ethics," *New Statesman*, February 8, 1941; Harold Strauss, "The Riddle of Moscow's Trials: Arthur Koestler's Dramatic Novel Illuminates That Fantastic Episode," *New York Times Book Review*, May 25, 1941, 1.

35. Zeisel, *A Soviet Prison Memoir*, 32; deposition of Bykhovskii, May 20, 1936, excerpted in Zeisel, *A Soviet Prison Memoir*, 38, 45; Kirkham, "Eva Zeisel," 28. For a foundational text on the purges, see Robert Conquest, *The Great Terror: Stalin's Purge of the Thirties* (New York: Collier Books, 1968).

36. Zeisel, *A Soviet Prison Memoir*, 90–97. On the likely reasons behind her release, see Kirkham, "Eva Zeisel," 29–30.

37. Kirkham, "Eva Zeisel," 31; Bruce Mays, "Hans Zeisel: The Time of His Life," *Student Lawyer* (American Bar Association), 1980, n.p.

38. Zeisel, *A Soviet Prison Memoir*, 83, 66, 73, 100; Lessard, "The Present Moment," 49; Kirkham, "Eva Zeisel," 30.

39. Lessard, "The Present Moment," 51; Eidelberg et al., "Eva Zeisel," 28–31, 43; Kirkham, "Eva Zeisel," 32–33, 222; Pat Kirkham and Lynne Walker, "Women Designers in the USA, 1900–2000: Diversity

and Difference," in *Women Designers in the USA, 1900–2000: Diversity and Difference*, ed. Pat Kirkham (New York: Bard Graduate Center for Studies in the Decorative Arts; New Haven, CT: Yale University Press, 2000), 58; Alexander J. Kostellow, "Design and Structure Program of the Pratt Institute Art School," *Design* 41 (May 1940), 6–9, 24; "Industrial Design at Pratt Institute," *Interiors* 106 (July 1947), 100–108, 132–134.

40. Eidelberg et al., "Eva Zeisel," 32, 69; Gordon Bruce, *Eliot Noyes* (New York: Phaidon Press, 2007).

41. Eidelberg et al., "Eva Zeisel," 36; "Modern Chinaware at the Modern Museum," *Art News of America*, May 1946, 13; Eugenia Sheppard, "China Service Is Displayed in Modern Shapes," *New York Herald Tribune*, April 17, 1946, 20; Mary Whitman Davis, "Castleton China Company: Museum, 1946," in Moore et al., *Eva Zeisel: Life, Design, and Beauty*, 66–73; Johnstone, *Throwing Curves | Eva Zeisel*.

42. Moore et al., *Eva Zeisel: Life, Design and Beauty*; Castleton China Museum, Promotional Brochure, Castleton China, Inc., New York, January 3, 1949; Scott A. Vermillion, "Eva Zeisel, MUSEUM," International Museum of Dinnerware Design, 2024.

43. Kirkham, "Eva Zeisel," 33, 222; Meri Villane, "Red Wing Potteries: Town and Country, 1947," in Moore et al., *Eva Zeisel: Life, Design, and Beauty*, 74–79; Earl Martin, "Hall China Company: Hallcraft Tomorrow's Classic, 1952," in Moore et al., *Eva Zeisel: Life, Design, and Beauty*, 96–101.

44. Eva Zeisel, "On Being a Designer," in Eidelberg, *Eva Zeisel: Designer for Industry*, 73–104, 73; Kirkham, "Eva Zeisel," 23–24; Zeisel, "Die Künstlerin hat das Wort," 173–174. By the 1940s, the modernist movement had become firmly associated with Louis Sullivan's immortal line: "Form ever follows function, and this is the law." The idea that form might instead come first had, to the modernist orthodoxy, come to seem almost unethical. Louis H. Sullivan, "The Tall Office Building Artistically Considered," *Lippincott's Magazine*, April 1896, 403–409, 408.

45. Hamilton, "Eva Zeisel, Ceramic Artist and Designer, Dies at 105."

46. Kirkham, "Eva Zeisel," 13–14; Zeisel, "On Being a Designer," 97; Eva Zeisel, "Essay: The Roots of 20th Century Design," in *On Design*, 15.

47. Lessard, "The Present Moment," 36.

48. Much later, in the summer of 2000, Zeisel accepted an invitation to visit a group of designers at the Lomonosov factory, where she herself had worked decades earlier in Leningrad with her family. The Russians, she said when she came back, were a "right-minded,

generous people." Linda Hales, "Unbreakable Porcelain," *Washington Post*, January 25, 2024.

49. Lessard, "The Present Moment," 51.

50. Zeisel, "On Being a Designer," 73; Eva Zeisel, "Introduction: The Magic Language of Design," in Zeisel, *On Design*, 13–14, 14.

51. "Eva Zeisel: Designer for Industry," Brooklyn Museum Archives, records of the Department of Public Information, press releases, 1971–1988, 1984, 023-24; Eidelberg, *Eva Zeisel: Designer for Industry*; Lessard, "The Present Moment," 58–59.

52. Karl Polanyi, *The Great Transformation: The Political and Economic Origins of Our Time* (Boston: Beacon Press, 2001 [1944]).

53. Polanyi, *The Great Transformation*, 48.

54. Lessard, "The Present Moment," 43.

55. Lessard, "The Present Moment," 36, 59; Zeisel, *On Design*.

56. Zeisel, "On Being a Designer," 97.

Chapter 2: Function

1. "Industrial artist": Usage dates from mid-1800s; early example, George Birdwood, "Sir George Birdwood writes:—," *Journal of the Society for Arts* 36, no. 1840 (1888): 359–400, 373.

2. All early life biographical details for Teague are from "Obituary: Mr. Walter Dorwin Teague," *Journal of the Royal Society of Arts* 109, no. 5054 (January 1961): 123; "Walter Dorwin Teague: Dean of Design—a Portrait," *Printers' Ink: The Weekly Magazine of Advertising and Marketing*, January 30, 1959, n.p., in Walter Dorwin Teague Papers, Special Collections Research Center, Syracuse University Libraries, Box 1, folder "Articles About Mr. Teague"; Arthur J. Pulos, *American Design Ethic: A History of Industrial Design to 1940* (Cambridge, MA: MIT Press, 1983), 285; Gilbert Seldes, "Industrial Classicist," *New Yorker*, December 15, 1934, 28–32; Russell Flinchum, "Why Teague Matters," North Carolina State University, Department of Graphic and Industrial Design (2010); Jeffrey L. Meikle, *Twentieth Century Limited: Industrial Design in America, 1925–1939* (Philadelphia: Temple University Press, 1979): 44; Jason Morris, *Teague: Design and Beauty* (film), IMDB, 2014.

3. Florence N. Levy, ed., *American Art Annual* 4 (1903–1904): 286, HathiTrust Digital Library; Seldes, "Industrial Classicist," 28.

4. On Teague's agency, see various sources in Walter Dorwin Teague Papers, Special Collections Research Center, Syracuse University Libraries, Box 1, folder "Biography of Mr. Teague"; on borders, see Walter Dorwin Teague, loose sketches and mockups for decorative borders, undated, in Walter Dorwin Teague Papers,

Special Collections Research Center, Syracuse University Libraries, Box 17, several folders titled "Teague Borders," and Clarence P. Hornung, ed., *Classic Border Designs by Twentieth-Century Masters: Bradley, Teague, Cleland, Rogers and Hornung* (New York: Dover Publications, 2011), 24–40; on advertising, see T. J. Jackson Lears, *Fables of Abundance: A Cultural History of Advertising in America* (New York: Basic Books, 1995), 196, and Roland Marchand, *Advertising the American Dream: Making Way for Modernity, 1920–1940* (Berkeley: University of California Press, 1985).

5. For the first (craft-related) usage (e.g., "design" as the planning of a calico print or a piece of fine furniture to be made by hand), see, e.g., the name of the Rhode Island School of Design, founded in 1877 (Rosanne Somerson and Mara Hermano, eds., *The Art of Critical Making: Rhode Island School of Design on Creative Practice* [Hoboken, NJ: Wiley, 2013]; Dawn and Andrew Martinez Barrett, *"Infinite Radius": Founding Rhode Island School of Design* [Providence: Rhode Island School of Design, 2008]). For the theological usage (referring both to God and to his subjects), see, e.g., Josiah Pratt, *Three Hundred and Fifty Portions of the Book of Psalms . . . with a Collection of Six Hundred Hymns Adapted for Public Worship* (Seeley and Son, 1829): "Why do the Jews and Gentiles join / To execute a vain design / Idly their utmost power engage / And storm with unavailing rage?" (orig. 1738). For the second (visual art) usage, see William Dunlap, *A History of the Rise and Progress of the Arts of Design in the United States* (C. E. Goodspeed & Company, 1918).

6. The Art Students' League taught exclusively "fine art" when Teague was there, although it was in the process of developing a more "applied" set of offerings. See Levy, *American Art Annual*, 205.

7. "Walter Dorwin Teague: Dean of Design," *Printers' Ink*, n.p.; Walter Dorwin Teague, "Proceedings of the Art Directors' Club," New York City, February 2, 1925, 8, 18, in Walter Dorwin Teague Papers, Special Collections Research Center, Syracuse University Libraries, Box 1, folder "Art Directors' Club, 1925."

8. William E. Leuchtenburg, *The Perils of Prosperity, 1914–1932*, 2nd ed. (Chicago: University of Chicago Press, 1993), 178; W. Dorwin Teague [Jr.], *Industrial Designer: The Artist as Engineer* (Lancaster, PA: Armstrong World Industries, 1998), 10, 15; Sarah Harrison Smith, "The Past Is Present," *New York Times*, October 19, 2018; Teague, *Industrial Designer*, 14–15; Seldes, "Industrial Classicist," 28–32, this detail at 31–32.

9. *Exposition internationale des arts décoratifs et industriels modernes, Paris* (exhibition catalog) (New York: Garland, 1977 [1925]); see also

J. Stewart Johnson, *American Modern, 1925–1940: Design for a New Age* (New York: Harry N. Abrams, in association with the American Federation of Arts, 2000).

10. *Report of Commission Appointed by the Secretary of Commerce to Visit and Report upon the International Exposition of Modern Decorative and Industrial Art in Paris 1925* (Washington, DC: Department of Commerce, 1926), 18–19; Johnson, *American Modern*, 8.

11. See Johnson, *American Modern*.

12. "Exhibit Lacks Americans,'" *New York Times*, March 5, 1925; Johnson, *American Modern*, 13; "Art in Industry," *New York Times*, March 20, 1925; "Names Delegates to Paris Exposition . . . ," *New York Times*, April 19, 1925; "Painleve Thanks Hoover . . . ," *New York Times*, August 1, 1925; Creange paraphrased in "Paris Exhibit Officers Honor American Press . . . ," *New York Times*, May 30, 1925; "Travel to Europe Breaks the Record . . . ," *New York Times*, April 26, 1925.

13. Kenneth Reid, "Walter Teague, Master of Design," *Pencil Points* 18, no. 9 (September 1, 1937), 539–571, 543; Lorraine Coons and Alexander Varias, *Steamship Travel in the Interwar Years: Tourist Third Cabin* (Stroud, UK: Amberley Publishing, 2016); Meikle, *Twentieth Century Limited*, 28, 46–47 (citing letter from W. Dorwin Teague [Jr.] to Meikle, November 3, 1976); self-portrait of Walter Dorwin Teague (and what he witnessed) in Europe, drawn upon return from his 1926 travels, shown in Morris, *Teague: Design and Beauty*; William J. R. Curtis, *Modern Architecture Since 1900*, 3rd ed. (London: Phaidon Press, 1996), 172–177; Le Corbusier, *Towards a New Architecture* (*Vers une architecture*), trans. Frederick Etchells (Mineola, NY: Dover Publications, 2013 [1923]), 107; Walter Dorwin Teague, *Design This Day: The Technique of Order in the Machine Age* (London: Studio Publications, 1941 [1940]), 228 (also cites Le Corbusier throughout).

14. Teague, *Industrial Designer*, 21; various unattributed and undated magazine clippings, marked "File under modern design" and similar, in Walter Dorwin Teague Papers, Special Collections Research Center, Syracuse University Libraries, Boxes 14–15, in folders titled, e.g., "Modern Design," "Modern Interiors, Exteriors, Furniture, Cities, Decorative Arts," and similar. See also Meikle, *Twentieth Century Limited*.

15. Meikle, *Twentieth Century Limited*, 44–46, citing letter from W. Dorwin Teague [Jr.] to Jeffrey L. Meikle, November 3, 1976; Reid, "Walter Teague, Master of Design," 539, 543–544; "Walter Dorwin Teague: Dean of Design," *Printers' Ink*, n.p.; Mary Siff, "A Realist in Industrial Design," *Arts and Decoration* 41 (October 1934), 44, 46–47, cited in Meikle, *Twentieth Century Limited*, 44–45.

16. Sarah Williams Goldhagen, "Something to Talk About: Modernism, Discourse, Style," *Journal of the Society of Architectural Historians* 64, no. 2 (2005): 144–167, 154, citing George Lakoff and Mark Johnson, *Philosophy in the Flesh: The Embodied Mind and Its Challenge to Western Thought* (New York: Basic Books, 1999), 27–28.

17. Walter Gropius, *Internationale Architektur* (Munich: Albert Langen Verlag, 1925).

18. Lewis Mumford, "Towards a Rational Modernism," *New Republic*, April 25, 1928.

19. Curtis, *Modern Architecture Since 1900*, 12; Walter Dorwin Teague, "Machine Age Aesthetics," *Advertising Arts*, July 1932, 8; Walter Dorwin Teague, "Art of the Machine Age," *Industrial Education Magazine* 38 (November 1936), 228.

20. Vitruvius, *De architectura / The Ten Books on Architecture*, trans. Morris Hicky Morgan (Cambridge, MA: Harvard University Press, 1914), 17 (note that Morgan translates these words as "durability," "convenience," and "beauty"); Heinrich Hübsch et al., *In What Style Should We Build? The German Debate on Architectural Style*, trans. Wolfgang Herrmann [orig. *In welchem Style sollen wir bauen?*, 1828] (Santa Monica, CA: Getty Publications, 1992), 70; Horatio Greenough, "Relative and Independent Beauty" (1852), 73, and "American Architecture" (1843), 61, in *Form and Function: Remarks on Art, Design, and Architecture*, ed. Harold A. Small (Berkeley: University of California Press, 1947); Eugène-Emmanuel Viollet-le-Duc, *Discourses on Architecture*, trans. Henry Van Brunt [orig. *Entretiens sur l'architecture*, 1863–1872] (Boston: Osgood, 1875).

21. On Greenough's influence on the American transcendentalists, see Francis Otto Matthiessen, *American Renaissance: Art and Expression in the Age of Emerson and Whitman* (Oxford: Oxford University Press, 1968); on the reception and influence of Sullivan's dictum, see Jonathan Bell and Ellie Stathaki, *The New Modern House: Redefining Functionalism* (London: Laurence King Publishing, 2010), 9; John Harwood, *The Interface: IBM and the Transformation of Corporate Design, 1945–1976* (Minneapolis: University of Minnesota Press, 2011), 18; Le Corbusier, *Towards a New Architecture*, 153.

22. On the rise of Nazism and the end of the Bauhaus, see Magdalena Droste, *Bauhaus* (Cologne: Taschen, 2015), 485–487; on the Deutscher Werkbund's embrace of industry (particularly the use of machines rather than handcraft to produce goods), see Droste, *Bauhaus*, 17–18.

23. Droste, *Bauhaus*, 98–99, 104, 252, 242, Greil citation at 244; Fiona McCarthy, *Gropius: The Man Who Built the Bauhaus* (Cambridge, MA: Belknap Press, 2019), 102–173 (particularly 147–148), 231.

24. Droste, *Bauhaus*, 104, 126, 246; McCarthy, *Gropius*, 174–210.

25. "Felt compromised": Christopher Turner, "Rethinking the Utopian Vision of the Bauhaus," *Apollo: The International Art Magazine*, July 20, 2018; Feininger cited at Droste, *Bauhaus*, 127; on Meyer's functionalism ("Building is not an aesthetic process"), see Droste, *Bauhaus*, 345–347, 350, 405; on "design" terminology, see Droste, *Bauhaus*, 126–127.

26. Ernő Kállai, "Ten Years of Bauhaus" (1930), trans. Wolfgang Jabs and Basil Gilbert, in *Between Two Worlds: A Sourcebook of Central European Avant-Gardes, 1910–1930*, ed. Timothy O. Benson and Éva Forgács (Cambridge, MA: MIT Press, 2002), 632–636; Philip Goad et al., eds., *Bauhaus Diaspora and Beyond* (Melbourne: Melbourne University Publishing, 2019); Steve Jobs quoted in Rob Walker, "The Guts of a New Machine," *New York Times*, November 30, 2003.

27. David M. Kennedy, *Freedom from Fear: The American People in Depression and War, 1929–1945*, rpt. ed. (New York: Oxford University Press, 2001), 203–204; see also Gene Smiley, *Rethinking the Great Depression* (Chicago: Ivan R. Dee, 2002), 60–61; Meikle, *Twentieth Century Limited*, 68–75.

28. Walter Dorwin Teague, "The Growth and Scope of Industrial Design in the United States," *Journal of the Royal Society of Arts* 107, no. 5037 (August 1959); Elisabeth Luther Cary, "Calling Art to Our Assistance: Thrift, as Well as Taste, Prompts the Modern Manufacturer to Enlist the Artist's Aid in Merchandising His Product," *New York Times*, June 12, 1932, 6; Elisabeth Luther Cary, "A Late Flowering: Industrial Art and Design," *New York Times*, November 18, 1934, 160; Raymond P. Calt, "A New Design for Industry," *The Atlantic*, October 1939; Kennedy, *Freedom from Fear*, 104; Alan Brinkley, *The End of Reform: New Deal Liberalism in Recession and War*, rpt. ed. (New York: Vintage, 1996), 72, 4.

29. Teague, "The Growth and Scope of Industrial Design in the United States," 640–651.

30. Henry Dreyfuss, *Designing for People* (New York: Allworth Press, 2003), 18; George Nelson, "Both Fish and Fowl," *Fortune* 9 (February 1934), 40, 88; on books of business, see Meikle, *Twentieth Century Limited*, 68–75, citing "Designs of Walter Dorwin Teague" (list provided by W. Dorwin Teague [Jr.]), "Brown Book" (Henry Dreyfuss archives), and Geddes, "Affidavit Regarding Activities," July 1946 (Norman Bel Geddes archives); for arguments for design as a differentiator, see, e.g., Nelson, "Both Fish and Fowl"; "Best Dressed Products Sell Best," *Forbes*, April 1, 1934.

31. Seldes, "Industrial Classicist," 31–32.

32. Seldes, "Industrial Classicist," 28 (cameras); Walter Dorwin Teague, Cocktail Glasses, 1920s, Museum of Modern Art, online collection; Meikle, *Twentieth Century Limited*, 94 (barometer).

33. Seldes, "Industrial Classicist," 28.

34. Seldes, "Industrial Classicist," 28; Steve Jobs quoted in Walker, "The Guts of a New Machine."

35. Walter Dorwin Teague, "Why Disguise Your Product?," *Electrical Manufacturing*, October 1938 (reprint/offprint), n.p., in Walter Dorwin Teague Papers, Special Collections Research Center, Syracuse University Libraries, Box 79, folder "Writings / Published material."

36. Seldes, "Industrial Classicist," 32.

37. Kennedy, *Freedom from Fear*, 139.

38. Kennedy, *Freedom from Fear*, 376; Brinkley, *The End of Reform*, esp. 8, 68, 269.

39. Brinkley, *The End of Reform*, 5; Daniel Ritschel, *The Politics of Planning: The Debate on Economic Planning in Britain in the 1930's* (Oxford: Oxford University Press, 1997); Richard Toye, *The Labour Party and the Planned Economy, 1931–1951* (London: Royal Historical Society, 2003); Tony Judt, *Postwar: A History of Europe Since 1945* (London: Penguin Books, 2006), 69, 67.

40. National Industrial Recovery Act, Pub. L. No. 73-67, 48 STAT 195 (1933), Archives.gov; US Congress, Senate Committee on Finance, *Investigation of the National Recovery Administration: Hearings Before the Committee on Finance . . .* (Washington, DC: US Government Printing Office, 1935); Walter Lippmann, "Authority in the Crisis," quoted in Arthur M. Schlesinger Jr., *The Coming of the New Deal* (Boston: Houghton Mifflin, 1959), 121.

41. George L. Harrison, "Letter to Hon. Marriner S. Eccles, Chairman, Board of Governors of the Federal Reserve System, Washington, D.C.," November 3, 1937, FRASER Digital History Library, 2–3.

42. Letter from Walter Dorwin Teague to Mrs. M. Worth, October 17, 1940, in Walter Dorwin Teague Papers, Special Collections Research Center, Syracuse University Libraries, Microfilm Collection, reel 16–10, quoted in Meikle, *Twentieth Century Limited*, 47–48.

43. Seldes, "Industrial Classicist," 32; letter from Teague to Mrs. M. Worth, quoted in Meikle, *Twentieth Century Limited*, 47–48.

44. Norman Bel Geddes, *Magic Motorways* (New York: Random House, 1940); Henry Dreyfuss and Gilbert Seldes, "10 Years of Industrial Design, 1929–1939," *Engineering Societies Library Collection (Library of Congress)*, 1939.

45. Dreyfuss, "Book on Industrial Design 1946," *Designing for People*, misc. files, Dreyfuss Collection, cited in Russell Flinchum, *Henry*

Dreyfuss, Industrial Designer: The Man in the Brown Suit (New York: Cooper Hewitt, National Design Museum, Smithsonian Institution, and Rizzoli, 1997), 79; Dreyfuss, *Designing for People*: travel, communication, nutrition, and culture, 232; health and comfort, 232–233; leisure, 237; security, 233.

46. "W. Dorwin Teague," *Aspen Times*, September 21, 2004; Walter Dorwin Teague, "Preface to the American Edition," in *Design This Day*, 19; Teague, *Design This Day*, 68.

47. Teague, *Design This Day*, 203.

48. Kennedy, *Freedom from Fear*, 204; Teague, *Design This Day*, 196.

49. Teague, *Design This Day*, 196; Margaret Thatcher, interview with Douglas Keay for *Woman's Own*, October 31, 1987, 8–10, in Thatcher Archive (THCR 5/2/262), COI transcript, Margaret Thatcher Foundation online.

50. Jeffrey L. Meikle, *Design in the USA* (Oxford: Oxford University Press, 2005), 131; Barry Katz, "The Arts of War: 'Visual Presentation' and National Intelligence," *Design Issues* 12, no. 2 (1996): 3–21.

51. Meikle, *Design in the USA*, 131ff.

52. Museum of Modern Art (MoMA) for the Society of Industrial Designers, minutes of "Conference on Industrial Design, a New Profession," MoMA, New York City, November 11–14, 1946, in MoMA Manhattan Library Archives.

53. MoMA, minutes, 4, 69.

54. MoMA, minutes, 67–76.

55. MoMA, minutes, 44, 63.

56. Louis Menand, "Academic Freedom Under Fire," *New Yorker*, April 29, 2024.

57. Shannan Clark, *The Making of the American Creative Class: New York's Culture Workers and Twentieth-Century Consumer Capitalism* (Oxford: Oxford University Press, 2020); "Dean": for one of many sources, see Jeffrey L. Meikle, review of *Industrial Strength Design: How Brooks Stevens Shaped Your World*, by Glenn Adamson, *Journal of Design History* 18, no. 1 (2005): 119–121.

58. "How a Big Design Office Works (an Article About the Industrial Design Organization Walter Dorwin Teague Associates)," in *Industrial Design*, n.d. [1950s] (reprint/offprint), n.p., in Walter Dorwin Teague Papers, Special Collections Research Center, Syracuse University Libraries, Box 79, folder "Writings / Published material."

59. Allen Andrews, "Teague," *Design for Industry: The Independent Journal of Industrial Design* 66, no. 398 (August–September 1959): 12–16, 14.

60. Andrews, "Teague," 14–15.

61. Note that Sottsass never considered himself a postmodernist. See Deyan Sudjic, "How the Memphis Design Movement Made a Comeback," *New York Times*, October 28, 2021. Note, too, that even as many professedly postmodern architects and designers claimed to reject modernist functionalism, some of postmodernism's greatest spokespeople—the architectural critics Denise Scott Brown and Robert Venturi—have professed themselves functionalists. See Denise Scott Brown, "The Redefinition of Functionalism," in *Architecture as Signs and Systems*, ed. Robert Venturi and Denise Scott Brown (Cambridge, MA: Belknap Press, 2004), 142–174; Denise R. Constanzo, "Venturi and Scott Brown as Functionalists: Venustas and the Decorated Shed," *Cloud Cuckoo-Land: International Journal of Architectural Theory* 30, no. 17 (July 2012): 10–25, 12.

62. George H. Marcus, *Functionalist Design: An Ongoing History* (Munich: Prestel, 1995), 152–165.

63. Walker, "The Guts of a New Machine."

64. Rebecca Davis O'Brien, "What to Know About R.F.K. Jr. and His Threat to Biden and Trump," *New York Times*, April 5, 2024; Jack Dorsey (@jack), "He can and he will," Twitter, June 4, 2023, 4:48 p.m.; Julia Jacobs, "Elon Musk Thinks a Mini-submarine Could Help in Thai Cave Rescue," *New York Times*, July 19, 2018; Matthew Weaver, Helen Davidson, and Michael Safi, "All 12 Boys and Coach Successfully Rescued from Thai Cave—as It Happened," *The Guardian*, July 10, 2018; Radhika Viswanathan, "Elon Musk's Plan to Bring a Mini-submarine to Rescue the Thai Boys," *Vox*, July 11, 2018; PR Thai Government, "Elon Musk Will Send . . . ," post of July 6, 2018, Facebook, https://www.facebook.com/thailandprd/photos/pb.180940151929407.-2207520000.1530975840./1852586424764763/?type=3&theater; Radhika Viswanathan, "Thai Cave Rescue: Elon Musk's Plan to Help Involved a Mini-submarine," *Vox*, July 22, 2018; Farhad Manjoo, "Silicon Valley's Politics: Liberal, with One Big Exception," *New York Times*, September 6, 2017, sec. Technology.

65. Karl Polanyi, *The Great Transformation: The Political and Economic Origins of Our Time* (Boston: Beacon Press, 2001 [1944]); Katy Lederer, "Meet the Leftish Economist with a New Story About Capitalism," *New York Times*, November 26, 2019; Mariana Mazzucato, *The Entrepreneurial State: Debunking Public Versus Private Sector Myths*, rev. ed. (New York: PublicAffairs, 2015 [2013]), 22.

66. Mazzucato, *The Entrepreneurial State*, 27, 93–107, 27.

67. Mazzucato, *The Entrepreneurial State*, 27, 24.

68. Martin Wolf, "A Much-Maligned Engine of Innovation," *Financial Times*, August 4, 2013; Mazzucato, *The Entrepreneurial State*, 14;

Congressional Research Service, "Defense Advanced Research Projects Agency: Overview and Issues for Congress," August 19, 2021, Project on Government Secrecy, 11.

69. Mazzucato, *The Entrepreneurial State*, 15f.

70. Derek Thompson (@DKThomp), "There are no libertarians in a pandemic," Twitter, March 2, 2020, 4:22 p.m.

71. George Packer, "We Are Living in a Failed State," *The Atlantic*, April 20, 2020.

Chapter 3: Problem Solving

1. All early life biographical details for Rand are from Jessica Helfand, *Paul Rand: American Modernist* (New York: William Drenttel, 1998); Steven Heller, "Thoughts on Rand," *PRINT Magazine* 51, no. 3 (May–June 1997): 106–109, 120; "Timeline," PaulRand.design, April 28, 2023.

2. Alessia Arosio et al., eds, *Paul Rand: Good Design Is Good Business* (Milan: Politecnico/designverso, 2018).

3. Helfand, *Paul Rand*, 17–18; Pat Kirkham, *Charles and Ray Eames: Designers of the Twentieth Century* (Cambridge, MA: MIT Press, 1995), 145; "The Beautiful and the Useful," in Paul Rand, *Thoughts on Design*, with a foreword by Michael Bierut (San Francisco: Chronicle Books, 2014 [1947]): 9–10.

4. Heller, "Thoughts on Rand," 106.

5. Paul Rand, "The Designer's Problem," in Rand, *Thoughts on Design*, 11–12.

6. "Bureau of Indian Affairs," PaulRand.design, accessed August 21, 2024.

7. Rand corporate identity presentation to Atlas Crankshaft Corporation, reproduced in Stanley Mason, "How Paul Rand Presents Trade-Mark Designs to Clients," *Graphis* 153 (1971–1972): 54–59, 54; Doug Evans, "1993 Interview re: Paul Rand and Steve Jobs" (interview with Steve Jobs), filmed 1993, YouTube, 3:10, https://www.youtube.com/watch?v=xb8idEf-Iak.

8. On the problem-centered architectural brief, see, e.g., William Peña, *Problem Seeking: New Directions in Architectural Programming* (Houston, TX: Caudill Rowlett Scott, 1969). Hawksmoor on Queen Mary: John Bold, "Comparable Institutions: The Royal Hospital for Seamen and the Hôtel des invalides," *Architectural History* 44 (2001): 136–144, 136.

9. Victor Horta, "Reminiscences of the Maison du Peuple" (undated), in *Architecture and Design, 1890–1939: An International Anthology of Original Articles*, ed. Tim Benton and Charlotte Benton (New York: Whitney Library of Design, 1975), 65; Spiro Kostof, *A History of*

Notes to Chapter 3

Architecture: Settings and Rituals, 2nd ed. (Oxford: Oxford University Press, 1995), 5, 7; Sigfried Giedion, *The Eternal Present: The Beginnings of Architecture* (New York: Pantheon, 1964), 13–27.

10. OED Online, s.v. "problem, n.," and "problem-solving, n. and adj.," accessed March 2023.

11. György Marx, *A marslakók legendája*, Magyar Elektronikus Könyvtár, accessed August 21, 2024; George Marx, *The Voice of the Martians: Hungarian Scientists Who Shaped the 20th Century in the West* (Budapest: Akadémiai Kiadó and István Hargittai, 2001); István Hargittai, *The Martians of Science: Five Physicists Who Changed the Twentieth Century* (New York: Oxford University Press, 2006).

12. George Pólya, *How to Solve It: A New Aspect of Mathematical Method* (Princeton, NJ: Princeton University Press, 1945).

13. Pólya, *How to Solve It*, v.

14. Allen Newell, "The Heuristic of George Pólya and Its Relation to Artificial Intelligence" (paper given to the International Symposium on the Methods of Heuristic, University of Bern, Bern Switzerland, July 1981 [1980]), 1; Alan H. Schoenfeld, "Pólya, Problem Solving, and Education," *Mathematics Magazine* 60, no. 5 (December 1987): 283–291, 283.

15. Pólya, *How to Solve It*, 113, 129–130.

16. Farewell address by President Dwight D. Eisenhower, January 17, 1961, Final TV Talk January 17, 1961 (1), Box 38, Speech Series, Papers of Dwight D. Eisenhower as President, 1953–1961, Eisenhower Library, National Archives and Records Administration.

17. All early life biographical details are from Herbert Simon's detailed autobiography, *Models of My Life* (Cambridge, MA: MIT Press, 1996).

18. Simon, *Models of My Life*, 37, 44, 60.

19. "Merriam's hand," wrote two political scientists in 1985, "can be seen in virtually every facet of modern political science." Raymond Seidelman, *Disenchanted Realists: Political Science and the American Crisis, 1884–1984*, with the assistance of Edward J. Harpham (Albany: State University of New York Press, 1985), 109; Simon, *Models of My Life*, 44, 60, 62.

20. Herbert A. Simon, *Administrative Behavior: A Study of Decision-Making Processes in Administrative Organization* (New York: Macmillan, 1947).

21. Michael D. Ward and Daniel Guetzkow, "Harold S. Guetzkow," *PS: Political Science and Politics* 42, no. 2 (2009): 413–414; Daniel Druckman, "Remembering Harold Guetzkow," *Simulation & Gaming* 42, no. 3 (June 2011): 290–293.

22. Simon, *Models of My Life*, 163.

23. K. Anders Ericsson, "The Acquisition of Expert Performance as Problem Solving: Construction and Modification of Mediating Mechanisms Through Deliberate Practice," in *The Psychology of Problem Solving*, ed. Janet E. Davidson and Robert J. Sternberg (Cambridge: Cambridge University Press, 2003): 31–84, 33; see also Dorit Wenke and Peter A. Frensch, "Is Success or Failure at Solving Complex Problems Related to Intellectual Ability?," in *The Psychology of Problem Solving*, 87–126, 88.

24. Immanuel Kant, "Preface," in *Metaphysical Foundations of Natural Science*, trans. Michael Friedman (Cambridge: Cambridge University Press, 2004 [1786]), 3–14; Andrew J. Reck, "The Influence of William James on John Dewey in Psychology," *Transactions of the Charles S. Peirce Society* 20, no. 2 (1984): 87–117, 89; Ericsson, "The Acquisition of Expert Performance as Problem-Solving," 36.

25. On behaviorism's dominance, see Roger L. Dominowski and Lyle E. Bourne, "History of Research on Thinking and Problem Solving," in *Thinking and Problem Solving*, ed. Robert J. Sternberg (San Diego: Academic Press, 1994), 1–35, 15, 18; Ericsson, "The Acquisition of Expert Performance as Problem Solving," 37–38. Note also that there were dissenters—see, e.g., William James, *The Principles of Psychology* (New York: Henry Holt and Company, 1890), 1:224–290, esp. 1:259–260, and John Dewey, *How We Think* (Boston: D. C. Heath & Co., 1910), 9–14—and that in Europe, even experimental psychology was more flexible.

26. Dominowksi and Bourne, "History of Research," 16–18.

27. Simon, *Models of My Life*, 189.

28. Simon, *Models of My Life*, 198; Edmund Callis Berkeley, *Giant Brains; or, Machines That Think* (New York: John Wiley & Sons, 1949), vii.

29. James Allen Smith, *The Idea Brokers: Think Tanks and the Rise of the New Policy Elite* (New York: Free Press, 1991), xiv; David Hounshell, "The Cold War, RAND, and the Generation of Knowledge, 1946–1962," *Historical Studies in the Physical and Biological Sciences* 27, no. 2 (1997): 237–267, 240, 244; Paul Erickson et al., *How Reason Almost Lost Its Mind: The Strange Career of Cold War Rationality* (Chicago: University of Chicago Press, 2015). Hounshell and Erickson et al. both note that RAND—through its development of systems analysis and related methods—"helped to foster the pervasive quantification of the social sciences in the postwar era" (Hounshell, "The Cold War, RAND, and the Generation of Knowledge," 265).

30. Erickson et al., *How Reason Almost Lost Its Mind*, 14.

31. Simon, *Models of My Life*, 131–139, 167–168, 199–202.

32. Simon, *Models of My Life*, 167–168, 199–202.

33. Simon, *Models of My Life*, 203–209.

34. Katherine Simon Frank, "Herbert A. Simon: A Family Memory," Carnegie Mellon University School of Computer Science, accessed June 22, 2023.

35. Simon, *Models of My Life*, 189–190, 204–209.

36. Simon, *Models of My Life*, 206–209; Pamela McCorduck, *Machines Who Think*, 2nd ed. (Natick, MA: A. K. Peters, Ltd., 2004), 167; for attributions as the first instance of AI, see, e.g., Daniel Crevier, *AI: The Tumultuous Search for Artificial Intelligence* (New York: Basic Books, 1993), 44–46; McCorduck, *Machines Who Think*, 123–125; Stuart J. Russell and Peter Norvig, *Artificial Intelligence: A Modern Approach*, 2nd ed. (Upper Saddle River, NJ: Prentice Hall, 2003), 17.

37. Hounshell, "The Cold War, Rand, and the Generation of Knowledge, 1946–1962," 261; Allen Newell, J. C. Shaw, and Herbert A. Simon, "Elements of a Theory of Human Problem Solving," *Psychological Review* 65 (1958): 151–166; Herbert A. Simon and Allen Newell, "Computer Simulation of Human Thinking and Problem Solving," *Monographs of the Society for Research in Child Development* 27, no. 2 (1962): 137–150.

38. Herbert A. Simon, *The Sciences of the Artificial*: Karl Taylor Compton Lectures (Cambridge, MA: MIT Press, 1969), 4, 22–26, 52, 55.

39. Simon, *The Sciences of the Artificial*, 5, xi, 55–56.

40. Erickson et al., *How Reason Almost Lost Its Mind*, 3, 5.

41. Simon, *The Sciences of the Artificial*, 57–58, 99; Xinya You and David Hands, "A Reflection upon Herbert Simon's Vision of Design in *The Sciences of the Artificial*," *Design Journal* 22, no. S1 (April 2019): 1345–1356, 1347.

42. Per Galle, "Foundational and Instrumental Design Theory," *Design Issues* 27, no. 4 (2011): 81–94, 82–84; Erickson et al., "Introduction," in *How Reason Almost Lost Its Mind*, 3.

43. Hugh Dubberly, "Why We Should Stop Describing Design as 'Problem Solving,'" in *After the Bauhaus, Before the Internet: A History of Graphic Design Pedagogy*, ed. Geoff Kaplan (Cambridge, MA: MIT Press, 2022), 275–276; Ivan Rupnik, "Projecting Space-Time: The Laboratory Method, Modern Architecture and Settlement-Building, 1918–1932" (PhD diss., Harvard University, 2015), cited at Dubberly, "Why We Should Stop Describing Design as 'Problem Solving,'" 276; Frederick Winslow Taylor, *The Principles of Scientific Management* (New York: Harper & Brothers, 1911); El Lissitzky and Ilya Ehrenburg, "Statement by the Editors of *Veshch/Gegenstand/Objet*" (1922), in *Art and Theory, 1900–1990*, ed. Charles Harrison and Ed Wood (Oxford: Blackwell, 1994), 321, cited at Dubberly, "Why We Should

Stop Describing Design as 'Problem Solving,'" 276; Walter Gropius, *Scope of Total Architecture* (New York: Harper & Row, 1955 [1943]), 20, 3.

44. On midcentury interest in design's meaning and methods, see Nigel Cross, "A History of Design Methodology," in *Design Methodology and Relationships with Science*, ed. M. J. de Vries, N. Cross, and D. P. Grant (Dordrecht: Kluwer Academic Publishers, 1993), 15–27. For an account of this interest's rise and origins, see interview with Rittel, "Son of Rittelthink: The State of the Art in Design Methods," DMG 5th Anniversary Report, DMG Occasional Paper No. 1 (1972), 5–10. On the Japanese Society for the Science of Design, see Japanese Society for the Science of Design (Nihon Dezain Gakkai), *Bulletin of Japanese Society for Science of Design* (Dezaingaku kenkyû), Japan, 1956–. See also Dubberly, "Why We Should Stop Describing Design as 'Problem Solving,'" 279; Victor Margolin, "Design Research: Towards a History," in *Design and Complexity—DRS International Conference*, ed. D. Durling et al., July 7–9, 2010, Montreal, Canada.

45. All details of Churchman's biography are drawn from W. Ulrich, "Obituary: C West Churchman, 1913–2004," *Journal of the Operational Research Society* 55, no. 11 (2004): 1123–1129; John P. van Gigch et al., "In Search of an Ethical Science: An Interview with C. West Churchman: An 80th Birthday Celebration," *Journal of Business Ethics* 16, no. 7 (1997): 731–744; Ernest Koenigsberg and John P. van Gigch, "Introduction: In Celebration of the 80th Birthday of C. West Churchman, Born Mount Airy, Pennsylvania, August 29, 1913," *Interfaces* 24, no. 4 (1994): 1–4; Arjang A. Assad, "C. West Churchman," in *Profiles in Operations Research: Pioneers and Innovators*, ed. Arjang A. Assad and Saul I. Gass (New York: Springer Science & Business Media, 2011), 171–200.

46. See biographical sources above and Jean-Pierre Protzen, "Design Thinking: What Is That?" (Cal Design Lab Lecture, Berkeley, California, 2010), 1.

47. Google ngram for "(problem solving + [problem-solving])," 1800–2019, English language (2019), books.google.com/ngrams.

48. J. Christopher Jones and D. G. Thornley, eds., *Conference on Design Methods: Papers Presented at the Conference on Systematic and Intuitive Methods in Engineering, Industrial Design, Architecture and Communications, London, September, 1962* (Oxford: Pergamon Press, 1963); L. Bruce Archer, "Systematic Method for Designers," in *Developments in Design Methodology*, ed. Nigel Cross (Chichester, UK: Wiley, 1984), 58, reprinted from a work published by The Design Council, London, in 1964; Christopher Alexander, *Notes on the Synthesis of Form* (Cambridge, MA: Harvard University Press, 1964).

49. D. J. Huppatz, "Revisiting Herbert Simon's 'Science of Design,'" *Design Issues* 31, no. 2 (2015): 29–40, 29.

50. Simon, *The Sciences of the Artificial*, 62; Nelson Goodman, *Ways of Worldmaking* (Indianapolis: Hackett Publishing Company, 1978).

51. It is this judgment process, Simon asserts, that produces what we understand as "style." Simon, *The Sciences of the Artificial*, 64, 75; Simon, "The Architecture of Complexity," *Proceedings of the American Philosophical Society* 106, no. 6 (December 1962): 467–482; Simon quoted in Byron Spice, "CMU's Simon Reflects on How Computers Will Continue to Shape the World," *Pittsburgh Post Gazette*, October 16, 2000.

52. Simon, *The Sciences of the Artificial*, 77; Goodman, *Ways of Worldmaking*, 6.

53. Rand, *Thoughts on Design*.

54. Simon, *Models of My Life*, 133, see also 119–122.

55. Simon, *Models of My Life*, 119–122.

56. Martin Lipton, Steven A. Rosenblum, and William Savitt, "On the Purpose and Objective of the Corporation," Harvard Law School Forum on Corporate Governance, August 5, 2020.

57. All biographical details for Charles and Ray Eames are from John Neuhart and Marilyn Neuhart, *Eames Design* (New York: Abrams, 1989); Ruth Bowman, "Oral History Interview with Ray Eames, 1980 July 28–August 20," Archives of American Art, Smithsonian Institution; Kirkham, *Charles and Ray Eames*; Donald Albrecht, ed., *The Work of Charles and Ray Eames: A Legacy of Invention* (New York: Harry N. Abrams Inc., 1997); Lotte Johnson et al., *The World of Charles and Ray Eames*, ed. Catherine Ince (New York: Rizzoli, 2016); Charles Eames and Ray Eames, *An Eames Anthology: Articles, Film Scripts, Interviews, Letters, Notes, and Speeches*, ed. Daniel Ostroff (New Haven, CT: Yale University Press, 2015); Pat Kirkham, "'In a Man's World,'" in *Women Designers in the USA, 1900–2000: Diversity and Difference*, ed. Pat Kirkham (New Haven, CT: Yale University Press, 2000), 269–290. On Saarinen's problem-solving vision, see Paul Goldberger, "The Cranbrook Vision," *New York Times Magazine*, April 8, 1984, 48; *Eames Celebration*, reprinted from *Architectural Design Magazine* (London: Architectural Design Magazine, 1966), 2; Kirkham, *Charles and Ray Eames*, 13. On Lounge Chair Wood problem statement and product, see "The Shapes of Progress," *Art Institute of Chicago Museum Studies* 27, no. 2 (2001): 70–103, 110–112; *Shaping the Modern: American Decorative Arts at the Art Institute of Chicago, 1917–65* (Chicago: Art Institute of Chicago, 2001), 70–103, 110–112, 71, 80.

58. Quote: "Think," presentation for IBM at 1964–1965 New York World's Fair, by Charles and Ray Eames (Los Angeles: Office of Charles & Ray Eames, 1964). See also Charles Eames, dir., *A Communications Primer*, short documentary (Los Angeles: Office of Charles & Ray Eames, 1953); Kirkham, *Charles and Ray Eames*, 379; Charles Eames to Ian McCallum, September 3, 1954, Part II: Speeches and Writings series, Charles and Ray Eames Papers, Manuscript Division, Library of Congress, Washington, DC, in Eames and Eames, *An Eames Anthology*, 136–137; Charles Eames, dir., *The Information Machine: Creative Man and the Data Processor*, short documentary (Los Angeles: Office of Charles & Ray Eames, 1958); John Harwood, *The Interface: IBM and the Transformation of Corporate Design, 1945–1976* (Minneapolis: University of Minnesota Press, 2011), 38–39, 162–163, 170–173, 183.

59. Harwood, *The Interface*, 173. For an excellent extended analysis of the Eameses' whimsical proclivities, see Pat Kirkham, "Functioning Decoration," in *Charles and Ray Eames*, 143–200.

60. Ray Eames, "Line and Color," *California Arts & Architecture* 60, no. 8 (September 1943): 16–17, reprinted in Eames and Eames, *An Eames Anthology*, 13; Charles Eames quoted in Greg Allen, "Modern Love," *Humanities* 32, no. 6 (November/December 2011).

61. Jacob W. Getzels and Mihaly Csikszentmihalyi, *The Creative Vision: A Longitudinal Study of Problem Finding in Art* (New York: John Wiley & Sons, 1976), 250.

62. Harold Taylor, "Problems and Solutions" (Keynote Address), 11th International Design Conference in Aspen, June 18–24, 1961, 1–11, in folder "Man/Prob. Solver: Conf. papers, 1961," International Design Conference in Aspen records, 1949–2006, The Getty Research Institute, Los Angeles, Accession no. 2007.M.7; "Speakers Invited to '61 Conference Who Could Not Make It This Year," folder "Man/Prob. Solver: Conf. papers, 1961," International Design Conference in Aspen records, 1949–2006, The Getty Research Institute, Los Angeles, Accession no. 2007.M.7.

63. Short and long programs for conference "Man/Problem Solver" and recording of conference sessions, folders "Man/Prob. Solver: Program, 1961" and "Man/Prob. Solver: Conf. papers, 1961," International Design Conference in Aspen records, 1949–2006, The Getty Research Institute, Los Angeles, Accession no. 2007.M.7.

64. Short and long programs for "Man/Problem Solver"; Gwendolyn Brooks, "kitchenette building," Poetry Foundation, 1963; W. H. Auden, "In Memory of W. B. Yeats," Poets.org, accessed August 10, 2023.

65. Charles Eames, speech and seminar transcript, October 10, 1952, American Institute of Architects, Kansas City, MO, Part II: Speeches and Writings series, Charles and Ray Eames Papers, Manuscript Division, Library of Congress, Washington, DC, in Eames and Eames, *An Eames Anthology*, 104–110, 110.

Chapter 4: Human-Centeredness

1. Nigel Cross, "A History of Design Methodology," in *Design Methodology and Relationships with Science*, ed. M. J. Vries, N. Cross, and D. P. Grant (Dordrecht: Kluwer Academic Publishers, 1993), 15–27; Jean-Pierre Protzen, "Design Thinking: What Is That?" (Cal Design Lab Lecture, UC Berkeley Department of Architecture, 2010), 1–2; Jean-Pierre Protzen and David J. Harris, *The Universe of Design: Horst Rittel's Theories of Design and Planning* (New York: Routledge, 2010); Herbert Simon and Allen Newell, *Human Problem Solving* (Englewood Cliffs, NJ: Prentice Hall, 1972).

2. C. West Churchman, *Challenge to Reason* (New York: McGraw Hill, 1968), 2; W. Ulrich, "Obituary: C West Churchman, 1913–2004," *Journal of the Operational Research Society* 55, no. 11 (2004): 1123–1129.

3. Chanpory Rith and Hugh Dubberly, "Why Horst W. J. Rittel Matters," *Design Issues* 23, no. 1 (January 2007): 72–74; Chanpory Rith and Hugh Dubberly, "Horst W. J. Rittel's Writings on Design: Select Annotations," *Design Issues* 23, no. 1 (January 2007): 75–88; C. West Churchman et al., "In Memoriam: Horst W. J. Rittel," *Design Issues* 23, no. 1 (January 2007): 89–91; Protzen and Harris, *The Universe of Design*; Robin Kinross, "Hochschule für Gestaltung Ulm: Recent Literature," *Journal of Design History* 1, nos. 3/4 (1988): 249–256.

4. C. West Churchman, "Free for All," *Management Science* 14, no. 4 (December 1, 1967): B141–B142; for Rittel on design as planning, see, in particular, Rittel, "The Reasoning of Designers," Arbeitspapier A-88-4 (Stuttgart: Institut für Grundlagen der Planung, Universität Stuttgart, 1988), 1.

5. Churchman, "Free for All"; Horst W. J. Rittel and Melvin M. Webber, "Dilemmas in a General Theory of Planning," *Policy Sciences* 4, no. 2 (June 1, 1973): 155–169. "Dilemmas" is a revision of a paper presented to the Panel on Policy Sciences, American Association for the Advancement of Science, Boston, December 1968.

6. Rittel and Webber, "Dilemmas," 163 ("traces"), 166–167 ("right").

7. Rittel and Webber, "Dilemmas," 155–169, 161.

8. Churchman, "Free for All," B141; Rittel and Webber, "Dilemmas," 160ff.

9. Rittel and Webber, "Dilemmas"; Rittel, "The Reasoning of Designers," 3.

10. Rittel, "The Reasoning of Designers," 5; John Chris Jones, "How My Thoughts About Design Methods Have Changed During the Years," *Design Methods and Theories* 11, no. 1 (1977), 48–62; Christopher Alexander interviewed by Max Jacobson, "The State of the Art in Design Methods," originally published in *DMG Newsletter* 5, no. 3 (1971): 3–7, reprinted in Nigel Cross, *Developments in Design Methodology* (Hoboken, NJ: Wiley, 1984): 309–316, 309, 312, 315.

11. American deaths: Peter N. Carroll, *It Seemed Like Nothing Happened: America in the 1970s*, rpt. ed. (New Brunswick, NJ: Rutgers University Press, 1990), 4; Vietnamese civilian deaths: Thomas C. Thayer, *War Without Fronts: The American Experience in Vietnam* (Boulder, CO: Westview Press, 1985), 125–128 (~182,700 Vietnamese civilians admitted injured to hospitals from 1967 to 1969; former assistant director of USAID public health division in Saigon estimates that hospital admissions represent 50 percent of all wounded Vietnamese civilians, producing an estimate of 365,000 total injured; USAID official also estimates one death per 2.5 seriously wounded during the period 1965 to 1972, producing an estimate of very roughly ~104,400 total dead during the period 1967 to 1969); Charles Hirschman, Samuel Preston, and Vu Manh Loi, "Vietnamese Casualties During the American War: A New Estimate," *Population and Development Review* 21, no. 4 (1995): 783–812; Nixon quote: Richard Nixon, "Address at the Dedication of the Karl E. Mundt Library at General Beadle State College, Madison, South Dakota," June 3, 1969, American Presidency Project.

12. Gloria Emerson, "British Mood Defiant Toward Tight Curbs," *New York Times*, January 13, 1969, 65; Mike Davis and Jon Wiener, *Set the Night on Fire* (New York: Verso, 2020), 11.

13. "Great social responsibility": Milner Gray, address to 11th International Design Conference in Aspen, CO, June 18–24, 1961, 5, in folder "Man/Prob. Solver: Conf. papers, 1961," International Design Conference in Aspen records, 1949–2006, The Getty Research Institute, Los Angeles, Accession no. 2007.M.7; "A new society": Dr. Harold A. Taylor, "Problems and Solutions" (Keynote Address), address to 11th International Design Conference in Aspen, CO, June 18–24, 1961, 11, in folder "Man/Prob. Solver: Conf. papers, 1961," International Design Conference in Aspen records; "Blast off": Edward C. Bursk, address to 11th International Design Conference in Aspen, June 18–24, 1961, 6, in folder "Man/Prob. Solver: Conf. papers, 1961"; Elena Dellapiana and Ramon Rispoli, "Which Way to Go? Some Complicated Crossroads Facing Design Culture in Aspen," *Design*

Culture(s): Cumulus Conference Proceedings Roma 2021, vol. 2 (Rome: Cumulus Association, 2021), citing IDCA papers, 1969; J. Michaels, "30 Years of Design for Designers," *Aspen: The Magazine* 6, no. 5 (1980): 32–38, 36.

14. Martin Beck, ed., *The Aspen Complex* (Berlin: Sternberg Press, 2012), 63–65.

15. Jean Baudrillard, "Statement Made by the French Group" [1970], 84–85, International Design Conference in Aspen Papers, Special Collections and University Archives Department, Richard J. Daley Library, University of Illinois at Chicago, reproduced in Beck, *The Aspen Complex*, 98–100, 99, 100; Reyner Banham, ed., *The Aspen Papers: Twenty Years of Design Theory from the International Design Conference in Aspen* (London: Pall Mall Press, 1974), 222.

16. Eliot Noyes, "Conclusion" [1970], International Design Conference in Aspen Papers, Special Collections and University Archives Department, Richard J. Daley Library, University of Illinois at Chicago, reproduced in Beck, *The Aspen Complex*, 66–67, 66.

17. Stuart Hall, "Introduction," in Wolfgang Fritz Haug, *Critique of Commodity Aesthetics [Kritik der Warenästhetik]: Appearance, Sexuality and Advertising in Capitalist Society*, trans. Robert Bock (Minneapolis: Polity Press of the University of Minnesota Press, 1986 [1971]): 1–4, 3; Haug, *Critique of Commodity Aesthetics*, 6.

18. Wolfgang Fritz Haug, "Appendices: Response to an Enquiry from the International Design Centre," in Haug, *Critique of Commodity Aesthetics*, 136–137, 136.

19. Alison J. Clarke, *Victor Papanek: Designer for the Real World* (Cambridge, MA: MIT Press, 2021), 6; "Victor Papanek," Papanek Foundation, University of Applied Arts Vienna.

20. Clarke, *Victor Papanek*, 14, 10.

21. Clarke, *Victor Papanek*, 17, 26, 29, 40.

22. Clarke, *Victor Papanek*, 33, 35, 53, 56–57, citing "The Pencil and the Plow: Personal Memories of Frank Lloyd Wright," original typed manuscript (1991), 1, Victor J. Papanek Foundation, University of Applied Arts Vienna.

23. Clarke, *Victor Papanek*, 65; Alison J. Clarke, "Design Provocateur: Revisiting the Prescient Ideas of Victor Papanek," *Metropolis*, January 24, 2019.

24. Clarke, *Victor Papanek*, 81 ("Why Contemporary"), 82 (California teaching), 91 (Toronto).

25. Clarke, *Victor Papanek*, 98; Buckminster Fuller, original source unknown; Henry Dreyfuss, *Designing for People* (New York: Allworth Press, 2003 [1955]), 23–24.

Notes to Chapter 4

26. Dreyfuss, *Designing for People*, 102, 103–106; Russell Flinchum, *Henry Dreyfuss, Industrial Designer: The Man in the Brown Suit* (New York: Cooper Hewitt, National Design Museum, Smithsonian Institution, and Rizzoli, 1997), 97, citing Sally Clarke, "Consumer Demand and Bell Labs' French Phone" (unpublished paper, Shelby Cullom Davis Center, History Department, Princeton University, Princeton, NJ, April 28, 1995).

27. Dreyfuss, *Designing for People*, 127, 102; Flinchum, *Henry Dreyfuss, Industrial Designer*, 21–22; Jeffrey L. Meikle, *Twentieth Century Limited: Industrial Design in America, 1925–1939* (Philadelphia: Temple University Press, 1979), 58; Sheldon Cheney and Martha Candler Cheney, *Art and the Machine: An Account of Industrial Design in 20th-Century America* (New York: Whittlesey House, 1936), 82.

28. Dreyfuss, *Designing for People*, 102–103.

29. Dreyfuss, *Designing for People*, 103.

30. Dreyfuss, *Designing for People*, 103; Model 302 Telephone, ca. 1937, made for Bell Telephone Laboratories (United States), USA, cast and enamel-coated metal, steel, printed paper, rubber-sheathed cord, Cooper Hewitt, Smithsonian Design Museum, New York; "Henry Dreyfuss, FIDSA," IDSA, accessed December 10, 2018; Model 500 Telephone, designed 1953, this example ca. 1980, made for Bell Telephone Laboratories (United States), USA, molded plastic, metal, rubber, Cooper Hewitt, Smithsonian Design Museum, New York, accessed December 10, 2018; AT&T and Associated Companies, "The Telephone Story" posters.

31. Victor Papanek, "Education of a Designer I," *Industrial Design* 10, no. 11 (November 1963): 36.

32. On the development of Papanek's design philosophy out of engagement with Finland as "an alternative economy of design," see Clarke, *Victor Papanek*, 187–189, 216; Papanek in *Industrial Design* cited at Clarke, *Victor Papanek*, 124; Victor Papanek, "Victor Papanek: Biographical Data" (Part 1 of 2), administrative record, date unknown (revised September 1970), CalArts Design School Archives, California Institute of the Arts, Valencia, California, 3; Victor Papanek, "Preface to First Edition," in Victor J. Papanek, *Design for the Real World: Human Ecology and Social Change* (New York: Pantheon Books, 1972), 14.

33. Papanek, *Design for the Real World*, 107–115.

34. Papanek, *Design for the Real World*, 335.

35. Roland Robertson, *Globalization: Social Theory and Global Culture* (London: Sage, 1992), 4; Sergio Conti and Paolo Giaccaria, "Globalization: A Geographical Discourse," *GeoJournal* 45, nos. 1/2 (1998): 17–25; OED Online, s.v. "globalization (n.)," accessed July 2023.

36. Papanek, *Design for the Real World*, 241.

37. Papanek, *Design for the Real World*, 159, 298.

38. Clarke, "The Anthropological Object in Design," 79; Clarke, *Victor Papanek*, 118 (citing profile in the *Buffalo Evening News*), 214; Papanek, "Victor Papanek: Biographical Data," 9–10.

39. Victor Papanek, "Northern Lights," *Industrial Design* 14, no. 8 (1967): 29, quoted in Clarke, *Victor Papanek*, 188.

40. Clarke, *Victor Papanek*, 219; Ida Kamilla Lie, University of Oslo, "'Make Us More Useful to Society!'—The Scandinavian Design Students' Organization (SDO) and Socially Responsible Design, 1967–1973," *Design and Culture* 8, no. 3 (2016): 327–361. Note that, later, ErgonomiDesignGruppen rebranded as Veryday, which in 2016 was incorporated into the McKinsey group: Maria Göransdotter, "Designing Together: On Histories of Scandinavian User-Centred Design" (2022), in *Nordic Design Cultures in Transformation, 1960–1980: Revolt and Resilience*, ed. Kjetil Fallan et al. (New York: Routledge, 2022): 157–177, 175.

41. Alison J. Clarke, "Introduction," in *Design Anthropology: Object Culture in the 21st Century*, ed. Alison J. Clarke (Berlin: Springer Vienna Architecture, 2010), 11; Peter Smithson, "Just a Few Chairs and a House: An Essay on the Eames-Aesthetic," *Architectural Design*, September 1966, 443, cited at Kirkham, *Charles and Ray Eames*, 143; see also Alison J. Clarke, "The Anthropological Object in Design: From Victor Papanek to Superstudio," in Clarke, *Design Anthropology*, 74–88.

42. Suzanne Stephens, "Design Deformed," *Artforum*, January 1977; Clarke, "The Anthropological Object in Design," 77; Hans Hollein, *MAN transFORMS: Konzepte einer Ausstellung* (Vienna: Loecker Verlag, 1989), 13; Hans Hollein, "Writings > MANtransFORMS," hollein.com, June 1974.

43. Ton Otto and Rachel Charlotte Smith, "Design Anthropology: A Distinct Style of Knowing," in *Design Anthropology: Theory and Practice*, ed. Wendy Gunn, Ton Otto, and Rachel Charlotte Smith (New York: Routledge, 2013), 1–29; see also M. Hammersley and P. Atkinson, *Ethnography Principles in Practice*, 2nd ed. (London & New York: Routledge, 1995).

44. William L. Partridge and Elizabeth M. Eddy, "The Development of Applied Anthropology in America," in *Applied Anthropology in America*, ed. E. M. Eddy and W. L. Partridge, 2nd ed. (New York: Columbia University Press, 1987), 3–56, 24–25, citing May Ebihara, "American Ethnology in the 1930s: Contexts and Currents," in *Social Contexts in American Ethnology, 1840–1984*, ed. June Helm (Proceedings of the American Ethnological Society, 1984) (Washington, DC:

American Anthropological Association, 1985), 101–121; Lawrence C. Kelly, "Why Applied Anthropology Developed When It Did: A Commentary on People, Money, and Changing Times, 1930–1945," in Helm, *Social Contexts in American Ethnology*, 122–138; Otto and Smith, "Design Anthropology," 1–30; Ronald Busse and Malcolm Warner, "The Legacy of the Hawthorne Experiments: A Critical Analysis of the Human Relations School of Thought," *History of Economic Ideas* 25, no. 2 (2017): 91–114.

45. Partridge and Eddy, "The Development of Applied Anthropology in America," 32–36, 39.

46. Partridge and Eddy, "The Development of Applied Anthropology in America," 40–41, 43, 47.

47. Partridge and Eddy, "The Development of Applied Anthropology in America," 48; Lucy Suchman, "Consuming Anthropology," Centre for Science Studies, Lancaster University (manuscript prepared for publication in *Interdisciplinarity: Reconfigurations of the Social and Natural Sciences*, ed. Andrew Barry and Georgina Born [New York: Routledge, 2013]), 4.

48. Lucy Suchman, "I Have, More Than Ever, a Sense of the Immovability of These Institutions," interview with C. Otto Scharmer on behalf of the Society for Organizational Learning, Xerox PARC, Palo Alto, California, August 13, 1999, 1–2.

49. Suchman, "I Have, More Than Ever," 2; Laura Nader, "Up the Anthropologist: Perspectives Gained from Studying Up," US Department of Health, Education and Welfare, Office of Education, Washington, DC, 1972; Hugh Gusterson, "Studying Up Revisited," *Political and Legal Anthropology Review* 20, no. 1 (1997): 114–119; Lucy Suchman, "Anthropological Relocations and the Limits of Design," *Annual Review of Anthropology* 40, no. 1 (2011): 1–18, 4, 16.

50. Suchman, "I Have, More Than Ever," 1–2; Lucy Suchman, interview with Daniela Rosner, October 26, 2015, cited in Daniela K. Rosner, *Critical Fabulations: Reworking the Methods and Margins of Design* (Cambridge, MA: MIT Press, 2020), 43–44; Lucy Suchman, "Emerging into Emerita: Celebrating the Work of Lucy Suchman and Maggie Mort," Centre for Science Studies, Department of Sociology, Lancaster University, Lancashire, UK, September 2021, video recording.

51. Suchman herself credits much of her own insight about the extraprocedural nature of office work to Eleanor Wynn, a doctoral student in linguistic anthropology who came to PARC before Suchman arrived, and Jeff Rulifson, the Office Research Group computer science and research manager who initiated PARC's engagement with

Wynn in 1976 after finding himself frustrated with the quality of the office-work models provided by consulting firms to inform Xerox's software design. "Searching for alternatives," Suchman writes, Rulifson was inspired by reading Claude Lévi-Strauss, "from whom he took the lesson that 'we are our tools.'" Rulifson turned to his Bay Area academic networks in search of an anthropologist to help study office work. At Berkeley, he met Wynn, who agreed to a summer contract. Suchman continued and expanded the larger project that Rulifson and Wynn began. See Suchman, "Consuming Anthropology," 4–5, citing an interview Suchman conducted with Jeff Rulifson on February 19, 2003, as part of a project funded by the ESRC Science and Society Program Award / Grant Reference: L144250006; Carole Browner and Michael Chibnik, "Anthropological Research for a Computer Manufacturing Company," *Central Issues in Anthropology* 1, no. 2 (1979): 63–76, 64; see also Suchman, "I Have, More Than Ever," 3; Suchman, "Anthropological Relocations and the Limits of Design," 14.

52. Todd R. Weiss, "Xerox PARC Turns 40: Marking Four Decades of Tech Innovations," *Computerworld*, September 20, 2010.

53. Michael A. Hiltzik, *Dealers of Lightning: Xerox PARC and the Dawn of the Computer Age* (New York: Harper Business, 2000); Margaret O'Mara, *The Code: Silicon Valley and the Remaking of America* (New York: Penguin Press, 2019).

54. Suchman, "Emerging into Emerita."

55. Suchman, "I Have, More Than Ever," 4.

56. Suchman, "I Have, More Than Ever," 3.

57. Suchman, "Emerging into Emerita"; Suchman, "Anthropological Relocations and the Limits of Design."

58. "Pressing the Green Button," advertisement for Xerox 8200 copier, ca. 1983, © Xerox Corporation, reprinted in Lucy Suchman, *Human-Machine Reconfigurations: Plans and Situated Actions* (Cambridge: Cambridge University Press, 2007), 9.

59. "Ethnography and the PARC Copier," video of experiment by Xerox PARC researchers Austin Henderson and Lucy Suchman, ca. 1983, posted to YouTube by PARC, December 22, 2016.

60. Lucy Suchman, *Plans and Situated Actions* (Cambridge: Cambridge University Press, 1987).

61. Suchman, *Plans and Situated Actions*, 36, viii, 52, ix.

62. Lucy Suchman, "Making Work Visible," *Communications of the ACM* 38, no. 9 (1995): 56–64, 58.

63. Alonso H. Vera and Herbert A. Simon, "Situated Action: A Symbolic Interpretation," *Cognitive Science* 17, no. 1 (1993): 7–8. For

scholarship reflecting the debate, see, e.g., R. J. Anderson, "'Representations and Requirements': The Value of Ethnography in System Design," *Journal of Human-Computer Interaction* 9, no. 3 (1994): 151–182; J. Blomberg et al., "Ethnographic Field Methods and Their Relation to Design," in *Participatory Design: Principles and Practices*, ed. D. Schuler and A. Namioka (Hillsdale, NJ: Lawrence Erlbaum Associates, 1993), 123–155; D. Shapiro, "The Limits of Ethnography: Combining Social Sciences for CSCW," in *CSCW '94, Proceedings of the Conference on Computer Supported Cooperative Work* (Chapel Hill, NC: ACM Press, 1994), 417–428; see also Suchman, "Consuming Anthropology," 13; Vera and Simon, "Situated Action," 7–48.

64. Suchman, "Consuming Anthropology," 10; Suchman, "Anthropological Relocations and the Limits of Design," 4.

65. Maria Bezaitis and Rick E. Robinson, "Valuable to Values: How 'User Research' Ought to Change," in Clarke, *Design Anthropology*, 185–201, 188.

66. Suchman, "Making Work Visible," 56.

67. Suchman, *Human-Machine Reconfigurations*, 9–10, 3; Suchman, "Emerging into Emerita."

68. Claudia H. Deutsch, "Coping with Cultural Polyglots," *New York Times*, February 24, 1991; Christina Elnora Garza, "Studying the Natives on the Shop Floor," *Bloomberg Businessweek*, September 30, 1991; Kate A. Kane, "Anthropologists Go Native in the Corporate Village," *Fast Company*, October 31, 1996; Spencer E. Ante and Cliff Edwards, "The Science of Desire," *Bloomberg Businessweek*, June 5, 2006, 98–106; Suchman, "Consuming Anthropology," 9; Clarke, "Introduction," 10; Lucy Suchman, "Anthropology as 'Brand': Reflections on Corporate Anthropology" (paper presented at the Colloquium on Interdisciplinarity and Society, Oxford University, February 24, 2007).

69. Bezaitis and Robinson, "Valuable to Values," 1–29; Jane Fulton Suri, "Poetic Observation: What Designers Make of What They See," in Clarke, *Design Anthropology*, 16–32.

70. Fulton Suri, "Poetic Observation," 17.

71. Jo-Anne Bichard and Rama Gheerawo, "The Ethnography in Design," in Clarke, *Design Anthropology*, 45–55, 48, citing Donald A. Norman, "Rapid Ethnography," in *The Method Lab: User Research for Design*, ed. H. Aldersey-Williams, J. Bound, and R. Coleman (London: Design for Aging Network, Royal College of Art, 1999), 24–25; see also Donald A. Norman, *The Invisible Computer* (Cambridge, MA: MIT Press, 1999), 195, 282n4.

72. Bezaitis and Robinson, "Valuable to Values," 192.

73. Bezaitis and Robinson, "Valuable to Values," 192; James Clifford and George E. Marcus, eds., *Writing Culture: The Poetics and Politics of Ethnography*, 2nd (25th anniv.) ed. (Berkeley: University of California Press, 2010 [1986]); see also Suchman, "Making Work Visible."

74. Haug, *Critique of Commodity Aesthetics*, 6, 53.

75. Suchman, "Anthropological Relocations and the Limits of Design," 14; Suchman, "Consuming Anthropology," 6, 13–14.

76. Suchman, "Anthropological Relocations and the Limits of Design," 2; Suchman, "I Have, More Than Ever," 14–15; see also Lucy Suchman and Ana Gross, "Lucy Suchman in Conversation with Ana Gross," *Sociologica* 15, no. 2 (September 30, 2021): 179–185, 180.

77. Weiss, "Xerox PARC Turns 40"; Suchman, "Anthropological Relocations and the Limits of Design," citing J. Adame, "PARCing Problems," *IEEE Spectrum*, September 2002.

Chapter 5: Experience

1. Wallace Stevens, "Connoisseur of Chaos" (1942), in *Wallace Stevens: Collected Poetry and Prose* (LOA #96), ed. Joan Richardson and Frank Kermode (New York: Library of America, 1997), 194–195, 194.

2. Greta R. Krippner, *Capitalizing on Crisis: The Political Origins of the Rise of Finance* (Cambridge, MA: Harvard University Press, 2012), 16, 19, 22, 28.

3. Krippner, *Capitalizing on Crisis*, 1–26, 138–150; Rana Foroohar, interview with Gary Gensler, cited in Rana Foroohar, *Makers and Takers: The Rise of Finance and the Fall of American Business* (New York: Currency, 2016), 35.

4. Examples are from Markus K. Brunnermeier and Martin Oehmke, "Complexity in Financial Markets," manuscript, September 2009, 4–5; "frontlines . . .": Philip Mader, Daniel Mertens, and Natascha van der Zwan, "Financialization: An Introduction," in *The Routledge International Handbook of Financialization*, ed. Philip Mader, Daniel Mertens, and Natascha van der Zwan (New York: Routledge, 2021): 1–16, 6; Foroohar, *Makers and Takers*, 1. For an example of what Simon meant by "bounded rationality," take the heads of two city agencies charged with collaborating to run a city program together. They might agree completely on the program's goals, but—given their differing qualitative notions of what it would mean to run it well—they might be unable to come to the conclusion that classical economics would expect. "How can human beings make rational decisions in circumstances like these?" Simon wrote. "How are they to apply the marginal calculus? Or, if it does not apply, what do

they substitute for it?" (Herbert Simon, "Rational Decision-Making in Business Organizations [1978 Nobel Lecture, Economics]," in *Nobel Lectures in Economic Sciences 1969–1980*, ed. Assar Lindbeck [Singapore: World Scientific Publishing Co., 1992], 352). For a discussion of financial complexity and bounded rationality, see Brunnermeier and Oehmke, "Complexity in Financial Markets."

5. Foroohar, *Makers and Takers*; Todd R. La Porte, ed., *Organized Social Complexity: Challenge to Politics and Policy* (Princeton, NJ: Princeton University Press, 1975), 3, 18.

6. On the scientific and cultural implications of the discovery of chaos (as well as the earlier study of complexity), see James Gleick, *Chaos: Making a New Science* (London: Penguin Books, 2008 [1987]); Melanie Mitchell, *Complexity: A Guided Tour* (New York: Oxford University Press, 2011); M. Mitchell Waldrop, *Complexity: The Emerging Science at the Edge of Order and Chaos* (New York: Simon & Schuster, 1992); Mark C. Taylor, *The Moment of Complexity: Emerging Network Culture* (Chicago: University of Chicago Press, 2003).

7. David E. Sanger, "Wall Street's Tomorrow Machine," *New York Times*, October 19, 1986; Heinz R. Pagels, *The Dreams of Reason: The Computer and the Rise of the Sciences of Complexity* (New York: Simon & Schuster, 1988); Brian Hayes, "Computers in Command," *New York Times*, August 14, 1988 (review of Pagels's *The Dreams of Reason*).

8. John Markoff, "Ideas and Trends: In Computer Behavior, Elements of Chaos," *New York Times*, September 11, 1988.

9. Alfred Balk, "Computers: A Necessary Insidiousness," *New York Times*, January 17, 1988.

10. Donald A. Norman, "The Trouble with Unix: The System Design Is Elegant but the User Interface Is Not," *Datamation* 4, no. 1 (January 1981): 37–41.

11. Norman, "The Trouble with Unix," 41.

12. Norman, "The Trouble with Unix," 37.

13. Norman, "The Trouble with Unix," 37–38; quotes from Donald A. Norman, "The Truth About Unix: The User Interface Is Horrid," draft manuscript prepared for *Datamation*, 1981, 1.

14. Don Norman and Jeffrey R. Yost, "Oral History Interview with Don Norman," Association for Computing Machinery, 2022, 10; Michael Lesk, "Another View," *Datamation* 4, no. 1 (January 1981), 40 (response to Norman, "The Trouble with Unix").

15. Stephen W. Draper and Donald A. Norman, "Introduction," in *User Centered System Design: New Perspectives on Human-Computer Interaction*, ed. Donald A. Norman and Stephen W. Draper (Hillsdale, NJ: Lawrence Erlbaum Associates, 1986), 1–6, 3.

Notes to Chapter 5

16. Donald Norman, "Don Norman on the Term 'UX,'" Nielsen Norman Group, video, 2016.

17. Norman used terms with slightly more specificity and preciseness than they're used here. The software's own version of the vision, in Norman's writing, was its "conceptual model," and the version the user would adopt was the user's "mental model." I've collapsed the terms here for simplicity and to reflect how they're used in the field today. Draper and Norman, "Introduction," 4; Norman, "Don Norman on the Term 'UX'"; Norman, "The Trouble with Unix," 41; Donald Norman, "Some Observations on Mental Models," in *Mental Models*, ed. D. Gentner and A. L. Stevens (Hillsdale, NJ: Lawrence Erlbaum Associates, 1983), 7–14; Donald Norman, "Cognitive Engineering," in Norman and Draper, *User Centered System Design*, 31–61, 46–48.

18. Norman and Yost, "Oral History Interview with Don Norman"; John Rheinfrank, "A Conversation with Don Norman," *Interactions* 2, no. 2 (April 1995): 47–55.

19. Kenneth J. W. Craik, *The Nature of Explanation* (Cambridge: Cambridge University Press, 1952 [1943]), 59, 61.

20. John Mollon, "On This Day . . . 7th May: Kenneth Craik (1914–1945)," University of Cambridge Department of Psychology, May 7, 2020; on behaviorism's dominance and decline, see Michiel Braat et al., "The Rise and Fall of Behaviorism: The Narrative and the Numbers," *History of Psychology* 23, no. 3 (2020): 252–280, preprint pp. 1–2; Philip N. Johnson-Laird, *Mental Models: Towards a Cognitive Science of Language, Inference, and Consciousness* (Cambridge, MA: Harvard University Press, 1983), 165, 97. Also in 1983, the psychologists Dedre Gentner and Albert L. Stevens published another book on the topic of mental models; in it, Gentner and a coauthor showed that experimental subjects tended to explain electricity to themselves using analogies that acted as inferential frameworks for making sense of the world. The evidence was clear: the mental-models theory was right. Dedre Gentner and Albert L. Stevens, eds., *Mental Models* (Hillsdale, NJ: L. Erlbaum Associates, 1983).

21. Norman, "Some Observations on Mental Models," 8, 12, 14; Don Norman, *The Psychology of Everyday Things* (New York: Basic Books, 1988), 189.

22. David Liddle, "Design of the Conceptual Model: An Interview with David Liddle," in *Bringing Design to Software*, ed. Terry Winograd (New York: ACM Press / Addison-Wesley, 1996), 17–36, 19–20; Charles Irby et al., "A Methodology for User Interface Design," Xerox Palo Alto Research Center, January 1977, 3–4.

23. Liddle, "Design of the Conceptual Model," 20, 21 (the Irby study became, as Liddle put it, "the basis for the whole Star design process" [20]); Jonathan Seybold, "Xerox's 'Star,'" in *The Seybold Report* (Media, PA: Seybold Publications, 1981).

24. On GUIs: a previous PARC/Xerox product, the Alto, released in 1973, had had one; so had a previous, early 1970s PARC experiment, Alan Kay's "Dynabook," its programming language "Smalltalk," and its interface "Pygmalion." On Star's GUI particularly: David Canfield Smith et al., "The Star User Interface: An Overview" (paper delivered at the National Computer Conference, 1982), 519.

25. Smith et al., "The Star User Interface," 519.

26. Liddle, "Design of the Conceptual Model," 26; Paul Atkinson, *Computer* (London: Reaktion Books, 2010), 68–69; Douglas K. Smith and Robert C. Alexander, *Fumbling the Future: How Xerox Invented, Then Ignored, the First Personal Computer* (New York: iUniverse, 1999), 235; Michael Tuck, "The Real History of the GUI," Sitepoint, August 2001.

27. Liddle, "Design of the Conceptual Model," 29.

28. Steve Wozniak and Gina Smith, *iWoz: Computer Geek to Cult Icon: How I Invented the Personal Computer, Co-founded Apple, and Had Fun Doing It* (New York: W. W. Norton, 2007); Walter Isaacson, *Steve Jobs* (New York: Simon & Schuster, 2011), 62ff; Laine Nooney, *The Apple II Age: How the Computer Became Personal* (Chicago: University of Chicago Press, 2023), 2.

29. Heath R., "What Really Happened: Steve Jobs @ Xerox PARC '79," Living Computers: Museum + Labs, April 2020; Wayne E. Carlson, "16.2 Apple Computer," in *Computer Graphics and Computer Animation: A Retrospective Overview* (Columbus: Ohio State University, 2017).

30. According to Larry Tesler, "There was a lot of influence from Xerox obviously on the user interfaces that were done on the Lisa and the Macintosh," though "maybe not as much as some people think." Larry Tesler and Chris Espinosa, "Origins of the Apple Human Interface," public lecture, Computer Museum History Center, October 28, 1997.

31. Morris B. Holbrook and Elizabeth C. Hirschman, "The Experiential Aspects of Consumption: Consumer Fantasies, Feelings, and Fun," *Journal of Consumer Research* 9, no. 2 (1982): 132–140, 139, 132.

32. Joseph B. Pine II and James H. Gilmore, "Welcome to the Experience Economy," *Harvard Business Review*, July 1998; see also Joseph B. Pine II and James H. Gilmore, *The Experience Economy: Work Is*

Notes to Chapter 5

Theater and Every Business a Stage (Boston: Harvard Business School Press, 1999).

33. Pine and Gilmore, "Welcome to the Experience Economy."

34. Pine and Gilmore, "Welcome to the Experience Economy"; see also Pine and Gilmore, *The Experience Economy*.

35. Donald Norman, "Design as Practiced," in *Bringing Design to Software*, ed. Terry Winograd (New York: ACM Press / Addison-Wesley, 1996), 233–251; Don Norman, "Where Did the Term User Experience (UX) Come From?," JND.org, April 15, 2023; Norman and Yost, "Oral History Interview with Don Norman."

36. Norman, "Where Did the Term User Experience (UX) Come From?"

37. Hartmut Esslinger, *Keep It Simple: The Early Design Years of Apple* (Stuttgart: Arnoldsche Verlagsanstalt, 2014), 259–261.

38. Rheinfrank, "A Conversation with Don Norman," 47–55, 50.

39. Rheinfrank, "A Conversation with Don Norman"; Don Norman, "The Four Fundamental Principles of Human-Centered Design and Application," JND.org, July 23, 2019; Norman and Yost, "Oral History Interview with Don Norman," 14.

40. John Markoff, "Why Apple Sees Next as a Match Made in Heaven," *New York Times*, December 23, 1996.

41. "Steve Jobs—Get Much Simpler, Be Really Clear—Sept. 23, 1997," video posted to YouTube by askphilipwilliams, January 16, 2015; Isaacson, *Steve Jobs*, 343. Neither Steve Jobs nor Jonathan Ive was naive about the proposition that complexity should be simplified. They both knew that simplification was extraordinarily difficult, sometimes even impossible, to achieve. Yet Apple's design culture became organized around the simplification of complexity.

42. Norman and Yost, "Oral History Interview with Don Norman," 17; Draper and Norman, "Introduction," 1–3, 4. Note also that, for example, Mitchell Kapor, one of the earliest software designers, was stating publicly by 1990 that he believed "computing professionals themselves should take responsibility for creating *a positive user experience*" (Mitchell Kapor, "A Software Design Manifesto" [1990], in *Bringing Design to Software*, ed. Terry Winograd [New York: ACM Press / Addison-Wesley, 1996], 1–9: 3; emphasis mine).

43. Don Norman and Bruce Tognazzini, "How Apple Is Giving Design a Bad Name," *Fast Company*, November 10, 2015; "Human Interface Guidelines," Apple Developer, accessed January 7, 2024.

44. Norman and Tognazzini, "How Apple Is Giving Design a Bad Name."

45. Federica Laricchia, "Apple iPhone Market Share 2007–2024," *Statista*, August 5, 2024.

46. Norman and Tognazzini, "How Apple Is Giving Design a Bad Name."

47. Dieter Rams, Alex Anderson, and Molly Mandell, "Dieter Rams: As Little Design as Possible," *Kinfolk*, February 21, 2017 (interview with Dieter Rams).

48. Initial qualitative study: Jen Cardello and Kathryn Whitenton, "Killing Off the Global Navigation: One Trend to Avoid," Nielsen Norman Group, February 9, 2014; follow-up quantitative study: Kara Pernice and Raluca Budiu, "Hamburger Menus and Hidden Navigation Hurt UX Metrics," Nielsen Norman Group, June 26, 2016. The 2016 (quantitative) study also studied task completion on mobile devices, with similar findings: people used the hidden navigation in 57 percent of cases and the nonhidden navigation in 86 percent of cases (1.5 times as often).

49. Christia Spiratos and Michaela Kořistová, "Navigation User Interface Design in e-Commerce and Its Impact on Customers' Satisfaction: A Mixed-Methods Study Analysing the Impact of Different Menu Styles and User Interface Elements" (PhD thesis, Jönköping University School of Engineering, May 2021).

50. Retrospective reflection in Donald A. Norman, *Living with Complexity* (Cambridge, MA: MIT Press, 2010), 285.

51. Norman, *Living with Complexity*, 118.

52. Norman, *Living with Complexity*, 10, 285.

53. Norman, *Living with Complexity*, 51, 40.

54. Jesse James Garrett, *The Elements of User Experience: User-Centered Design for the Web* (New York: Peachpit Press, 2002), 3, 51; Jesse James Garrett, "The Elements of User Experience," diagram, jjg.net, March 30, 2000, http://www.jjg.net/elements/pdf/elements.pdf.

55. Elizabeth (Dori) Tunstall, *Decolonizing Design: A Cultural Justice Guidebook* (Cambridge, MA: MIT Press, 2023), 39, 45; "NASDAQ Composite Index (COMP) Historical Data | Nasdaq," NASDAQ, accessed January 3, 2024.

56. Tunstall, *Decolonizing Design*, 45, 39.

57. Tunstall, *Decolonizing Design*, 72, 50.

58. Paul Basken and Dori Tunstall, "Interview with Dori Tunstall," *Times Higher Education*, December 8, 2022, n.p.; Tunstall, *Decolonizing Design*, 9, 10.

59. Tunstall, *Decolonizing Design*, 64.

60. Tunstall, *Decolonizing Design*, 11, 50–51; see also Elizabeth (Dori) Tunstall, "The Yin and Yang of Seduction and Production: Social

Transitions of Ethnography Between Seductive Play and Productive Force in Industry," EPIC, September 6, 2014; Tunstall, *Decolonizing Design*, 11, 72.

61. Dori Tunstall, Dana Arnett, and Kevin Bethune, "S10E11: Dori Tunstall," *The Design of Business | The Business of Design*, Design Observer, February 14, 2023, n.p.

62. International Interior Design Association (IIDA), "Dori Tunstall: Design Anthropologist," *IIDA Perspective*, issue "IIDA Hybrid Professionals" (ca. 2015), 21.

63. Tunstall, *Decolonizing Design*, 69; Ron Fanfair, "Black Leaders Recruited to Support OCAD U Students, Staff & Community Partners," November 18, 2019; OCAD Faculty of Design, "Position: Open Call for Black Applicants in the Faculty of Design," International Council of Design, January 2020.

64. Tunstall, *Decolonizing Design*, 84; remarks of OCAD Faculty Association president Min-Sook Lee, in "Cluster Hiring at OCAD University," Canadian Association of University Teachers, accessed January 5, 2024.

65. Tunstall, *Decolonizing Design*, 85–86, citing David A. Harrison, Kenneth H. Price, and Myrtle P. Bell, "Beyond Relational Demography: Time and the Effects of Surface- and Deep-Level Diversity on Work Group Cohesion," *Academy of Management Journal* 41, no. 1 (February 1998): 96–107, and Hui Liao, Aichia Chuang, and Aparna Joshi, "Perceived Deep-Level Dissimilarity: Personality Antecedents and Impact on Overall Job Attitude, Helping, Work Withdrawal, and Turnover," *Organizational Behavior and Human Decision Processes* 106, no. 2 (July 2008): 106–124.

66. Sasha Costanza-Chock, *Design Justice: Community-Led Practices to Build the Worlds We Need* (Cambridge, MA: MIT Press, 2020), xviii.

67. Costanza-Chock, *Design Justice*, 10.

68. Costanza-Chock, *Design Justice*, xvii, 9, citing Sandra G. Harding, ed., *The Feminist Standpoint Theory Reader: Intellectual and Political Controversies* (New York: Routledge, 2004), and James I. Charlton, *Nothing About Us Without Us: Disability Oppression and Empowerment* (Berkeley: University of California Press, 1998), 84.

69. "Design: Soul & Body," Matt Kahn's Classic Stanford Design Lectures, Stanford.edu, accessed January 10, 2024.

Chapter 6: Thinking

1. David M. Kelley, "Oral History of David M. Kelley," conducted by Barry Katz, July 11, 2011, Computer History Museum, 2; Dinah

Eng, "How IDEO Brings Design to Corporate America," *Fortune*, April 11, 2013.

2. Kelley, "Oral History," 2–3.

3. Daniel Kahneman, *Thinking, Fast and Slow* (New York: Farrar, Straus and Giroux, 2011), 13 (and full text).

4. David Kelley, interview by Alex Soojung-Kim Pang, Palo Alto, CA, "Making the Macintosh: Technology and Culture in Silicon Valley," Stanford.edu, July 2000, accessed December 28, 2023, 1; Eng, "How IDEO Brings Design to Corporate America."

5. Kelley, interview by Pang, 2.

6. Kelley, "Oral History," 4–5.

7. Kelley, "Oral History," 4–5.

8. Kelley, interview by Pang, 3; Kelley, "Oral History," 4.

9. Marion Buchenau and Jane Fulton Suri, "Experience Prototyping," *Proceedings of the Conference on Designing Interactive Systems: Processes, Practices, Methods, and Techniques* (2000): 424–433, 424.

10. Buchenau and Fulton Suri, "Experience Prototyping," 425; Bill Moggridge, *Designing Interactions* (Cambridge, MA: MIT Press, 2007), 241; see also Jeremy Myerson, *IDEO: Masters of Innovation* (London: Te Neues Pub Group, 2001), 88–89 and throughout; Tim Brown, *Change by Design: How Design Thinking Transforms Organizations and Inspires Innovation* (New York: HarperBusiness, 2009); Tim Brown, "Design Thinking," *Harvard Business Review*, June 2008.

11. On this point, see Linda Tischler, "Ideo's David Kelley on 'Design Thinking,'" *Fast Company*, February 1, 2009, particularly remarks of Roger Martin, dean of the University of Toronto's Rotman School of Management.

12. Thomas J. Sugrue, *The Origins of the Urban Crisis* (Princeton, NJ: Princeton University Press, 1996); Malcolm Harris, *Palo Alto: A History of California, Capitalism, and the World* (New York: Little, Brown, 2023), 363.

13. Myerson, *IDEO*, 21; Moggridge, *Designing Interactions*, 9.

14. Moggridge, *Designing Interactions*, 9–11.

15. Moggridge, *Designing Interactions*, 11–12; note that (as Moggridge acknowledges) there were some precedents (Alan Kay's Dynabook concept in 1968, several portable data terminals, several "luggable computers more the size of a sewing machine than a laptop" (11).

16. Katz quoted in Kelley, "Oral History," 11, 7–8; Kelley, interview by Pang, 5.

17. Kelley, interview by Pang, 5; Kelley, "Oral History," 11–12.

18. Kelley, "Oral History," 14; Moggridge, *Designing Interactions*, 107–108; Katz quoted in Kelley, "Oral History," 14–15.

19. Kelley, interview by Pang, 8; Myerson, *IDEO*, 32; Moggridge, *Designing Interactions*, 108–111.

20. Myerson, *IDEO*, 21–23; Kelley, "Oral History," 9–10, 18; Tom Kelley and Jonathan Littman, *The Art of Innovation: Lessons in Creativity from IDEO, America's Leading Design Firm* (New York: Currency, 2001), chap. 2.

21. Scott Underwood, history of IDEO logo, Underwood portfolio, synopsized by David Seliger as "The History of the IDEO Logo," Core77, August 26, 2011.

22. Underwood in Seliger, "The History of IDEO Logo"; Myerson, *IDEO*, 23.

23. Anthony Lyons, telephone interview with author, unpublished, conducted January 21, 2020.

24. Lyons, interview; Anthony Clark, "Ready to Revitalize," *Gainesville Sun*, December 17, 2006.

25. Lyons, interview; Clark, "Ready to Revitalize."

26. Lyons, interview; Clark, "Ready to Revitalize."

27. NASDAQ Composite Index (.IXIC) forty-five-year historical data, accessed via Google Finance, January 26, 2024; Margaret O'Mara, *The Code: Silicon Valley and the Remaking of America* (New York: Penguin Press, 2019), 329, 359; Joe Kukura, "Throwback Thursday: Remembering the Last Big Tech Layoff Bloodbath, the Dot-Com Bust of 2000–2001," *SFist*, November 11, 2022; "Layoffs near 2 Million in 2001," *Silicon Valley Business Journal*, January 3, 2002, citing data from outplacement firm Challenger, Gray & Christmas, Inc.

28. Bruce Nussbaum, "The Power of Design," *Businessweek*, May 17, 2004; Eng, "How IDEO Brings Design to Corporate America"; "History of IDEO Inc.," FundingUniverse, accessed April 12, 2019; Ted Koppel, "The Deep Dive," *Nightline*, July 13, 1999, cited in Myerson, *IDEO*, 8.

29. Nussbaum, "The Power of Design"; Weng Cheong, "International Design Firm IDEO Is Cutting Up to 8% of Its Workforce in North America and Europe," *Business Insider*, December 10, 2020; Myerson, *IDEO*, 148.

30. Myerson, *IDEO*, 30, 33; Brown, *Change by Design*, 177.

31. Tim Brown quoted in Ann Grimes, "An Idea Firm Finds Growth amid an Economic Slowdown," *Wall Street Journal*, March 7, 2002; Brown quoted in Ernest Beck, "It Was a Dark and Stormy Year: Top Designers Share Strategies for Surviving the Recession," *I.D. Magazine*, April 2009; Tischler, "Ideo's David Kelley.'"

32. Tischler, "Ideo's David Kelley"; Brown, *Change by Design*, 12–13.

33. Tischler, "Ideo's David Kelley."

34. Jake Knapp, "How Does Creativity Really Work? I'm Going Inside IDEO to Find Out," *Medium*, May 22, 2017.

35. Bruce Archer, "Whatever Became of Design Methodology?," *Design Studies* 1, no. 1 (1979): 17–18, 17; Peter G. Rowe, *Design Thinking* (Cambridge, MA: MIT Press, 1991 [1987]), 2.

36. Brown, "Design Thinking," 2.

37. Brown, *Change by Design*, 1.

38. "Redesigning Theater > The Design Thinking Process," Stanford d.school, accessed March 1, 2019.

39. Brown, *Change by Design*, 177–179; Brown, "Design Thinking," 2–4.

40. Emily Steel, "The Ads Making Colombian Guerrillas Lonely This Christmas," *Financial Times*, December 12, 2013.

41. Lyons, interview.

42. Lyons, interview.

43. Lyons, interview; Jeff Feingold, "Cerberus Partners Acquires Red River Technology," *NH Business Review*, June 3, 2021.

44. Vintage 2018 Population Estimates, Gainesville City, US Census, Census.gov; "Data USA: Gainesville, FL," US Census, Source 2017 ACS 5 Year, accessed June 8, 2019; Deborah Strange and Jim Ross, "Study Finds Nearly Half of Alachua County Households at Financial Risk," *Gainesville Sun*, February 23, 2017; "2017–2018 UF Graduation Survey: University of Florida Graduates Outcomes," University of Florida Career Connections Center, accessed June 8, 2019; Carla Vianna, "Battling the Brain Drain: Career Fairs Aim to Employ More Students in Gainesville," *Independent Florida Alligator*, April 8, 2015.

45. Anthony Clark, "Downtown Reborn," *Gainesville Sun*, March 29, 2013.

46. Chad Smith, "CRA Manager Leaving for Job in Idaho," *Gainesville Sun*, October 25, 2011; Ed Braddy, "Letter from Mayor Ed Braddy," 2014 City of Gainesville Popular Annual Financial Report, January 10, 2024, 4; April Warren, "Braddy to Voters: Focus on My Accomplishments," *Gainesville Sun*, February 27, 2016; Richard Florida, *The Rise of the Creative Class—and How It's Transforming Work, Leisure, Community, and Everyday Life* (New York: Basic Books, 2002); Ron Cunningham, "City Manager Lyons: 'Revolutionary-in-Chief,'" *Gainesville Sun*, April 26, 2017.

47. Lyons, interview; Diana Budds, "How One Florida City Is Reinventing Itself with UX Design," *Fast Company*, October 31, 2016.

48. Lyons, interview; Dubai: Nathan Crabbe, "A City Designed for the People" (editorial), *Gainesville Sun*, July 19, 2015; "Singapore's Road

to a Human-Centered Government" (case study), IDEO, accessed February 1, 2024; Claire Martin, "Shaping a School System, from the Ground Up," *New York Times*, July 5, 2014.

49. Bob Sutton, "Rave Review for Change by Design in *New York Times*," *Bob Sutton: Work Matters*, September 28, 2009; "Insights for Innovation," IDEO U, accessed February 3, 2024; "Design Thinking Bootcamp," Stanford d.school, accessed February 3, 2024; "Design Thinking Bootcamp: Make Impact and Drive Growth in Your Organization," Stanford Graduate School of Business, accessed February 3, 2024.

50. Rebecca Ackermann, "Design Thinking Was Supposed to Fix the World. Where Did It Go Wrong?," *MIT Technology Review*, February 9, 2023; Alice Rawsthorn, "Expanding the Definitions of Design," *New York Times*, October 19, 2018; Peter N. Miller, "Is 'Design Thinking' the New Liberal Arts?," *Chronicle of Higher Education*, March 26, 2015.

51. Mike Lin et al., "Nurse Knowledge Exchange Plus: Human-Centered Implementation for Spread and Sustainability," *Joint Commission Journal on Quality and Patient Safety* 41, no. 7 (July 2015): 303–312; Barbara Blakeney et al., "Unlocking the Power of Innovation," *OJIN: The Online Journal of Issues in Nursing* 14, no. 2 (May 31, 2009); Brown, *Change by Design*, 177–179; Thomas Lockwood and Edgar Papke, "How Kaiser Solved the Problem of Hospital 'Ghost Towns,'" *Fast Company*, November 10, 2017.

52. Brown, *Change by Design*, 3, citing Jane Fulton Suri and R. Michael Hendrix in *Rotman Management* magazine; problem identified by the winning team ("Aquaduct") in the "Innovate or Die Pedal-Powered Machine Contest," cited in Brown, *Change by Design*, 28.

53. Brown, *Change by Design*, 267; Tim Brown and Roger L. Martin, "Design for Action," *Harvard Business Review*, September 2015, 2–3; Brown, *Change by Design*, 14. On the knowledge economy, see Fritz Machlup, *The Production and Distribution of Knowledge in the United States* (Princeton, NJ: Princeton University Press, 1962); Peter Drucker, *The Effective Executive: The Definitive Guide to Getting the Right Things Done* (New York: Harper Business, 2006 [1967]); Peter Drucker, *The Age of Discontinuity* (New Brunswick, NJ: Routledge, 1992 [1969]); Roberto Mangabeira Unger, *The Knowledge Economy* (Brooklyn, NY: Verso, 2019).

54. Lyons, interview.

55. Lyons, interview; Gainesville Blue Ribbon Advisory Committee on Economic Competitiveness, "The Gainesville Question," City of Gainesville, fall 2015, accessed February 1, 2024.

56. Gainesville Blue Ribbon Advisory Committee, "The Gainesville Question," 12.

57. Gainesville Blue Ribbon Advisory Committee, "The Gainesville Question," 26.

58. Gainesville Blue Ribbon Advisory Committee, "The Gainesville Question," 16–36, 26, 31.

59. April Warren, "Report: City Must Be Friendlier to Citizens, Business," *Gainesville Sun*, December 3, 2015; "Editorial: The Department of Doing," *Gainesville Sun*, October 8, 2015; Budds, "How One Florida City Is Reinventing Itself."

60. Lyons, interview; April Warren, "Gainesville Commission Selects Anthony Lyons as New City Manager," *Gainesville Sun*, April 21, 2016; Andrew Caplan, "Bowie Suggested as Interim City Manager," *Gainesville Sun*, December 31, 2018; Cunningham, "City Manager Lyons."

61. April Warren, "Some Blue Ribbon Changes in the Works," *Gainesville Sun*, May 19, 2016; Budds, "How One Florida City Is Reinventing Itself."

62. Andrew Caplan, "Gainesville Aims to Be 'New American City,'" *Gainesville Sun*, June 24, 2018; "Gainesville as the New American City," *Business in Greater Gainesville*, April 1, 2017, accessed January 15, 2024; "Editorial: The Department of Doing."

63. Andrew Caplan, "City Hires Assistant City Manager," *Gainesville Sun*, June 7, 2017; NAACP of Alachua County, "Alachua County Branch of the NAACP Files Complaint on Behalf of City Employees," June 7, 2017; Jenese Harris, "NAACP Complaint Filed Against Gainesville City Manager," *WJXT*, July 12, 2017; Andrew Caplan, "Report: City Policy Not Followed in Search," *Gainesville Sun*, October 11, 2017; Andrew Caplan, "Gainesville's Assistant City Manager to Resign," *Gainesville Sun*, November 21, 2018; Andrew Caplan, "Commission Discusses Report Largely Clearing Lyons," *Gainesville Sun*, January 18, 2018.

64. Caplan, "Gainesville's Assistant City Manager to Resign"; Andrew Caplan, "Gainesville City Commission Accepts City Manager's Resignation," *Gainesville Sun*, December 13, 2018; Ron Cunningham, "Gainesville Has Designed Our Mayor to Fail," *Gainesville Sun*, December 14, 2018; Andrew Caplan, "Gainesville City Manager Submits Resignation," *Gainesville Sun*, December 11, 2018.

65. "Gainesville City, Florida," QuickFacts, US Census, accessed September 20, 2021; Plan East Gainesville, Final Report, Metropolitan Transportation Planning Organization (MTPO) for the Gainesville Urbanized Area, February 2003; 2013–2017 American

Community Survey 5-Year Estimates, Gainesville City, Race, Total Population, US Census, accessed September 20, 2021; University of Florida Bureau of Economic and Business Research (BEBR), "Understanding Racial Inequality in Alachua County," report, January 2018, 10–13; Instagram for Gainesville East, post of November 14, 2018; Andrew Caplan, "'New American City,'" *Gainesville Sun*, June 24, 2018.

66. "Editorial: Resignation of Anthony Lyons Is City's Loss," *Gainesville Sun*, December 12, 2018.

67. Lyons, interview.

68. Caplan, "Gainesville City Commission Accepts City Manager's Resignation"; Dana Cassidy, "Gainesville City Manager Anthony Lyons Resigns from Position," *Independent Florida Alligator*, December 16, 2018.

69. Nicole Perlroth, "Solving Problems for Real World, Using Design," *New York Times*, December 30, 2013.

70. Hasso Plattner Institute of Design (d.school), Stanford University School of Engineering, accessed July 10, 2024; Ackermann, "Design Thinking Was Supposed to Fix the World."

71. Alex Calamia, "The Director of the Department of Doing Steps Down from Health Concerns," WCJB TV 20, February 5, 2019; John Henderson, "Can Local Firm AMJ Finally Bring Lot 10 to Life?," *Gainesville Sun*, May 7, 2021; John Henderson, "Gainesville Commission Agrees to Sell Lot 10 Property to Developer for Multi-story Project," *Gainesville Sun*, October 26, 2021; Lee Malis, "Is Gainesville Development Out of Control?," *Gainesville Iguana*, May 9, 2022.

72. Horst Rittel, "The Reasoning of Designers," Arbeitspapier A-88-4 (Stuttgart: Institut für Grundlagen der Planung, Universität Stuttgart, 1988), 3–5.

73. For extensive discussion of this relationship, see coda of Brown and Martin, "Design for Action."

74. Lyons, interview.

75. Brown, *Change by Design*, 251–252.

76. For more, see (in chronological order) Dan Saffer, "Design Schools: Please Start Teaching Design Again," Adaptive Path, March 2007; Don Norman, "Design Thinking: A Useful Myth," Core77, June 25, 2010; Christo Sims, "The Politics of Design, Design as Politics," in *The Routledge Companion to Digital Ethnography*, ed. Larissa Hjorth et al. (New York: Routledge, 2017); Meg Miller, "Want to Fight Inequality? Forget Design Thinking," *Fast Company*, February 16, 2017; Natasha Jen, "Design Thinking Is B.S.," *Fast Company*, April 9, 2018; Natasha Iskander, "Design Thinking Is Fundamentally

Conservative and Preserves the Status Quo," *Harvard Business Review*, September 5, 2018; Lilly Irani, "'Design Thinking': Defending Silicon Valley at the Apex of Global Labor Hierarchies," *Catalyst: Feminism, Theory, Technoscience* 4, no. 1 (May 7, 2018): 1–19; Lilly Irani, *Chasing Innovation: Making Entrepreneurial Citizens in Modern India* (Princeton, NJ: Princeton University Press, 2019); Darin Buzon, "Design Thinking Is a Rebrand for White Supremacy," Medium, January 14, 2021; Tricia Wang, "Design Thinking's Most Popular Strategy Is BS," *Fast Company*, June 28, 2021; Antionette Carroll and Tania Anaissie, "How Design Thinking Protects White Supremacy," SXSW 2024, Austin, Texas, for presentation in March 2024.

77. Ackermann, "Design Thinking Was Supposed to Fix the World."

78. Rittel, "The Reasoning of Designers," 2; see also Horst Rittel, "Son of Rittelthink: The State of the Art in Design Methods," *DMG 5th Anniversary Report*, DMG Occasional Paper No. 1.7.2 (1972): 143–147.

Afterword

1. Roberto Mangabeira Unger, *The Knowledge Economy* (Brooklyn, NY: Verso, 2019); Alvin Hansen, "Capital Goods and the Restoration of Purchasing Power," *Proceedings of the Academy of Political Science* 16 (1934): 11–19.

2. Brian Braiker, "The Dust-Kicker: Artist Timothy Goodman on Life, Love and Work," *Brooklyn Magazine*, January 30, 2023; Timothy Goodman, "Shop," tgoodman.com, accessed July 15, 2024.

3. Sagmeister Inc., "Levi's Gears Billboard," September 16, 2010, YouTube video, https://www.youtube.com/watch?v=bjpiP8o5CFI.

4. Angus Montgomery, "The Playful Jessica Walsh," *Design Week*, May 8, 2013.

5. Thomas Piketty, *Capital and Ideology*, trans. Arthur Goldhammer (Cambridge, MA: Belknap Press of Harvard University Press, 2020), 415.

6. Piketty, *Capital and Ideology*, 415, 424.

7. Piketty, *Capital and Ideology*, 492, 656, 687, 693.

8. Piketty, *Capital and Ideology*, 415–417, 454–455,

9. Piketty, *Capital and Ideology*, 417; Martín Espada, "Imagine the Angels of Bread," in *Imagine the Angels of Bread: Poems* (New York: W. W. Norton, 1997).

10. Erik Olin Wright, *Envisioning Real Utopias* (London: Verso, 2010), 6.

11. Wright, *Envisioning Real Utopias*, 2–5, 194–203, 217–222.

12. Wright, *Envisioning Real Utopias*, 192–193, 80.

13. Jessica Helfand, "Sylvia Harris: 1953–2011," *Design Observer*, July 25, 2011; Steven Heller, "Remembering Sylvia Harris," *PRINT Magazine*, July 26, 2011.

14. Office of the US Census Bureau Public Information, "Preliminary Estimates Show Improvement in Census 2000 Coverage," Census.gov Newsroom, February 14, 2001; "Historic Census Undercount of Black Americans Robs Communities of Billions in Funding and Fair Political Representation," National Urban League, October 15, 2021; "2002 Public Budget Database," Fiscal Year 2002 Public Budget Database, United States Office of Management and Budget, Receipts: Public Budget Database, accessed March 15, 2015.

15. Helfand, "Sylvia Harris."

16. Dana Chisnell, "Home," danachisnell.com, accessed July 15, 2024.

INDEX

Aalto, Alvar, 135
ABC, 88, 218
Accenture, 14
Acer, 221
Ackermann, Rebecca, 231, 241–242, 245–246
Adaptive Path, 14
Administrative Behavior (Simon), 97–98
Adorno, Theodor, 133
advertising
  growth of, 52
  Teague and, 52, 53*fig*, 54
AEG assembly hall, 59
Agricultural Adjustment Administration, 69
AIGA Gold Medal, 88
Alexander, Christopher, 112, 127, 129
Altman, Sam, 16
Altran, 14
Aluminum Company of America, 120
American Institute of Graphic Arts, 202
AMJ, 242
Amoeba Music, 16
&Walsh, 251

anthropological impulse, 146–148
anthropology, field of, 148–152, 159–161
Antonelli, Paola, 42
Apple Computer, 184–185, 188–192, 196–197, 216–217. *See also* Jobs, Steve
Apple Lisa, 185, 185*fig*, 217
applied anthropology, 149–151
apprentices, 22–23, 135–136
Arc Worldwide, 201
Archer, Bruce, 112, 223
architectural brief, 92
Argodesign, 14
Arnold, John E., 136
ARPANET (Advanced Research Projects Agency Network), 174, 176
Arrow Collars, 52
art deco, 56
Art Directors Club of New York, 54
Art et Industrie, 58
Art League of California, 136
Art Students League of New York, 52, 87
Arthur Andersen, 162
artificial intelligence (AI), 106–107, 154, 159

Index

Arts & Architecture, 15–16
Arts and Crafts movement, 28
arts of design, 26–27
Atlas Crankshaft, 91, 218
Auden, W. H., 123
Austro-Hungarian Empire, 20–22
automation, 154

Bach, Richard, 65
Bains, Angela, 204
Baldwin, James, 140
Banham, Rayner, 132
Barcelona Chair, 28
basic research, 153
Baudrillard, Jean, 132
Bauhaus, 56, 58, 61–64, 193, 199
Bay Ridge Specialty Company, 38
beautification, 25
beauty, Striker (Zeisel) and, 35
"Beauty: The New Business Tool" (Calkins), 26
behaviorism, 99–100, 179–180
Behrens, Peter, 59
Bel Geddes, Norman, 72
Bell Labs, 137–139, 162, 174, 175–176
Berkeley, Edmund, 102
Bezaitis, Maria, 160, 163, 164
birthday cakes, evolution of, 187
Black Panthers, 131
black pottery, 24
Blu Dot, 14
Blue Ribbon Committee on Economic Competitiveness, 229–230
BlueFocus, 14
BMW, 221
Boeing, 78, 210
Boudreau, James C., 76–77
Braddy, Ed, 229–230, 235
Bradley, Tom, 130–131
Breuer, Marcel, 28
Brinkley, Alan, 65, 69

Brooklyn Museum, 45
Brooks, Gwendolyn, 121–123, 122*fig*
Brown, Tim, 14–15, 221–222, 224, 227, 231, 233–234, 244
Brown Berets, 131
Buchenau, Marion, 213

Calder, Alexander, 87
California Arts & Architecture magazine, 120
California Institute of the Arts (CalArts), 139, 144
Capgemini, 14
Capital One, 14
capitalism
  design and, 2–3, 16
  Haug on, 134
  New Deal and, 69
  Polanyi on, 47
  rational choice theory and, 171
  Striker (Zeisel) and, 47–48
Carnegie Institute of Technology, 38, 98
Carnegie Mellon University, 38, 98, 106, 209
Carson, Rachel, 140
"Case Study Apartment," 15
Castleton China, 39, 40, 45
Cavendish, Margaret, 17–18
Change by Design (Brown), 231
chaos, 172–173
Chisnell, Dana, 257
Christian Carstens KG, 27, 29
Chronicle of Higher Education, 232
Chuang, Aichia, 205
Churchman, C. West, 110–112, 125–126, 128, 151
Citizen Research & Design, 256
City Lights, 16
Civilian Conservation Corps, 69
Claremont, New Hampshire, 220, 228

Index

Clarke, Alison J., 146
Clifford, James, 164
Cold War, 101, 102–103, 214, 249
Cold War rationality, 107–109
Colliers, 25
Colombia's Ministry of National Defense, 226–227
colonialism, 149
commoditization, 186
communism, 31, 44
community land trusts, 255
complexity
   acceptance of, 194–195
   confusion and, 195–196
   increase in, 169, 171–176, 181–182, 189
   lived experiences and, 207
   simplification and, 192–194
computer science, 101–102, 104–106, 112, 119
computing, growth of, 172–176, 181–182
conceptual model (mental model), 177–181, 182–184, 186, 190, 191, 196
Conference on Design Methods, 112
"Conference on Industrial Design: A New Profession," 75–76
confusion, as problem, 195–196
consumers, concept of, 65
Cooper Hewitt, 146–148, 147fig
Cooper Union, 135
Corning, 66
Cornwall, Kestin, 204
corporations, anthropologists in, 159–161, 165–166
corporations, study of, 152–156
Costanza-Chock, Sasha, 205–207
COVID-19 pandemic, 84–85
Craik, Kenneth, 179–180
Cranbrook Academy of Art, 118

Creange, Henry, 56
Creative Engineering Laboratory, 136
Creative Vision, The (Getzels and Csikszentmihalyi), 121
Csikszentmihalyi, Mihaly, 121

Darkness at Noon (Koestler), 35–36, 45, 116
Daston, Lorraine, 107
Datamation, 176
David Kelley Design, 218
De architectura (Vitruvius), 60, 91–93
Death and Life of Great American Cities, The (Jacobs), 140
decision-making processes, study of, 98
decolonization movements, 142, 149
Decolonizing Design (Tunstall), 203fig
Dee, John, 93
Defense Advanced Research Projects Agency (DARPA), 84
defibrillator, portable, 221
Description of a New World, Called the Blazing-World, The (Cavendish), 18
design
   beauty and, 19–49
   capitalism and, 2–3, 16
   codifying method of, 109–110, 111
   education in, 108
   experience and, 169–208
   as fragmented discipline, 212–213
   function and, 51–85
   human-centeredness and, 125–167

Index

design *(continued)*
  as marriage of aesthetics with function, 9
  as megaconcept, 1
  modernist conception of, 9
  outsized investment in, 10–11
  problem solving and, 5, 9–10, 87–123
  rationalizing, 110, 117, 126–127, 129
  simplification as approach to, 112
  use of term, 10–11, 52–53
  as way of thinking, 9–10, 209–247
design ABILITIES, 225*fig*
design brief. *See* architectural brief
Design Clinic, 135, 136
Design for Democracy, 202
Design for the Real World (Papanek), 134, 140–141
design justice, 206–207
Design Justice (Costanza-Chock), 205–206
Design Methods Movement, 110, 212
design modernism, 11–12
Design of Everyday Things, The (Norman), 194
design thinking, 9–10, 113, 222–227, 231–238, 241–247
Design Thinking (Rowe), 223
Design This Day (Teague), 73–74
Design Within Reach (DWR), 7–8, 12–14, 15–16, 42–43
designers, origin of term, 26–27
"Designer's Problem, The" (Rand), 89
DesignGruppen, 146
Designing for People (Dreyfuss), 72–73, 137
Deutscher Werkbund, 28, 58, 62
disability justice movement, 207

discourse
  role of, 3–4
  use of term, 3
discoverability problems, 193–194
distributive justice, 116
Domino, 8
Doorley, Scott, 241–242
dot-com bubble, 220
Dreyfuss, Henry, 72–73, 75, 137–139
Droste, Magdalena, 63
Dubberly, Hugh, 109
Dublin Group, 162
Duncker, Karl, 101
DuPont, 78
Dwell, 8
DXC, 14

Eames, Charles and Ray, 42, 115, 117–120, 118*fig*, 120*fig*, 123, 146, 147
Earnest Elmo Calkins, 26
Eastman Kodak, 66, 78
Eccles, Marriner, 71
Eichler, Joseph, 215
Einstein, Albert, 93
Eisenhower, Dwight D., 95
E-Lab LLC, 162, 199
elections, design guidelines and, 202
Elements (Euclid), 93
Ellenby, John, 215
Emerson, Ralph Waldo, 61
empiricism, 96–97, 137
encoding, 114–115
Engelbart, Doug, 217
Entrepreneurial State, The (Mazzucato), 82–84
Equal Exchange, 255
ErgonomiDesign, 145–146
ErgonomiDesignGruppen, 146
Erickson, Paul, 107, 108
Ericsson, K. Anders, 99

Index

"esoteric interiors," 28
Espada, Martín, 254
Esquire, 88
ethnographic impulse, 142–143
ethnographic studies/research, 149, 159, 161–162, 164
Euclid, 93
Evers, Medgar, 130
everything principle, 177, 213
experience, defining, 187–188

Fanon, Frantz, 142
FARC (Revolutionary Armed Forces of Colombia), 226–227
"Farm Bill," 74
Fascism, 36, 37
Fast Company, 13
fast-thinking operations, 210
Federal Art Project, 69
Federal Emergency Relief Administration, 69
Federal Reserve Board, 71
Federal Theatre Project, 69
Federal Writers' Project, 69
Feininger, Lyonel, 63–64
finance, industry of, 169–173
Financial Times, 83
financialization, 2, 170–171
Fire Next Time, The (Baldwin), 140
first-person experience, 176–178
Fjord, 14
Flextronics International, 14
Florida, Richard, 229
Folkers, Paul, 238
Forbes, Robert, Jr., 7–8, 13, 14
Ford, 25–26, 78
Ford, Henry, 25
Ford Foundation, 98
Foroohar, Rana, 170
Franco, Francisco, 35
Frankford Arsenal, 110
Franz Joseph, 20–21, 22

Free Willy, 221
frog design, 14
Fuhlbrügge, Hermann, 27, 32, 33
Fuller, Buckminster, 137, 139
Fulton Suri, Jane, 162–163, 213
function, modernism and, 30, 59–61, 80
functionalism
  rise of, 61–62, 75
  in United States, 64–68
Fuseproject, 14

Gainesville, Florida, 227–231, 234–241, 242, 243, 246
Gainesville Blue Ribbon Report, 235–236
Gainesville Community Redevelopment Agency, 229, 241
game theory, 103, 119
Garrett, Jesse James, 197, 197*fig*
gas compressors, 67
Gehry, Frank, 80
General Electric, 78
General Motors, 26, 162
General Problem Solver, 106
Gensler, Gary, 170–171
Gestalt School, 100–101
Getzels, Jacob, 121
Giant Brains (Berkeley), 102
Gilmore, James, 187
Glenhill, 13
globalization, 2, 142
Goebbels, Joseph, 31
Goldhagen, Sarah Williams, 3, 59
"Good Design" exhibitions, 40, 147
Goodman, Nelson, 114, 115, 252*fig*
Goodman, Timothy, 250–251
Grand Designs, 8
"Granit" collection (Zeisel), 42–43
graphical user interfaces (GUIs), 154, 183, 185, 188, 217

Index

Great Depression, 64–66, 87, 249
Great Purge, 36
Great Transformation, The (Polanyi), 46–47, 82
Greece, redesign of export economy of, 78–79
Greenough, Horatio, 60–61
Greil, Max, 63
GRiD Systems, 215
Gropius, Walter, 58, 59, 61–62, 63–64, 109
Grosz, George, 87
Guetzkow, Harold, 96–97, 98
Guggenheim Fellowship, 121
guild system, 22, 47

Hall, Stuart, 133
Hall China Company, 41
hamburger menus, 193–194, 196
Harrell, Cyd, 246, 257
Harris, Sylvia, 256–257
Harvard Council on Foreign Relations, 107
Harwood, John, 119
Hasso Plattner Institute of Design, 241–242. *See also* Stanford d.school
Haug, Wolfgang Fritz, 133–134, 165
Hawksmoor, Nicholas, 92
Hawthorne Study, 149–150
Helfand, Jessica, 257
Heller (company), 14
Heller, Steven, 89, 256
heritage brands, 8
Herman Miller, 14, 15
heuristics/heuristic analysis, 94–95, 105, 114
hexagon diagram, 224–225, 225*fig*, 226
Hirschman, Elizabeth, 186

Hitler, Adolf, 100
Hochschule für Gestaltung Ulm, 126
Hoek van Holland housing blocks, 59
Hoffman, Dan, 238, 240
Holbrook, Morris, 186
Hollein, Hans, 147, 147*fig*, 148
Hoover, Herbert, 55, 56
Horkheimer, Max, 133
Houseman, William, 131
Hovey, Dean, 216–218
How to Solve It (Pólya), 93–95, 101, 105
Hubsch, Heinrich, 60, 193
human cognition, theory of, 106–107
human factors analysis, 150
"Human Interface Guidelines" (HIG), 191–192
human-machine interface, 160
Hungarian Democratic Republic, 22
Hungarian Guild of Chimney Sweepers, Oven Makers, Roof Tilers, Well Diggers, and Potters, 22–23
Hungarian Royal Academy of Fine Arts, 20
Hungarian Soviet Republic, 22
Hungary, 19–24, 45

IBM, 61, 88, 162, 218
ID Two, 218
IDEO, 9–10, 14–15, 162–163, 218–224, 226–227, 230–232, 234–236, 239, 243
IDEO U, 221
Illinois Institute of Technology, 95–96
"illusion industry," 133

Index

industrial design
  after World War II, 77–78
  books on, 72–73
  first courses in, 38
  MoMA exhibitions and, 40
  professionalization of, 75–77
  Teague on, 68
  World War II and, 75
Industrial Design, 139
Industrial Revolution, 1, 46, 249
inequality, 2, 253–254
innovation, state and, 82–84
integrated circuits, 214
Intel, 162
International Design Conference in Aspen (IDCA), 121–122, 122*fig*, 131–133, 212
International Exposition of Modern Industrial and Decorative Arts, 28–29, 55–56
"International Style" show, 16
Internationale Architektur (Gropius), 59
interventionism, 44–45
intuitive mind, 210
iOS, 191
iPad, 191, 192
iPhone, 191, 192, 230
Irby, Charles, 182
Irby study, 182
Ive, Jonathan, 190

Jacobs, Jane, 140
Jameson, Fredric, 17
Japanese Society for the Science of Design, 110
Jeanneret, Pierre, 56
Jobs, Steve, 3, 4, 64, 80, 91, 184–185, 188, 190–191, 217, 218. *See also* Apple Computer
Johnson, Philip, 80

Johnson-Laird, Philip, 180
Joint Chiefs of Staff, 75
Jones, John Chris, 129
Joshi, Aparna, 205
Judt, Tony, 70

Kahn, Matt, 208
Kahneman, Daniel, 210
Kaiser Permanente, 226, 232–233
Kállai, Ernő, 64
Kandinsky, Wassily, 31
Kant, Immanuel, 99
Kaplan, Ron, 156, 157
Karapancsik, Jakob, 24
Katz, Barry, 216
Kaufmann, Edgar J., Jr., 40, 75, 135
Kelley, David, 209–212, 214, 216–219, 221–222, 241
Kennedy, John F., 130
Kennedy, Robert F., 130
Képzőművészeti Akadémia, 20
King, Martin Luther, Jr., 47, 130
Kirkham, Pat, 89
Kispester-Granit, 24–25
"kitchenette building" (Brooks), 123
Klee, Paul, 87
Knapp, Jake, 223
knowledge economy, 250
knowledge work, 154, 155–156
Koch, Carl, 131–132
Koestler, Arthur, 35–36, 44, 45, 116
Koffka, Kurt, 100
Kohler, Wolfgang, 100
Koppel, Ted, 221
Kriegspiel, 103
Krippner, Greta, 169
Kritik der Warenästhetik (*A Critique of Commodity Aesthetics*; Haug), 133

Index

La Mer, 136
labor laws, 2
Lafargue Clinic, 135
Language Dept., 15
laptops, 216
Latour, Bruno, 10
Le Corbusier, 11–12, 29, 40, 55, 56–57, 57*fig*, 59, 61, 136
lean research, 163
Lears, T. J. Jackson, 52
Lesk, Michael, 176
"less but better" philosophy, 190, 193
Lessard, Suzannah, 44
Levi's, 250–251, 252*fig*
Liao, Hui, 205
Liddle, David, 182
linear programming, 119
Lippmann, Walter, 70
lived experiences, 204–207, 213
Living with Complexity (Norman), 194
Loewy, Raymond, 72, 75–76
Logic Theorist, 105, 154
logical positivism (empiricism), 96–97
Lomonosov State Porcelain Factory, 32
Loos, Adolf, 193
"Lounge Chair Wood" (Eames and Eames), 118, 118*fig*
Lowe SSP3, 226
Lunar Design, 14
Lyons, Anthony, 219–220, 227–232, 234–243, 237*fig*

Macintosh, 185, 188, 189, 191, 217–218. *See also* Apple Computer
Made by Design line, 8
Magic Motorways (Bel Geddes), 72
Maier, Norman R. F., 98

Maison La Roche, 56
Maison Ozenfant, 56, 57*fig*
Malaysia, race riot in, 130
Malinowski, Bronislaw, 149
Malkin, Janet, 151
"MAN transFORMS" exhibition, 146–148, 147*fig*
Manock, Jerry, 216
Marcus, George H., 80
Marcus, George E., 164
market liberalism, 81
market society, rise of, 46–47, 48
markets
  regulation of, 2
  unregulated, 1
  See also capitalism
Markos, Stephen, 9
Mars, Roman, 8
"Martians, the," 93
Marxism, 17
Mary, Queen, 92
Massachusetts Institute of Technology (MIT), 136–137
mathematics, problem solving and, 93–95
Mayo, Elton, 149
Mazzucato, Marianna, 82–84
McBride, Cheryl, 238
McCorduck, Pamela, 105
McKim, Bob, 211, 218
McKinsey & Company, 14
means-ends analysis, 106
medical passports, 211
medical records, 211
Meikle, Jeffrey, 66
Memphis, 80
Menand, Louis, 77
mental model, 177–181, 182–184, 186, 190, 191, 196
Merriam, Charles E., 97
"Methodology for User Interface Design, A," 182

Index

Meyer, Hannes, 64
microprocessor industry, 214
Microsoft Research, 162
Mies van der Rohe, Ludwig, 28, 40, 59
military-industrial complex, 95
Millett, Kate, 140
Miró, Joan, 87
Mobilier et Décoration, 58
modernism
    concept of, 58–59
    function and, 59–61, 80
    International Exposition of Modern Industrial and Decorative Arts and, 55–56
    Papanek and, 136–137
    Rand and, 88–89
    simplification and, 193
    Striker (Zeisel) and, 28–30, 41
    Teague and, 58, 60
    in United States, 59–60, 61
    utopian thinking and, 11–12
Moggridge, Bill, 213–216, 218
monopoly, problem of, 69
Moscou, Kathy, 204
mouse, computer, 217–218
Mumford, Louis, 59–60
Murad Turkish Cigarettes, 52
Murry, Fred, 239
"Museum" collection (Zeisel), 39–41, 40*fig*, 45
Museum of Modern Art (MoMA), 16, 39–40, 75, 118, 135, 147
Musk, Elon, 81–82

Nader, Laura, 152
National Association for the Advancement of Colored People (NAACP), 238
National Institutes of Health, 84
National Recovery Administration, 69, 70

Native Americans, 152
Nazi Party, 31, 100, 134
Nelson, George, 131, 147
Nestlé, 162, 221
New Deal, 68–72, 81, 116, 249
New School, 100
New York Federal Reserve Board, 71
New York Society of Ceramic Arts, 39
New Yorker, 66–67, 71
Newell, Allen, 94, 103–106, 156, 157
Newton, Isaac, 172
NeXT Computers, 91, 190, 218
Nielsen, Jakob, 191
Nielsen Norman Group, 191, 196
Nightline, 221
Nike, 230
99% Invisible, 8
Nissan, 162
Nixon, Richard, 130
Noguchi, Isamu, 115
Nokia, 162
non-Western cultures, designers' turn to, 142–144, 146–149
Nooney, Laine, 184
Nordic design practice, 145
Norman, Donald A., 163, 174–177, 179, 180–181, 188–192, 194–196, 207, 213
Northern Ireland Riots, 131
Notes on the Synthesis of Form (Alexander), 112, 127, 129
Noyes, Eliot, 39, 61, 132–133
Nurse Knowledge Exchange, 232–233
Nuttall, Mike, 218

Obama, Barack, 231
Objective Gallery, 9
Ohrbach's, 88
Olmstead, Frederick Law, 54

Index

On Problem-Solving (Duncker), 101
Ontario College of Art (later OCAD University), 136
Ontario College of Art and Design (OCAD) University, 202–205
OpenIDEO community, 223
Operation Christmas, 226–227
operations research, 95, 110, 111, 126
orca, mechanical, 221
organicism, 41–42, 61
ornament
    postmodernism and, 80
    Teague on, 54, 68
Oud, J. J. P., 59

Packard, 25–26
Packer, George, 84–85
PalmPilot, 221
pandemic, 84–85
Papanek, Victor, 134–137, 139–145, 146, 162
PARC (Palo Alto Research Center, Xerox), 153–155, 159–160, 165–167, 181–182, 184–185, 215, 217
Parsons School of Design, 87
participatory city budgeting, 255–256
participatory design, 160
patient capital, 83
Pavillon de l'Ésprit Nouveau, 29, 56
PayPal, 81
Peji, Bennett, 256
Pentagram, 8
Phoenix Hosiery, 52
Picasso, Pablo, 87
Piketty, Thomas, 252–254
Pine, Joseph, 187
"planning," 70, 78

Plans and Situated Actions (Suchman), 156–157
poetry, 121–123
Polanyi, Karl, 19, 22, 46–47, 75, 82, 93, 256
Polanyi, Michael, 19, 22, 44, 93
Polaroid, 78
political science, 97
Pólya, George, 93–95, 101, 105, 121
postmodernism, 80
pottery
    black, 24
    in the Soviet Union, 31–34
    Striker (Zeisel) and, 23–25, 27–28, 29–30, 29*fig*, 38, 39–41, 40*fig*, 42–43, 43*fig*
poverty, problem of, 128
power
    focus on, 4
    United States and, 4–5
Poy, Michael Lee, 204
Pratt Institute, 38–39, 87
Principia Mathematica (Russell and Whitehead), 104, 105
problem solving
    as concept, 92–93
    design and, 5, 9–10, 87–123
    heuristic analysis and, 94–95
    problem articulation and, 91–92
    psychology and, 98–101
    Rand on, 89–91
product design, 210–212
productive thinking, 101, 108
Productive Thinking (Wertheimer), 101
Project Runway, 8
Prouvé, Jean, 15
provenance, passion for, 8
psychology
    mental model and, 179–180
    problem solving and, 98–101

Index

Psychology of Everyday Things, The (Norman), 180–181, 194
Pulitzer Prize, 121
Pyrex, 66

race relations, 130–131
Rams, Dieter, 190, 193
RAND, 102–103, 104, 106, 107
Rand, Paul (Peretz Rosenbaum)
  background of, 87–88
  Eameses and, 117–118
  Kelley and, 218–219
  modernist aesthetics and, 88–89
  problem solving and, 89–91, 113, 115
  work of, 88–89, 88*fig*
rapid ethnography, 163
rational choice theory, 171
rationality, Cold War, 107–109
Red River Solutions, 228
Red Wing Pottery, 41
redistribution, Polanyi on, 49
reproductive thinking, 101, 108
research
  basic, 153
  lean, 163
Revlon, Inc., 88
Revolutionary Armed Forces of Colombia (FARC), 226–227
Rittel, Horst
  background of, 126
  on designers, 246–247
  on designer's reasoning, 242–243
  rationalizing design and, 126–127, 129, 162
  Suchman and, 151
  West's seminar and, 125
  wicked problems and, 128–129, 242
Robinson, Marton, 204
Robinson, Rick E., 160, 163, 164
Romanisches Café, 30

Roosevelt, Franklin, 65, 68–71, 74
Rosenbaum, Peretz (later Paul Rand), 87
Rowe, Peter, 223
Royal Hospital for Seamen, 92
Royal Society of London, 88
Russell, Bertrand, 104

Saarinen, Eliel, 118
safety nets, social, 2
Sagmeister & Walsh, 251
Sagmeister Inc., 250
Sakier, George, 77
SAP, 241
Sapient Corporation, 162, 198–201, 207
Saval, Nikil, 17
Scandinavian Design Students' Organization, 145
Scandinavian modernism, 56
Schapiro, Meyer, 16
Schoenfeld, A. H., 94
School of Design, CalArts, 139
Schramberger Majolikafabrik, 27, 29
Schumacher, E. F., 140
Schumpeter, Joseph, 3
Sciences of the Artificial, The (Simon), 106–109
Scope of Total Architecture (Gropius), 109
Scully, Emma, 9
Seldes, Gilbert, 67, 68, 71
Servel Refrigerators, 78
Sexual Politics (Millett), 140
Seybold, Jonathan, 182–183
Shao, Chris, 9
Shaw, Cliff, 104, 106
Silent Spring (Carson), 140
Silicon Valley, 214, 215, 220–221, 231
Simon, Arthur, 95–96

Index

Simon, Dorothea, 104
Simon, Herbert
  background of, 95–96
  photograph of, 96*fig*
  politics of, 116–117
  as powerful voice, 4
  problem solving and, 101–102, 103–109, 110, 113, 114–115, 154
  rational choice theory and, 171
  symbolic action and, 159
  work of, 96–98
simplification
  as approach to design, 112, 190–193
  arguments against, 195–196
situated actions, 156–159, 202
situated knowledge, 206
Skinner, B. F., 179
slow-thinking operations, 210
Small Is Beautiful (Schumacher), 140
small-scale model, 179–180
Smith, James Allen, 102
social anthropologists, 148–149
Social Democratic Party (Hungary), 22
social dislocations, 46
social insurance systems, 2
Solar Do-Nothing Machine, 120, 120*fig*
SonicRim, 162
Sottsass, Ettore, 80
soul contact, 30, 42–43, 49
Soviet Union
  pottery and, 31–32
  Striker (Zeisel) and, 31, 44–45, 47–48
Spanish Civil War, 35
Staatliches Bauhaus (Bauhaus State School), 62
Stalin, Joseph, 34, 36–37
Stalinism, 116

Stanford d.school, 224, 225*fig*, 231, 241–242
State China and Glass Industries of the Russian Republic, 32
Steelcase Inc., 14–15
Stevens, Wallace, 169, 189
Stewart, Potter, 187
Stormoguide Weather Station, 67
Striker, Eva (later Zeisel)
  after release from prison, 37–38
  arrest and imprisonment of, 33–37, 44
  background of, 19–20, 21–23
  beauty and, 41, 42, 45, 48–49
  capitalism and, 47–48
  in Germany, 27–31
  later life of, 43–46
  modernism and, 28–30, 41
  in New York, 37–39
  pottery and, 23–25, 27–28, 29–30, 29*fig*, 38, 39–41, 40*fig*, 42–43, 43*fig*
  self-portrait by, 21*fig*
  in Soviet Union, 31–36, 47–48
Striker, Laura Polanyi, 19, 22, 28
structuralism, 146
Suchman, Edward, 151
Suchman, Lucy, 151–161, 165–167, 202
Sullivan, Louis, 61, 193
Superhouse, 9
Superstudio, 146
Sutton, Robert, 10, 231
symbolic action, 159
symbolization, 179
symbols processing, 104–105, 106–107, 159
systems analysis, 111, 112
Systems Research Laboratory, 103

320

Index

Taliesin Studios, 135–136
"Tall Office Building Artistically Considered, The" (Sullivan), 61
Target, 8
Tatlin, Vladimir, 31
taxes, redistributive regime for, 2
Taylor Instrument, 67
Teague, Walter Dorwin
   advertising and, 52, 53fig, 54
   background of, 51–52
   design book by, 73–74
   education of, 52
   in Europe, 55, 56–58
   firm of, 77–78
   functionalism and, 68
   Greek economy and, 78–79
   home of, 54
   methods of, 66–67
   modernism and, 60
   New Deal and, 71
   as powerful voice, 4
   on role of industrial designers, 76
   sketches by, 79fig
   Wilkie and, 71–72
   World War II and, 75
techno-utopianism, 16, 71–72, 73, 81. *See also* utopian thinking
telephone, redesign of, 137–139
Ten Years of Industrial Design (Dreyfuss), 72
Tennessee Valley Authority, 69
Texas Instruments, 78
Thatcher, Margaret, 17, 74
Thiel, Peter, 81–82
Thomas, Wendy, 240
Thompson, Derek, 84
Thoughts on Design (Rand), 89
Tognazzini, Bruce, 191, 192
"Tomorrow's Classic" (Zeisel), 41
"Towards a Rational Modernism" (Mumford), 59–60

"Town and Country" set (Zeisel), 41, 43, 43fig
"Trouble with Unix, The" (Norman), 174–176
Troubles, 131
Tunstall, Elizabeth "Dori," 198–205, 203fig, 207, 257
Turing Award, A. M., 106
Type Directors Club Medal, 88

UC Berkeley, 111, 151–152
Ukrainian Porcelain and Glass Trust, 32
UNESCO, 144
United States
   functionalism in, 64–68
   government of as innovator, 82–84
   modernism in, 59–60, 61
United Students Against Sweatshops, 255
universal basic income (UBI), 255–256
University of Chicago, 97
Unix, 174–176
"Up the Anthropologist" (Nader), 152
UPS, 88, 218
US Air Force Academy, 78
US Army, 201–202
US Bureau of Indian Affairs, 90, 218
US Census, 256–257
US Centers for Disease Control and Prevention, 162
US military-industrial complex, 95
US Ordnance Laboratory, 110
usability
   Apple Computer and, 188
   graphical user interfaces (GUIs), 183, 185, 188, 217
   studies on, 193–194

Index

user experience (UX) design, 186, 189–191, 196–198, 199, 200, 207–208
user interfaces, 42, 154, 174, 176–177, 182–185, 188, 217
user research, 162–165
utopian thinking, 11–12, 16–17, 255. *See also* techno-utopianism

Value of Everything, The (Mazzucato), 82
Vasari, Giorgio, 26
Vaszary, János, 20
Venturi, Robert, 80
Vers une architeture (*Towards a New Architecture*; Le Corbusier), 11–12, 57, 61
Vietnam War, 130
Viollet-le-Duc, Eugène-Emmanuel, 61, 193
Vitruvius, 60, 91–93

Wahlforss, Henrik, 145–146
Wallace, Henry A., 74
Wallpaper, 8
Walsh, Jessica, 250–251, 252*fig*
Warner, Lloyd, 149
wealth inequality, 2, 253–254
Webber, Alan, 230
Webber, Melvin, 128–129
Weintraub, William H., 88
Weissberg, Alexander, 31
"Welcome to the Experience Economy" (Pine and Gilmore), 187
Wellman, David, 160
Wertham, Fredric, 135
Wertheimer, Max, 100, 101, 108
Western Electric Company, 149
Westinghouse, 88, 218

West's seminar, 111–112, 125–126
Whitehead, Alfred North, 104
whitewater canoeing example, 157–158
Whitman, Walt, 61
"Why Contemporary?" (Papanek), 136
wicked problems, 128–129, 242, 246, 257
Wikipedia, 255
Wilkie, Wendell, 71–72
Work Practice & Technology research group, 159–160
Work, Susan, 16
Works Progress Administration, 69
World War II, 75, 100, 150
worldmaking, 114, 115
Wozniak, Steve, 184
Wretched of the Earth, The (*Les damnés de la terre*: Fanon), 142
Wright, Erik Olin, 255–256
Wright, Frank Lloyd, 42, 61, 135–136
Wright, Russel, 42

X, Malcolm, 130
Xerox, 152–155, 159–160
Xerox Palo Alto Research Center (PARC), 153–155, 159–160, 165–167, 181–182, 184–185, 215, 217
Xerox Star, 182–185, 191, 217

Yale University, 218
Yorty, Sam, 131

Zeisel, Eva. *See* Striker, Eva (later Zeisel)
Zeisel, Hans, 37–38
Zeisel, Jean, 39

Credit: Ryan Duffin

Maggie Gram is a writer, cultural historian, and designer. She leads an experience-design team at Google. She has taught at the Maryland Institute College of Art, Washington University in St. Louis, Ca' Foscari University of Venice, and Harvard University, and she has written for *n+1* and the *New York Times*. She lives in New York.